Melancholy and the Archive

CONTINUUM LITERARY STUDIES SERIES

Also available in the series:
Active Reading by Ben Knights and Chris Thurgar-Dawson
Adapting Detective Fiction by Neil McCaw
Beckett's Books by Matthew Feldman
Beckett and Phenomenology edited by Matthew Feldman and Ulrika Maude
Beckett and Decay by Katherine White
Beckett and Death edited by Steve Barfield, Matthew Feldman and Philip Tew
Canonizing Hypertext by Astrid Ensslin
Character and Satire in Postwar Fiction by Ian Gregson
Coleridge and German Philosophy by Paul Hamilton
Contemporary Fiction and Christianity by Andrew Tate
English Fiction in the 1930s by Chris Hopkins
Ecstasy and Understanding edited by Adrian Grafe
Fictions of Globalization by James Annesley
Joyce and Company by David Pierce
London Narratives by Lawrence Phillips
Masculinity in Fiction and Film by Brian Baker
Modernism and the Post-colonial by Peter Childs
Milton, Evil and Literary History by Claire Colebrook
Novels of the Contemporary Extreme edited by Alain-Phillipe Durand and Naomi Mandel
Postmodern Fiction and the Break-Up of Fiction by Hywel Dix
Post-War British Women Novelists and the Canon by Nick Turner
Seeking Meaning for Goethe's Faust by J. M. van der Laan
Sexuality and the Erotic in the Fiction of Joseph Conrad by Jeremy Hawthorn
Such Deliberate Disguises: The Art of Phillip Larkin by Richard Palmer
The Imagination of Evil by Mary Evans
The Palimpsest by Sarah Dillon
The Measureless Past of Joyce, Deleuze and Derrida by Ruben Borg
Women's Fiction 1945–2000 by Deborah Philips

Melancholy and the Archive
Trauma, Memory, and History in the
Contemporary Novel

Jonathan Boulter

continuum

Continuum International Publishing Group
The Tower Building   80 Maiden Lane
11 York Road   Suite 704
London SE1 7NX   New York, NY 10038

www.continuumbooks.com

© Jonathan Boulter 2011

All rights reserved. No part of this publication may be reproduced or transmitted in any form or by any means, electronic or mechanical, including photocopying, recording, or any information storage or retrieval system, without prior permission in writing from the publishers.

Jonathan Boulter has asserted his right under the Copyright, Designs and Patents Act, 1988, to be identified as Author of this work

British Library Cataloguing-in-Publication Data
A catalogue record for this book is available from the British Library.

ISBN: 978-1-4411-2412-8 (hardcover)

Library of Congress Cataloging-in-Publication Data
A catalog record of this book is available from the Library of Congress.

Typeset by Newgen Imaging Systems Pvt Ltd, Chennai, India
Printed and bound in Great Britain

The concept of the archive must inevitably carry in itself, as does every concept, an unknowable weight.

—Derrida, *Archive Fever*

Keep watch over absent meaning.

—Blanchot, *The Writing of the Disaster*

Contents

Acknowledgments	viii
Introduction	1
Chapter 1. Archiving Trauma: Paul Auster	21
Chapter 2. Burying History: Haruki Murakami	59
Chapter 3. Humanizing History: David Mitchell	101
Chapter 4. Archiving Melancholy: José Saramago	140
Conclusion	183
Notes	186
Bibliography	198
Index	204

Acknowledgments

For Mitra Foroutan

My thanks to Rhian Atkin, Anna Klobucka, and David Frier for help at various points in the preparation of this book.

Early versions of parts of Chapters 2 and 4 appeared in *English Studies in Canada* (32.1.2006) and *Genre* (XXXVIII, Number 1–2, Spring–Summer 2005). My thanks to the editors for permission to reprint this work.

Introduction

In mental life nothing which has once been formed can perish.
—Freud, *Civilization and Its Discontents*

Thought cannot welcome that which it bears within itself and which sustains it, except by forgetting.
—Blanchot, *The Writing of the Disaster*

The archive always works, and a priori, against itself.
—Derrida, *Archive Fever: A Freudian Impression*

Preamble

Melancholy and the Archive finds its impetus and inspiration in a series of frustrations. I have been a serious reader of Freud and Derrida for decades; their work, specifically that dealing with ideas of loss, memory, and mourning, has deeply informed my readings of a variety of modern and contemporary writers. It is safe to say that without *Beyond the Pleasure Principle*, "Mourning and Melancholia," *Archive Fever*, or *The Ear of the Other*, I (and of course others) would not have been able to begin to think carefully about the complex protocols of memory and trauma at work in contemporary writing. It is Freud who allows us to begin thinking about how loss, as such, may in fact be an event that defines the subject as subject: without the experience of radical separation from a prior state of narcissistic self-sufficiency (as he suggests in "Mourning and Melancholia") the subject truly has no understanding of the intricacy and necessity of its own finitude. It is Derrida, following from Freud, who allows us to begin thinking about the subject precisely as a site, a topos, of loss. His work, in *The Ear of the Other*, *The Work of Mourning*, and *Specters of Marx* (among others) fashions an image, discomfiting perhaps, of the subject as always already inhabited by its own loss: the subject, in effect, becomes an archive, a site, where loss is maintained and nourished. From Freud and Derrida, thus, I have derived my key terms: melancholy and the archive. But, and here is where my frustration begins, a careful reader of Freud and Derrida will notice that these central terms are never fully worked out or defined in their work. Freud makes it clear that his understanding of the relation between his key terms, mourning and melancholia, is troubled by the fact that he cannot understand how mourning or melancholia, as such, work. To be more precise, Freud admits that he cannot understand the economic mechanism by which the subject breaks free of his or her attachment to the lost object. Mourning works, if it does, if the subject is able to sever her attachment to the lost object: her narcissistic attachment to that lost object is directed elsewhere and thus mourning occurs. Freud, however, is puzzled about how this process works:

> [N]ormal mourning, too, overcomes the loss of the object, and it, too, while it lasts, absorbs all the energies of the ego. Why, then, after it has run its course, is there no hint in its case of the economic condition for a phase of triumph? I find it impossible to answer this objection straight away. It also draws our attention to the fact that we do not even know the economic means by which mourning carries out its task. (Freud 1984, 264–5)

Earlier in his essay Freud has admitted that, in the case of melancholia, a similar (if pathological) process of severing attachment is at work: "We may imagine that the ego is occupied with analogous work during the course of a melancholia; in neither case have we any insight into the economics of the course of events" (262).

A similar process of mystification is at work in Derrida's *Archive Fever*. If Freud is frustrated by the fact that he cannot understand—and thus define—his key terms, Derrida rather blithely admits that he will not offer a definition of the concept of the archive. His task, he maintains, is merely to offer an "impression":

> We have no concept, only an impression, a series of impressions associated with a word. To the rigor of the *concept*, I am opposing here the vagueness or the open imprecision, the relative indetermination of such a *notion*. "Archive" is only a *notion*, an impression associated with a word. (Derrida 1995, 29)

Derrida will offer a justification for his refusal to descend into definition, but even that justification—having to do with allowing the word to stand open to the possibility of the future—leaves the reader with some degree of puzzlement.[1]

And here my task begins. *Melancholy and the Archive*, in some elaborate sense, is an attempt to understand what Freud claims not to understand

and what Derrida refuses to disclose. That is to say, I am attempting, via the work of some central contemporary writers, to understand how, first, the economies of mourning and melancholy work and, second, how these economies relate to a conception of the archive. A central element of my argument is that my fictional and theoretical texts have a crucial dialogical function; that is, I tend to read these authors—Auster, Mitchell, Saramago, and Murakami—not "through" theory but, in essence, "as" theory. It strikes me, and I make these specific arguments in the chapters to follow, that some of these novels stand as acute and uncanny commentary on critical lacunae in Freud or Derrida. The work of art, in my reading, becomes a thought experiment: it asks questions that the scientist and philosopher (can ask but) cannot answer: How does the subject respond to radical loss? How does the process of mourning and melancholy work, economically? What are the implications of the idea that the subject, *in loss*, becomes an archive *of loss*, a site where the memory of loss and trauma is maintained in a kind of crypt? What would this archive look like? These writers of fiction, I argue, give specific, if troubling, answers to these (and other) questions.

The Archive, Melancholy, Disaster

The archive, as traditionally conceived, is a location of knowledge, a place where history itself is housed, where the past is accommodated. The archive is intimately conjoined with cultural memory, with its preservation, perhaps even with its supplementation.[2] Thus, the archive, as Derrida argues in *Archive Fever*, is oriented to, just as it is defined by, a peculiar structure of temporality. We perhaps conceive of the archive as a response, material or affective, to the past, as working toward a preservation of what has been, but Derrida wishes to emphasize the degree to which the archive works authoritatively to mark out the space of beginnings and futurity. In his elaborate reading of Yosef Yerushalmi's *Freud's Moses* (and we need to remember that Derrida's theory of the archive emerges out of a reading of another's reading of the Freudian archive: his theory of the archive thus takes the form of what he might call a "dangerous supplement" to the thoughts of another), he draws our attention to the etymology of the word "archive," noting that the term itself means a place of commandment and commencement. The archive thus operates to assert a kind of juridical control:

> *Arkhe*, we recall, names at once the *commencement* and the *commandment*. The name apparently coordinates two principles in one: the principle

according to nature or history, *there* where things *commence*—physical, historical, or ontological principle—but also the principle according to the law, *there* where men and gods *command*, *there* where authority, social order are exercised, *in this place* from which *order* is given—nomological principle. (Derrida 1995, 1)

Note Derrida's insistence on what we could call the spatial claims of the archive: it is a place—*there, there*, he insists—of geographical, phenomenal, reality; it is a place from which the order of things—let us call it for now the order of history—is governed.[3] I wish to highlight Derrida's emphasis on the spatial reality of the archive: it is a space, a site, a phenomenal presence just as it becomes a temporal and spectral entity. The archive in Auster, Mitchell, Saramago, and Murakami at times marks itself precisely in these material terms: we have libraries (Mitchell), cemeteries (Saramago, Murakami), underground bunkers (Auster), actual texts (Auster, Mitchell, Saramago), all of which function in a specific relation to some conception of the past.

The archive, for Derrida, marks a space of anxiety, precisely, an anxiety about the possibility of loss: the archive exists only as an anticipation (and we note the futurity of this concept) of the loss of history; as such, it works proleptically to preserve what will inevitably be lost. The temporal valence of the archive thus is precisely futural: "the archive takes place at the place of originary and structural breakdown of the said memory" (11). Derrida speaks of the technical archive: "the archive . . . is not only the place for stocking and for conserving an archivable content *of the past* . . . the technical structure of the *archiving* archive also determines the structure of the *archivable* content even in its very coming into existence and in its relationship to the future" (16). It is precisely here, in the anxious relation to what *will be*, that the spectrality of the archive comes into play:

It is a question of the future, the question of the future itself, the question of a response, of a promise and of a responsibility for tomorrow. The archive: if we want to know what that will have meant, we will only know in times to come. Perhaps. Not tomorrow but in times to come, later on or perhaps never. A spectral messianicity is at work in the concept of the archive and ties it, like religion, like history, like science itself, to a very singular experience of the promise. (Derrida 1995, 36)

[T]he structure of the archive is *spectral*. It is spectral *a priori*: neither present nor absent "in the flesh," neither visible nor invisible, a trace always referring to another whose eyes can never be met. (Derrida 1995, 84)

In Derrida's complex reading of Yerushalmi's reading of Freud—in this way setting *Archive Fever* up as a kind of archive of Yerushalmi and Freud—the specter of Freud is instantiated (like the *arkon*) as an authority, but a spectral authority, a phantom to which Yerushalmi (and Derrida) orient their own temporal positions of coming *after*: after the Father, indebted to the Father, working perhaps to assert their own archiving gesture of authority over the figure who cannot be effaced. This "impossible archaeology" (85) of return can only figure history within a logic of the spectral inasmuch as the origin is both past but uncannily, and insistently, always returning as the trace (of the trace). We note here how Derrida shifts from emphasizing—at least etymologically—the phenomenal reality of the archive (it is a *place, there*) to a reading that insists on its inevitable spectrality. The archive is neither present nor absent in time: it perhaps will never be present; it is no longer, or ever was, a material entity, neither present nor absent *in the flesh*.[4]

I, too, wish to emphasize the spectral quality of the archive in what follows. And I begin by suggesting that while the subject in these fictional texts does move within and through the material archive—libraries, cemeteries, wells—he himself is continually marked as the archive: the subject, in other words, becomes the archive. And he becomes an archive specifically inasmuch as he becomes melancholic, in the Freudian sense of the term. In "Mourning and Melancholia," Freud attempts to come to an understanding of how the subject deals with trauma and loss. There are, he theorizes, two responses to loss, to the loss of a loved one, or the "loss of some abstraction that has taken the place of one, such as one's country, liberty, an ideal, or so on" (252). The first, and most healthy, is what he calls mourning. Mourning is a process by which the loss is comprehended and accepted, "worked through," to use his terminology. Mourning is the "normal" way one must deal with trauma and loss, with what Freud beautifully terms the "economics of pain" (252). Precisely how the subject overcomes loss is, as we recall, not known by Freud. It is a difficult process—it is "work"—but eventually the subject accepts that the loved one, with whom the subject may have identified, is no longer here to make claims on the subject. Melancholia, on the other hand, is an abnormal response to loss and situates the subject in a continual position of narcissistic identification with the lost object. In other words, the melancholy subject cannot accept that her loved one is, in fact, gone and works pathologically "to establish an *identification* of the ego with the abandoned object" (258). What this means is that the past—loss, trauma—continually works its way into the present moment because the subject cannot move past it. More troubling is the idea that the subject does not *wish* to allow loss to recede into history but desires continually to maintain a connection to the traumatic moment. In some ways the subject maintains this pathological state—which may, in fact, not be so pathological after all—because the traumatic moment is important for her, may, in fact, have shaped who she is.[5] In *The Ego and the Id*, in fact, Freud notes that melancholia may structure the ego itself: the incorporation of the lost object "has a great share in determining the form taken by the ego and [. . .] makes an essential contribution towards building up what is called its 'character'" (368). In *The Psychic Life of Power*, Judith Butler glosses Freud's notion: "[I]dentifications formed from unfinished grief are the modes in which the lost object is incorporated and phantasmatically preserved in and as the ego" (132). She suggests that Freud's position toward melancholia has shifted—Butler suggests he "reverses" (133) his position—between "Mourning and Melancholia" (1917) and *The Ego and the Id* (1923). She suggests that between these essays lies a reversal of Freud's attitude toward the overcoming of grief: in the earlier essay, grief is overcome by breaking attachments to the lost object; in the later essay, Butler suggests, Freud leaves open the possibility that melancholia may itself be a way of overcoming grief precisely in that the subject lets the lost object go by identifying with it. Butler's reading of Freud is intriguing, but I think she overstates matters here for the sake of strengthening her claims on melancholia's centrality. Freud has not "reversed" positions here so much as widened his range, to borrow his own phrase (367). Melancholia, for Freud, is never a means to overcoming grief: mourning is always his favored means to work through loss. The identification and incorporation of the lost object is a kind of narcissistic sublimation of loss: Butler would have us believe that sublimation and mourning are identical categories.

We can here turn again briefly to Derrida and his reading of melancholia in *The Ear of the Other* to clarify Freud's position on the centrality of the lost object to the melancholic subject. Here, drawing on the work of Freud, as well as Abraham and Torok, Derrida offers an image of melancholia that is uncannily fleshy; it is an image of history as a kind of viral, material presence, working its way into the body of the melancholy subject, who becomes, in its turn, a kind of cryptological archive; it is an image, I wish to suggest, particularly suited to a reading of certain of our authors:

> Not having been taken back inside the self, digested, assimilated as in all "normal" mourning, the dead object remains like a living dead abscessed in a specific spot in the ego. It has its place, just like a crypt in a cemetery or temple, surrounded by walls and all the rest. The dead object is incorporated in this crypt—the term "incorporated" signaling precisely

that one has failed to digest or assimilate it totally, so that it remains there, forming a pocket in the mourning body. The incorporated dead, which one has not really managed to take upon oneself, continues to lodge there like something other and to ventrilocate through the "living." (Derrida 1988, 57–8)

Here, in Derrida's image of the encrypted, now archived, subject, history speaks; history, more precisely, speaks through the subject from within the subject, fashioning the subject as *subject to* history just as it becomes the *subject of* history. As crypt, as archive ventrilocated by history, the subject begins to offer itself as a site to be heard, to be read, to be interpreted. And as such, as speaking archive, the subject offers itself to the reader—the reader who becomes now a kind of tomb raider—to be analyzed, more precisely, psychoanalyzed.

Melancholy and the Archive is a form of cultural psychoanalysis in the sense that it offers a reading of texts that reflect symptomatically various cultures' desires and anxieties about the role of the archive, of the subject as (uncanny) archive. I am using the notion of culture here to refer both to the national origins of the writers (American, English, Portuguese, Japanese) but also, crucially, to their place within a generalized global economy of melancholia (defined, via my reading of Freud's topography of melancholia, as a kind of historical nostalgia for what *has been*, what has been *lost*). But I am intrigued to notice how the subject—the self; his/her interiority—is often placed under some kind of threat even as she pursues the ideal of the archive, pursues, that is, some measure by which to preserve her history, her historical consciousness. Contemporary novelists offer analyses of the phenomenal archive (houses, crypts, holes, vaults, open spaces) and thus reify the very object within which memory—and history—itself is continually erased. It is here that these authors confirm Derrida's most troubling ideas about the archive: the archive is not the site of the preservation of the past, of history, of memory, but of the inevitable loss of these things. The archive thus is doubly inflected by loss: it is a response to loss—we build memorials to loss, to trauma; the subject remembers and, melancholically, becomes that loss—and it anticipates, perhaps creates, the conditions of future loss:

> The archive, if this word or this figure can be stabilized so as to take on a signification, will never be either memory or anamnesis as spontaneous, alive and internal experience. On the contrary: the archive takes place at the place of originary and structural breakdown of said memory. (Derrida 1995, 11)

My sense here is that this dynamic—a fascination with the idea of the real archive combined with an acute anxiety about how the self can respond ethically, really, to the demands of history—is the central trope in contemporary fiction, a trope, moreover, that urgently requires extended analysis.[6]

Disaster and the Archive

Derrida's sense that the archive takes place at the moment of the erasure of history—at the site where the archive loses its claims to maintaining history by reproducing history—is a crucial aspect to what follows in my analysis.[7] A simple way to express this is to say that the archive—be it material or affective (the subject as archive)—is continually calling itself into question. The archive defines itself by interrogating what it is doing with and to history; the archive defines itself by interrogating the claims of history on the subject. This is to say that if the archive is defined by a doubly inflected loss—the loss in the past, the loss to come—then the archive is marked, if not defined, by its specific relation to the *disaster*. And here I turn to my third thinker, Maurice Blanchot. Blanchot's *The Writing of the Disaster* (1995) is a crucial text in the analyses that follow; crucial for its contribution to thinking about what remains after loss; crucial for its thinking about what loss does to the subject; crucial, precisely, for its thinking about how subjectivity or interiority is mapped out—indeed, it offers itself as a cartographic, archivic space—after trauma. Moreover, Blanchot's text compels us to begin thinking about the *writing* of the disaster—disaster's writing—in relation to the specific workings of textuality in these novels. We need to keep in mind that these texts do not merely thematize loss: often, that loss is figured precisely as part of the impetus to writing itself. Auster's characters are all writers, for instance, as are Saramago's Raimundo Silva (*The History of the Siege of Lisbon*) and Ricardo Reis (*The Year of the Death of Ricardo Reis*); Mitchell's *Cloud Atlas* directly thematizes the relation of writing to the disaster (in fact, the central narrative, "Sloosha's Crossin' an' Ev'rythin' After," explicitly explores the relation between the disaster and its archiving in memory and story); Murakami's *Underground*, finally, is an overt attempt to represent the aftereffects of disaster in the archival form of the personal testimony. What I am interested in exploring here, with Blanchot, is his sense that the disaster produces some kind of shift—covert or otherwise—in the subject's sense of his or her interiority: the disaster, in Blanchot's sense, may in fact, rupture the subject's ability to stand in ethical relation to history, to the past. This is to say that the disaster fractures the archival possibility for the subject: he cannot any longer stand to history as witness or memorial, cannot, that is, become the workable archive, because his interiority, his sense that there is a space for history, for the event of history, is no longer continuous or stable. I wish here to quote a passage from *The Writing of the Disaster* that plays a key role in my thinking about the various forms of post-traumatized subjectivities in *Melancholy and the Archive*:

> Levinas speaks of the subjectivity of the subject. If one wishes to use this word—why? but why not?—one ought perhaps to speak of a *subjectivity without any subject*: the wounded space, the hurt of the dying, the already dead body which no one could ever own, or ever say of it, *I, my body.* (Blanchot 1995, 30)

It is my argument in what follows that this idea, subjectivity without any subject (*subjectivite sans sujet*), is particularly useful for thinking about the subject as he begins to negotiate a relationship to his memory, his history; specifically, as the subject negotiates a relationship to a disastrous history, to a past marked by loss and trauma, the subject becomes more than merely an individual reflecting on a particular kind of economy of tragic loss. The disaster, as I have said, produces some shift in the psyche, in the self, in the interiority of the subject, to the point where the subject finds himself to have become a trace of what he was, a cinder marking the passing of the disaster. We can see a variety of versions of this idea: Mitchell's *Ghostwritten*, for instance, tracks and traces the passage of a single consciousness through a variety of temporary subjects. This core consciousness is a precise, and uncanny, version of the idea of subjectivity without any subject: the consciousness has those things that mark it as a subject—memory, emotion, history—but it cannot attach fully to the human, to *a* human. As such, it remains a free-floating consciousness searching for an anchored subject. In an altogether different register, Saramago will thematize the idea of subjectivity without any subject in his analysis of the figure of Ricardo Reis, a heteronym of another writer (Fernando Pessoa) who Saramago creates as a character and chooses to animate; Reis, however, is never fully present to himself as a subject: he is merely an assumed personality—twice assumed, actually—with no claim on his own experience. Murakami, again in another register, offers an analysis of Aum Shinrikyo cult members (*Underground*) that makes clear that the cult member is precisely another version of Blanchot's traumatized individual: the cult member is not fully present to her or himself but has given up his self to a consciousness that precedes and exceeds his own. How, Murakami asks, can we understand this peculiar entity of the cult member except as someone who has forfeited any claims to being responsible as a fully integrated subject?

All of these examples of subjectivity without any subject play out against the backdrop of history, all are formed as the subject enters into the space of the disastrous event. My question thus becomes: how can a radically decentered subject respond to history? What happens to history, to the event of the disastrous past, when it only produces a decentered subject? My real question is obviously this one: what happens to the real of history if it only produces shattered subjectivities incapable of responding to the past in any coherent way? And here I can turn, briefly, back to my quotation from Blanchot and note that this subjectivity without any subject is described as being a *wounded space* (*la place blessee*). This peculiar, traumatized, fractured sensibility becomes explicitly materialized, spatialized, in contemporary literature. If subjectivity—the self's sense of what or who she is—is an immaterial process or function (call it mental or spiritual), what we find in these novels is a tendency to reify or materialize that process: subjectivity becomes material, becomes spatialized, becomes a wounded space, or a space of the wound. I am emphasizing this word *wound* (Blanchot's adjective *blessee* follows from the French for wound, *blessure*), because the word means "trauma": a traumatized space is one continually marked by its relation to the disaster that preceded it and provided its foundations and ground. A traumatized space, in other words, is always already a space of melancholy. We will see in what follows how subjectivity is materialized, finds its expression within, various spaces of melancholy, and we will attempt, as we observe how these spaces become archival, to make sense of the aporia at the heart of this process: the disaster produces a subject radically at ontological odds with itself; and yet that fractured subject, that subjectivity without any subject, becomes archival or projects an archival sensibility onto spaces surrounding him. How can the archive function in relation to damaged subjectivities? How can the archive be thought of as itself a damaged interiority?[8]

I want to begin to point to answers to these questions—questions more fully fleshed out in my chapters—by attempting to connect the Derridean reading of the archive with Blanchot's understanding of the nature of the disaster. In some ways the simplest beginning point is to notice that the archive and the disaster have similar energies and temporalities. The disaster, as Blanchot writes in the first sentence of *The Writing of the Disaster*, "ruins everything" (1), but that ruination is not available to the subject, cannot be known:

> There is no reaching the disaster. Out of reach is he whom it threatens, whether from afar or close up, it is impossible to say: the infiniteness of the threat has in some way broken every limit. We are on the edge of

disaster without being able to situate it in the future: it is rather always already past, and yet we are on the edge or under the threat, all formulations which would imply the future—that which is yet to come—if the disaster were not that which does not come, that which has put a stop to every arrival. (Blanchot 1995, 1)

We might, given the contortions of Blanchot's thinking here, add his theory of the disaster to our list of initiatory frustrations: the disaster ruins everything, but cannot be known; the disaster has always already occurred, yet is always already out of reach; the disaster, he writes later, is the experience that "none can undergo" (120). My own reading of the Blanchotian disaster relates it to Derrida's idea of the impossible event: the impossible, he notes in texts as various as "Force of Law," "As If It Were Possible," or "Nietzsche and the Machine," is an event that is unquantifiable, undecidable, aporetically conflictual, yet (ethically) unavoidable. The impossible thus links up with concepts that Derrida considers "undeconstructible" like justice, hospitality, friendship. The disaster, inasmuch as it "occurs" in an impossible temporality—it has happened; it is always about to occur—and inasmuch as it impinges on every aspect of the subject—defines the subject as a post-traumatic subjectivity without any subject—is another idea or figure that cannot be avoided but forever remains at the limits of thought.

Derrida's own thinking about the archive, in many ways, is disastrous, in Blanchot's sense of the term. The archive, like the disaster, is situated in an aporetic, or at least double, temporality: it is about the preservation of the past, and yet its full ontology, its true ontology, is futural. Moreover, for Derrida, the archive's function is not preservative or conservative, but is a destructive, ruinous one: the archive, he writes, articulates itself on and as the very possibility of its own destruction. How does Derrida get to this idea? From Freud. Derrida, following a reading of Freud's notion of the death drive in *Beyond the Pleasure Principle*, sees a similar economy of the death drive at work in the archive. If, as Freud maintains, the death drive—that drive he is forced to hypothesize given the human's inerrant taste for destruction—functions in the logic of repetition (we repeat unconsciously acts that are harmful to us or give displeasure), Derrida posits that this repetition feeds into the a priori desire for the archive. The archive, in other words, stands as a site of the repetition of the disaster of history. Thus, Derrida's most important observation:

> If there is no archive without consignation in an *external place* which assures the possibility of memorization, of repetition, of reproduction, or

of reimpression, then we must also remember that repetition itself, the logic of repetition, indeed the repetition compulsion, remains, according to Freud, indissociable from the death drive. And thus from destruction. Consequence: right on that which permits and conditions archivization, we will never find anything other than that which exposes to destruction, and in truth menaces with destruction, introducing, *a priori*, forgetfulness and the archiviolithic into the heart of the monument. Into the "by heart" itself. The archive always works, and *a priori*, against itself. (Derrida 1995, 11–12)

If we read Derrida's notion of the archive together with Blanchot's idea of the inevitable effect of the disaster on the subject, we can begin to see how complicated the figure of the archive, the subject-as-archive, becomes in contemporary fiction, fiction that is obsessed with the need to figure the subject precisely as the site for history, for the event of history. In contemporary fiction, there is, to state it baldly, a thematization of a desire to negotiate a relation with history. That desire presupposes at least two things: one, that the event as such has occurred; two, the subject must find a site, be it within himself or some externalized material location, for that history to be archived. This desire, however, is continually threatened by precisely the ideas that Derrida and Blanchot articulate: the archive, as such, is an impossibility; the subject, as such, is an impossibility.[9] And yet, the desire, which now is fully realized as a melancholic attachment to an impossible idea of history, persists, despite itself, perhaps *to* spite itself. This aporia—history must be preserved; history cannot be preserved—is what defines the project of the novelists I study here; this aporia, moreover, is precisely that which defines the project of the archive, *all archival projects*, as indissociably and forever, melancholic.

Auster, Mitchell, Saramago, Murakami

No choice of the object of study is an arbitrary one. The authors analyzed here are, in my estimation, four of the most important writers currently working. Their collective list of awards is perhaps testimony enough to their importance, as is the influence their work wields on other writers.[10] I have chosen them for reasons of recognition and influence but also because there is an uncanny link binding their work together. That is to say, I believe that when read together, the work of these writers speaks to a large, and needless to say, international, concern with issues of loss, memory, subjectivity, and the archive. In some ways this work speaks to Pierre Nora's claim that we inhabit a time obsessed with the idea of the archive. As Pierre Nora suggests, we live in an archival culture: "No society has ever produced archives as deliberately as our own, not only by volume, not only by new technical means of reproduction and preservation, but also by its superstitious esteem, by its veneration of the trace" ("Between History and Memory". 13). Nora is, in 1984, speaking of contemporary French culture, but his idea resonates out, in terms of geography and time: the idea of the archive, as a site of memory, of memory's supplementation, is perhaps the central trope in contemporary literature and philosophy. Nora, of course, is suspicious of the archive's claim on memory, of the archive's tendency to eradicate memory's strength: "Memory has been wholly absorbed by its meticulous reconstitution. Its new vocation is to record; delegating to the archive the responsibility of remembering, it sheds its signs upon depositing them there, as a snake sheds its skin" (13). The archive, in other words, is a threat to memory, to a kind of organic relation to history. Nora, in some ways wholly in agreement with Derrida's reading of the destructive capacities of the archive, wishes to call attention to what is lost in the archive, in the process of archivization, but he also wishes to alert us to what exceeds the archive: "Record as much as you can," he writes, "but something will remain." (14)[11] Something exceeds the archive, remains after the archive is closed. It is precisely this remainder, this lost kernel of the Real (to inflect this idea through Lacan for one moment) that concerns our writers. This lost kernel of the Real is the indivisible remainder of history, of the event: that aspect of the experience of history that cannot be accommodated within the traditional structure of either the archive as material topos (library, museum) or the immaterial topos of the subject-as-archive. Blanchot puts it thusly: "The disaster, unexperienced. It is what escapes the very possibility of experience—it is the limit of writing" (7). It is the indivisible remainder of history, of the experience of the impossible event of loss, which transforms the subject as he responds to its traumatic claims on him: he thus becomes, as we have discussed, Blanchot's subjectivity without subject, an archival affect without archive. It is this remainder (of history, of subjectivity), what Heidegger may call the placeholder (*Platzhalter*) of Nothingness, which must in some ways, at all cost, be accommodated, somehow, must somehow be given a place, a site, a home.[12]

I am fascinated by the very fact that this process of accommodating that which cannot be accommodated in the archive finds expression in such a wide variety of authors, from such a wide variety of cultural and national backgrounds. What does it say about contemporary ideas about history, about the subject's relationship to history, that the anxiety of the archive,

Derrida's *mal d'archive*, finds expression in American, Japanese, Portuguese, and British writings? Or in French and German psychoanalysis and philosophy? That history's claims are universal (essential)? That melancholia is a globalized phenomenon or condition? That the subject qua subject is always already fully melancholic at the moment he remembers? I am prepared to stand beside these universalist, even essentialist, claims (even though such claims perhaps are threatened by the general inflection of my prevailing theoretical influences [Blanchot, Derrida]) on the condition that we note that the various authors' responses to history are, at first, responses to a localized, or what appears to be a localized, condition. Thus, Saramago, in *The Year of the Death of Ricardo Reis* and *The History of the Siege of Lisbon* inflects his reading of the archive through a specific cultural context (Lisbon, historical and contemporary); Murakami's *Underground* and *The Wind-Up Bird Chronicle* can only have been written against the background of the Japanese view of the nature of the catastrophe (Aum Shinrikyo; the build-up to the Second World War); Auster's view of the archive, while perhaps less overtly dependent upon an historical long-view, is articulated against a specifically American backdrop; Mitchell perhaps presents the strongest case for a universalist (or a desire for a universalist) view of things: *Ghostwritten* takes place over a variety of countries, within a variety of national subjects; *number9dream* is set in Japan and features a Japanese protagonist; *Cloud Atlas*, again like *Ghostwritten*, unfolds over a sprawling and global vision of history and geography. For Mitchell, the idea of the archive, and archive fever as such, are always already global phenomena.

But what precisely does this claim to a globalized economy of the archive mean? It means, first, that the subject as such, as he responds to history, is always already something other than the (fantasy of) the fully integrated humanist subject.[13] That is, if we follow the implications of Derrida's and Blanchot's thinking, the relation to history, the response to history's unbearable claims (to witness, to record, to archive), is one that always defines the subject as merely an effect of history and never one fully present to himself. What this shattered subject(ivity) can offer to the archive, *as the archive*, is never the event itself, never history as such, but history's specter: "*When all is said, what remains to be said is the disaster. Ruin of words, demise writing*," as Blanchot puts it (33). The writer of the disaster, the *written* of the disaster—the subject of disaster's writing—will always be in the condition of ruin, the trace. And it is here that I can make my strongest claim to a (paradoxical) universalism or essentialism. My reading of these novels does confirm the idea that in contemporary international fiction the subject can never be, can never even hope to be, an integrated self-coincidental entity:

the archival subject—and this is the term for the main "characters" of all these novels—stands as a stark negation of the humanist claims for subjectivity as such. And this gives rise to my paradox: the archival subject (nonintegrated, nonself-coincidental) is a universal subject; there is, in other words, a universalizing antihumanism in all of the works of these writers. The archival subject is universal, but this in itself is not an essentialist claim because this subject can never rise to the condition of the "essence" as such: the archival subject is an *essential nonessentialist* subject. My responsibility here is to think through the implications of this version of interiority as it plays out against and within its international representation. What are, I ask, the implications of the idea that the contemporary subject is without "essence," is without that which we (perhaps still insist) articulates him as subject? If, as we perhaps still claim, the subject is the product of his/her experience, what happens when the idea of "experience," as such, is detonated within the disaster?

Melancholy and the Archive is divided into four chapters. In the first, I analyze three recent novels from Paul Auster: *The Book of Illusions* (2002), *Oracle Night* (2003), and *Travels in the Scriptorium* (2007). My concern here will be to explore how Auster will represent the archive as a phenomenological, real space in which memory is housed yet perpetually threatened with erasure. I think here, for instance, of the role of the Bureau of Historical Preservation in *Oracle Night*, a space clearly reminiscent of the Freudian conception of the unconscious: here, a character, Nick Bowen, is able to find traces of a past history, yet this discovery can only confirm that his present existence will inevitably, and in its turn, become only a trace of itself. In our reading of Auster we must also consider that narrative itself always functions as a kind of (compromised) archive: *Travels in the Scriptorium* certainly functions in this way, offering itself as it does as a site where memories (of trauma, loss, guilt) are represented and preserved but in the most provisional, tentative ways; *The Book of Illusions*, with its concern with the archival potential of film, neatly ties the question of narrative to other media, suggesting a desire to displace the weakness of traditional narrative onto other (inevitably vitiated) forms. Indeed, Auster asks a series of acute questions: What *would* the most effective archive look like? Can narrative—discourse open to shaping, displacement, distortion—ever offer itself as a viable space where trauma—and the *memory* of trauma—is preserved? Auster's real focus in all his novels is the specific relation between narrative—story telling—and interiority, how narratives work to shore up a sense of the fading self. We will see this trope at play in all the novels under scrutiny here. Ultimately, however, I am concerned with tracing how, for Auster, the archive—a place where history and the self is believed to be preserved—inevitably and repeatedly *fails*: the self will find it has lost its history even in the attempt to communicate that very history (*Oracle Night*, *The Book of Illusions*); narrative will only ever be revealed as a deliberate fantasy, working to displace unbearable historical truths (*Travels in the Scriptorium*). In precise ways Auster suggests that history can never itself be witnessed successfully and that all our attempts to preserve the historical sense—and the attempt must be made; there is no ethical choice *not* to act as impossible witness—stand as compromised testimony to a complex, and melancholy, failure.

In my second chapter I analyze four texts by Haruki Murakami: *Hard-Boiled Wonderland and the End of the World* (1991), *The Wind-Up Bird Chronicle* (1997), *Underground* (2000), and *after the quake* (2002). Murakami's work represents a fascinating counterpoint to my other novelists for a number of reasons, not the least being that one of his works under scrutiny is nominally nonfictional. *Underground* emerges from Murakami's fascination with the 1995 Aum Shinrikyo gas attacks in Tokyo and testifies to his interest in the twinned economies of trauma and memory; specifically, *Underground* emerges as a text, insofar as it is made up of interviews with victims and terrorists, *itself* functioning as an archive and thus as an ethical attempt to preserve some memory of history. I pair *Underground* with a reading of *after the quake*, arguing that both texts attempt to find the narrative means to archive, to represent, trauma and guilt. Ultimately, I wish to suggest that both texts share a similar economy of guilt: the archival representation of trauma can only be a guilty one inasmuch as representation displaces, perhaps violently, the Real of trauma. Similar economies of the archive are at work in other texts: characters themselves will offer complex archived responses to various traumas, from earthquakes (*after the quake*), to the savagery of war (*The Wind-Up Bird Chronicle*), to real or imagined apocalypse (*Hard-Boiled Wonderland and the End of the World*). What emerges in all of Murakami's texts is a sense that the archive—be it a human, a (psycho-)geographical location, an architectural structure—is always a spectral site, a ghostly zone where history is preserved in a fluctuating, fluid, yet *inevitably returning* form. In Murakami, the archive—be it the archive of memory or the material, psychogeographical archives in the material, real world—functions as a space where history, spectralized, yet insistently here, nostalgically returns, and will never be effaced, despite the desire precisely for this forgetting. This is Murakami's paradox: the archive functions as space into which trauma is displaced in order for it to be erased; inevitably, however, the archive cannot—will not—erase history and thus that which must be mourned, if not forgotten (trauma, loss, pain), asserts itself insistently as a radical form of *psychic debt*. In this way Murakami's work confirms Derrida's idea that the archive is always doubly spectral, a melancholic space where ghosts are housed and desire agonizingly and perpetually accommodated in its perpetual return.

Chapter Three offers a reading of three David Mitchell novels. Although I will obviously treat each of Mitchell's novels separately, tracing their individual complexities, ironies, and displacements, I will argue that there is a common thread linking them all. Mitchell's *Ghostwritten* (1999), *number9-dream* (2001), and *Cloud Atlas* (2004) all figure the subject, the self, as itself a kind of archive: the self becomes an unknowing/unknowable archive precisely as he or she "becomes" memory; that is, we often see an uncanny image of the human subject as virally infected by history, by memory, by the memory of trauma and loss, to the point where individual interiority is radically threatened with erasure. These novels, in various ways, are precisely about how historical traumas are transmitted from person to person without any necessary connection between subjects. I think here, for instance, of how the individual narratives in *Ghostwritten* are linked by spectral, ghostly fragments of discourse, how one line or phrase from one story is virally present in another; or, for instance, how, again, the individual narratives of *Cloud Atlas* form an architectural model of linked experiences: each narrative folds into and blends with the others. In this way *Cloud Atlas* conceives of itself, offers itself, as an architectural model of the archive preserving past and future histories. Through his various texts, Mitchell seems to argue that history has a kind of inevitability to it. Because of these structural, architectural linkages, the novels argue that history *will* be communicated, *must* be communicated, and that the human subject—as she becomes history's unwitting archive—is merely (but we need to consider carefully the resonance of this word) a site for its expression. Precisely, I am concerned here with demonstrating how melancholy—an inability to remove oneself from trauma and loss, from history *itself*—is conferred upon the subject, forced onto the subject, and I wish to analyze how the self negotiates a space for her own agency in the face of this compelled indebtedness to the past, to what Nietzsche calls the "greatest weight" of history.

My fourth and final chapter presents an analysis of three novels by José Saramago. In one way or another, Saramago has always been concerned with the weight of and indebtedness to history and thus, within the Freudian economy of loss, Saramago's works have always been about the "logic" (this word takes on a specific meaning here) of melancholy. We see the theme of the melancholy weight of history played out in *The Year of the Death of Ricardo*

Reis (1991), *The History of the Siege of Lisbon* (1996), and *All the Names* (1997). Saramago's deeply challenging novels work to suggest that while the individual must negotiate a real relation to history, must, that is, offer a response to the call of history (and in Saramago this is always an ethical response and responsibility), the individual always stands in for, perhaps speaks for, larger cultural and ideological concerns: these concerns—displacing the facts of history consciously and deliberately (*The History of the Siege of Lisbon*); imagining the historical reality of events even in the face of contrary accounts (*All the Names*)—in some crucial ways precede and exceed the subject, rendering him irrelevant to the passage of the very histories he witnesses or creates (a central theme in *The Year of the Death of Ricardo Reis*). I am fascinated by Saramago's suggestion that the archive is more than simply a geographic location, more than the space of memory within an individual, but that the archive is fully and finally *virtual*. That is to say, Saramago is careful to examine how history has no location separate from its Imaginary representation in the various interiorities of its subjects: simultaneously, however, this Imaginary space is represented as always already evacuated of essential presence or truth, evacuated, more precisely, of all *potential* claims to truth. (Saramago and Mitchell, although vastly dissimilar in tone, share a theoretical concern here). *All the Names* in some ways provides the sharpest analysis of the Imaginary archive, as it is here that we see how one man, Senhor José, a clerk in the labyrinthine General Registry, is brought to grief by his insistent imagining of a possible history of a *dead* woman. My reading of Saramago will extend my analyses of the spectral nature of the archive that we find in Murakami and Auster into a consideration of how *spectral and virtual* archives paradoxically become spaces where *real* ethical, political, and religious concerns are played out.

I am fascinated by the implications of how and where the archived is situated in these authors' works. It is my argument that the various locations of the archive—real space, imaginary space, subjective space—need to be analyzed individually as themselves revealing crucial aspects of each narratives' "reading" of the economy of the archive. Murakami's choice to locate the archive within the earth itself (for example, in *The Wind-Up Bird Chronicle*) speaks to a sense that archive has a kind of chthonic logic and appeal: the earth can be the only appropriate place for the (hidden) archive because geography, the land itself, has an authority that precedes and exceeds that of the human subject. Murakami's analysis of the archive thus has a kind of ecological resonance that suggests that the archive's place of commandment and commencement (as Derrida puts it) has a natural authority. Auster, by contrast, inevitably chooses to materialize the archive within human-constructed spaces like bunkers (*Oracle Night*), rooms (*Travels in the Scriptorium*), or the material site of film (*The Book of Illusions*). I am interested in the cultural differences between, here, Murakami and Auster: both materialize the archive, but each chooses different sites with vastly different cultural resonances within which to house the archive. I wish to suggest that Auster's materialization of the archive within human-constructed spaces—or human-produced texts like film—indicates a desire to control the economy and shape of the archive, to assert a kind of mastery over the shape history can take; Murakami, by contrast, clearly offers the possibility that history is a force—in Hegel's sense—that cannot be controlled as such, certainly not by human agency.

Mitchell and Saramago, on the other hand, in some ways stand as the metaphysicians in this analysis. Both figure the archive within spaces not immediately recognizable as material or geographic. Mitchell wishes, over the course of his novels, to work out a complex relationship between history and the manner of history's transmission: that is, he works to suggest that the text—novel, written historical document—is only the initial site of history's archiving. The textual location and representation of history is often overwritten in favor of locating history—and history's *effect*—within the "space" of human consciousness itself; this consciousness, moreover, can, in its turn, be transmitted and translated to others. It is for this reason—that the archive of history moves from the material to the immaterial—that I wish to examine Mitchell's archives as (complex and perhaps even paradoxical) forms of psychogeography: the topography of the archive becomes the topography of the mind. And indeed, Saramago's novels share a similar economy; and this similarity suggests fascinating connections between contemporary British and Portuguese responses to the burdens of history. Saramago, like Mitchell, moves the "house" of history from the material to the Imaginary realm (most brilliantly in *All the Names*): Saramago's texts argue that the material archive—the book, the real archive—is simply not a fully viable location for history as such. I am interested in exploring the possible reasons why both Mitchell and Saramago—as Europeans—feel that the text as such, the archive as such (library or bureaucratic office), is not able to house history effectively or safely. It strikes me that in Mitchell and Saramago we have a complicated, nuanced valorization of the human as archive, a return to (a kind of) humanism: where Auster and Murakami consistently figure the human as the site of failure to maintain history (hence history's materialization in the real space of earth, rooms, bunkers, film), Mitchell and Saramago see the human—its consciousness—as the only space for the archive, for history. And yet, for all this, the archival project must, according to Derrida, remain a failure: "the archive," we must recall, "always works, and *a priori*, against itself." My argument here, however, must be that if the archival project remains a failure, it is an enormously productive failure. These authors have produced massively complicated archival responses to the debts and burdens of history. Our task, as we sift through the cinders of the disastrous archive, is to acknowledge the persistence, the inevitability, of the experience of the event of history, the experience of loss, if only in the compromised, spectral form of the archival trace. Our reading of the trace, in its turn an archival gesture, may find its authority questioned by the aporetic conditions of its own possibility; but this aporia, the attempt to comprehend the archive in its condition of impossibility, must be, to borrow once more and finally from Derrida, our response and our responsibility.

Chapter 1

Archiving Trauma: Paul Auster

And each lost thing—a memory of what has never been.
—Auster, *Effigies*

In his 1917 essay "Mourning and Melancholia," a work that is the inspiration for a great number of contemporary discussions of trauma and mourning, Freud makes a startling, though perhaps not unexpected, admission: he does not understand how mourning works. Freud admits, several times in fact, that the mechanism of mourning, what he calls "the economics of pain" (252), remains unknown and that he therefore must warn against "any overestimation of the value of our conclusions" (251). Toward the end of the essay, Freud states bluntly: "we do not even know the economic means by which mourning carries out its task" (265). It seems thus that the effects of the process of mourning can be observed but the process itself, the means by which loss is incorporated and metabolized, cannot be known. Freud's essay is profoundly ambivalent, testifying as it does to the fact that something unknowable is at work in the very process the essay wishes to anatomize. Moreover, this unknowability is transparently mapped onto the essay itself, transforming "Mourning and Melancholia" into an almost perfect narrative mirror of the process it wishes, but fails, to comprehend. And, of course, it is possible to radicalize Freud's ambivalence. Despite the fact that mourning, as characterized by Freud, *does work*, does allow the subject to overcome loss, the repeated assertion that the work of mourning cannot be understood *as such* suggests that mourning, successful mourning, is a desired illusion. That is to say, Freud raises the issue of the unknowability of the process of mourning while simultaneously effacing that unknowability by valorizing the end, the desirable effects, of that process: the end of mourning, in other words, is predicated on (and predicted by) an absence, an unknowable space, from which successful mourning turns and melancholy incessantly (and nostalgically) returns.

Freud's description of mourning grants the difficulty of the process of overcoming loss—he speaks of its "great expense of time and cathectic energy" (253)—but posits the normalcy of the process as opposed to the "pathological disposition" (252) of the melancholic. Freud's repeated gestures towards the normalcy of mourning speaks to a deep ambivalence—here in the true psychoanalytical sense of the term—about mourning, as does the fact that the process itself cannot be known: how can normalcy be based on an unknowability unless unknowability is transformed into a principle of (healthy) subjectivity? That is to say, what Freud seems to be suggesting here is that the subject, who will inevitably experience loss, cannot understand itself even and especially through its most profound experiences: the experience of mourning is thus always a *failure* in the sense that it begs the question of its own results. Or, to put it in slightly different terms, Freud cannot anatomize the process of mourning because the process (of mourning) always fails. The energy of Freud's essay is precisely the result of his refusal to confront the fact that mourning may be an illusion: what he emphasizes is the *unknowability* of the process of mourning, not the fact that mourning may actually not work. Moreover, this ambivalence about mourning's effectiveness is a symptom of Freud's unconscious acknowledgement that mourning, as a working-through of past history, is not a proper ethical—or epistemological—response to trauma. The melancholic, she, who Freud admits, "has a keener eye for the truth than other people who are not melancholic" (255), represents the (aporetically) ideal ethical position vis á vis the historical past. In other words, Freud's ambivalence about mourning can be read as his refusal ethically to accept the process of forgetting that mourning must, if effective, facilitate. The economy of Freudian psychoanalysis, ostensibly working toward a management of the traumas of the past, working that is toward an eventual erasure of the past—or at least its resonance—is at explicit odds with Freud's own sense, repeatedly demonstrated, that the past truly is inescapable, that it truly does articulate the subject *as* subject. It is in this sense that we can characterize the entire Freudian project as melancholic, valorizing as it does the necessity of maintaining a link to the past in order to uncover the "truth" of the subject. I read Freud's ambivalence about the knowability of the process of mourning as a tacit admission that the process *as such* cannot serve to reveal the true link between the subject and the trauma that defines her. That is, if the goal of psychoanalysis is knowledge of history—and the subject's relation to that history—mourning as such cannot *be* known and, crucially, it erases the traces of its therapeutic process, thereby erasing its epistemological value as a source of historical knowledge. Melancholia, on the other hand, because it maintains in clear relief the trajectory and traces of the subject's trauma, explicitly serves to delineate and *make known* the (historical) subject to herself.

As an entry point into these late Auster novels, I wish thus to ask a simple question: How does mourning occur? That is to say, how does one overcome loss? Paul Auster's late novels are remorselessly, relentlessly, concerned with loss: *The Book of Illusions* traces how one man overcomes the death of his entire family; *Oracle Night* is about a man who has lost his own sense of place in the world; *Travels in the Scriptorium*, a radical investigation into the nature of writing, is about a man who has lost his authority, his sense of history and memory. Auster, then, would seem to argue that there is one theme and one theme only: loss and its possible overcoming. I began with a reading of Freud's "Mourning and Melancholia" precisely because I think that Auster's novels, with their ambivalent representation of mourning, interrogate the very idea of successful mourning, much in the same way as the ambivalence in Freud's essay itself is a marker of an anxiety over the possibility of overcoming loss. This is to say, I wish—especially in my reading of *The Book of Illusions* and *Oracle Night*—to read the novels as, in some senses, oblique commentaries on Freud's ambivalence. And in some crucial ways, Auster's representation of mourning's ambivalence begins with his figuration of the subject's relation to the archive: it is precisely here, in tracing how Auster himself traces how loss is overcome—how and where loss is mourned or only folded into a kind of perpetual, static melancholy—that we begin to see how carefully Auster interweaves the economies of mourning and the archive. In what follows, I am deliberately claiming that Auster's late novels figure the archive as the central *site*, or *affect*, where loss is catalogued and (possibly) metabolized. By "site" I mean that the archive is, at times, a material location or object (or objects): *The Book of Illusions* traces one man's negotiation of grief in relation to a series of secret, hidden, and eventually decrypted documents; *Oracle Night* places its protagonist literally within the archive, the crypt, arguing that it is only when the archive—as literalized site of melancholy—is materialized that loss can be comprehended as such. By "affect" I mean that Auster will transform the subject himself into an archive; the subject, the author-figure in *Travels in the Scriptorium*, becomes an archive in as much as he is archived by melancholy, marked by loss; the author-figure translates that loss into narrative, attempting to comprehend that mark of loss itself, attempting, that is, to understand how history can at once escape the subject and mark itself indelibly on his unconscious.

1.1 *The Book of Illusions* (2002)

Without question, in the depths of the crypt unspeakable words buried alive are held fast, like owls in ceaseless vigil.
—Abraham and Torok, "*The Topography of Reality*"

The Book of Illusions explores a simple trajectory: it traces one man's overcoming of the loss of his family in an airline accident. This loss (of a wife and two children) is initially presented as an unbearable one, a loss unable to be comprehended, let alone mourned. Auster's representation of David Zimmer's grief makes it clear that nothing, neither the "protocols of communal mourning" (7), nor the temporary oblivion of alcohol and sleep, will allow the forgetting of loss, so crucial to mourning, to occur. Zimmer's mourning, rather, begins with the chance viewing of a television program about silent comedians, one of whom is Hector Mann, an actor long presumed dead. Mann's film, a comedy, manages to amuse Zimmer; his smile signals that perhaps some instinct for survival is still in place: his laugh forces Zimmer to conclude that "there was something inside me I had not previously imagined, something other than just pure death . . . It meant that I hadn't walled myself off from the world so thoroughly that nothing could get in anymore" (9–10). Zimmer's mourning, thus, begins with the perception of a world beyond his own; his mourning begins with the perception of an Other, and most precisely, it begins with the perception of and fascination with the *work* of the Other. Because it is Mann's work as an actor—as comedian, as mime, as body artist—that captivates Zimmer. This fascination with the work of the Other inspires a reciprocal response: Zimmer decides to write a scholarly analysis of Mann's known oeuvre (amounting to 12 films). And thus we have arrived at the crucial beginning of Auster's analysis of the protocol of mourning: mourning is initiated by the work—and we can call it an archival body of work; an archive of work—of the Other. Indeed, Mann's archive inspires a reciprocal archive, for what is Zimmer's analysis but in its own way an attempt to offer some kind of authoritative statement about Mann's work? Given that Zimmer's analysis will be the only book-length analysis of Mann's films to date, Zimmer's book does operate as a kind of recuperative archive. We recall Derrida on the archive: it is a place of commandment and commencement. Zimmer's asserts a kind of authority, a kind of scholarly command over the work, and thus becomes what Derrida would call the "first archivist," he who "institutes the archive as it should be . . . not only in exhibiting the document but in establishing it" (55). What, of course, is fascinating about Zimmer's archival response to Mann's work is that at one level it is, at least from his initial perception, purely spectral; that is, it is an analysis of an artist and an art form (the silent film) that are both long dead.[1] Mann, as Zimmer makes clear in his first paragraph of *The Book of Illusions*, disappeared in 1929 and has not been heard of since. Moreover, Mann's art, film, is itself wholly spectral. Film, as such, perhaps only slightly less than music, is the most ephemeral of art forms: in its play of light, in its illusion of movement, it is never really, fully, present as such.[2] Derrida's description of the archive is resonant here: "The structure of the archive is spectral. It is spectral a priori: neither present nor absent 'in the flesh,' neither visible nor invisible, a trace always referring to another whose eyes can never be met" (84).[3]

Zimmer's book, *The Silent World of Hector Mann*, perhaps like most academic works, suffers its own spectral fate: it is duly reviewed and duly shelved. Indeed, Zimmer himself forgets about his work as soon as it is complete. He discovers that the distraction produced by the book was only temporary and thus he moves on to another writing project, a translation of Chateaubriand's *Memoires d'outre-tombe*; Chateaubriand's book is a more obviously spectral work, just as it obviously echoes the spectrality of Zimmer's book on Mann (and just as it obviously echoes the spectrality of *The Book of Illusions* itself: both Chateaubriand's and Zimmer's books are published after the authors' death). Auster thus establishes the idea of spectrality early in the novel: Zimmer's family is as spectral as the objects of his academic—and mourning—work. I am fascinated by how Auster signals the link between mourning and spectrality here, for surely one of the central trajectories of this novel is the peculiar claim the specter, as such, holds over the (mourning) subject. The specter is neither present nor absent: like memory itself, the specter is never fully present enough to eradicate or absent enough to forget. As such, memory—and specifically, memory of the specter—can only, perhaps, return, lethally as nostalgia, or melancholy.

But Zimmer's *The Silent World of Hector Mann* does catch the attention of a crucial reader: Hector Mann. And thus, the true trajectory of *The Book of Illusions* begins, the trajectory towards the ultimately spectral, the truly spectral, because unseen, filmic oeuvre of Hector Mann. Just over a year after *The Silent World of Hector Mann* is published Zimmer receives a letter from Frieda Spelling, Mann's wife, claiming that Mann is alive and living in New Mexico; after Zimmer expresses doubt about this claim, Spelling writes a more tantalizing letter, inviting him to Tierra Del Sueno to meet Hector:

Dear Professor . . . If I told you that [Hector] wrote and directed a number of feature films after leaving Hollywood in 1929—and that he is willing to screen them for you here at the ranch—perhaps that will entice you to come. Hector is almost ninety years old and in failing health. His will instructs me to destroy the films and the negatives of those films within twenty-four hours of his death, and I don't know how much longer he will last. Please contact me soon. (Auster, 2002, 77–8)

It is here, in this letter, that the true archival quest begins. And it is a complex archive being offered to Zimmer, to us. At the point of receiving the letter, the idea of the films is just that, an idea; Spelling's characterization of the films as being essentially at risk renders them always already doubly spectral: unseen films about to be destroyed.

As Zimmer travels to New Mexico, accompanied by Alma Grund, the daughter of the cameraman on Mann's Hollywood films (and, as he discovers, his secret films), Zimmer discovers that these films—there are 14 secret films in total—have an origin in Mann's deeply traumatic past. Zimmer's journey from New England to New Mexico is lengthy enough to allow Alma to fill in the details of Mann's disappearance and life subsequent to his Hollywood career, what Zimmer calls "Hector's destiny as a hidden man" (127). It is a complex story but finds it origins in a love affair gone badly wrong: Zimmer, a notorious philanderer, was engaged to an actress, Dolores Saint John; he also carried on a love affair with a journalist, Brigid O'Fallon; both women love him, and after being rejected by Mann, O'Fallon, now mentally unstable and pregnant, decides to confront Saint John; she appears at Saint John's house, and Saint John, perhaps accidentally, shoots her dead with a pistol. Mann, stricken with grief over this death, agrees to help hide the body of his dead lover, and it is this act of secret, guilty burial that essentially motivates his own disappearance. Mann changes his name to Hermann Loesser and begins a journey that clearly functions as a kind of penance: he travels to O'Fallon's home town, befriends her family, works for the family business, and, at the point of romantic involvement with O'Fallon's younger sister, again disappears, his penance incomplete. Following this failed penance, Mann deliberately degrades himself for several months by playing a role in a private sex show: he has sexual relations with a woman in front of paying customers. After it becomes clear that this ritualized humiliation is also failing as an act of true penance, Mann again disappears, soon to find himself once again enmeshed romantically with a woman, Frieda Spelling, whose life he has saved foiling a bank robbery.

It is against this background narrative—a narrative verging on the absurd when presented in raw outline—and the effects of one more traumatic event in Mann's life that we can begin to make sense of Mann's hidden film archive. Mann and Spelling marry and have a son; in events uncannily echoing those in Zimmer's life, this son dies (he is stung by a bee and has a fatal allergic response):

> Hector collapsed. Months went by, and he didn't do anything at all. He sat in the house; he looked at the sky through the bedroom window; he studied the backs of his hands ... Hector saw it [his child's death] as a form of divine punishment. He has been too happy. Life has been too good to him, and now the fates had taught him a lesson. (Auster 2002, 206–7)

Frieda convinces Mann to begin working on a project as a way of managing his grief, and thus, the idea of the secret film is born. The films will have to be secret for at least two reasons, one practical, one psychological. Mann has disappeared from the world and his reappearance after all these years later would be major disruption in their lives. More importantly, however, Mann has taken a personal vow never to make films again; as Alma puts it, while narrating Mann's life story to Zimmer[4], all Mann ever wanted to do was to make films, craft them precisely and perfectly. After his involvement with O'Fallon's death, Mann decides, as his penance, never to makes films again:

> That was all he had ever wanted for himself: to be good at that one thing [making films]. He had wanted only that, and therefore that was the one thing he would never allow himself to do again. You don't drive a girl insane, and you don't make her pregnant, and you don't bury her dead body eight feet under the ground and expect to go on with your life as before. A man who had done what he had done deserved to be punished. If the world wouldn't do it for him, then he would have to do it himself. (Auster 2002, 145–6)

Mann is able to work around his vow never to make films by planning never to show the films to any audience; the films, in other words, would have an a priori spectrality, would, in fact, perhaps not function as films in any real, philosophical sense. I quote Alma again:

> If someone makes a movie and no one sees it, does the movie exist or not? That's how he justified what he did. He would make movies that would never be shown to audiences, make movies for the pure pleasure of making movies. It was an act of breathtaking nihilism, and yet he's stuck to the bargain ever since ... It took great concentration and rigor to do what Hector did—and also a touch of madness ... As far as I know, Hector is

the first artist to make his work with the conscious, premeditated intention of destroying it . . . The day after Hector dies, [Frieda will] take his films into the garden and burn them all—every print, every negative, every frame he ever shot. That's guaranteed. And you and I will be the only witnesses. (Auster 2002, 207–8)

Mann's films, shot with obscure, unknown actors, are themselves created expressly with the intention of making them unreleasable to the general public; they feature explicit sexuality as well as other acts considered taboo: "Childbirth. Urination, defecation" (209). In other words, Mann's secret archive is marked by the absence of the very thing that motivates it: an audience, a witness. The films, more importantly, are no longer the comedies Mann once produced: they are uncanny, strange films, always with an "element of the fantastical running through them" (208). These films—with titles like *Report from the Anti-World* or *Travels in the Scriptorium*[5]—are clearly deeply personal, deeply subjective works, which can only be read as Mann's attempt to come to terms not only with the loss of O'Fallon and his son, but also with the lost possibility of work he might have been able to produce had he stayed in Hollywood. The films thus function as a trace of a lost life just as they are marked indelibly by the traces of lost lives. It is, perhaps, because the films are marked so deeply by guilt that they require being viewed by at least one outsider, David Zimmer: grief, in other words, needs a witness; mourning needs a witness if it is to work, if it is to be worked through.

Zimmer is able to view only one of Mann's films. Mann dies after Zimmer meets him for the first, and only, time and Frieda immediately sets about destroying the films. The film Zimmer does view is called *The Inner Life of Martin Frost* and it is about, perhaps not surprisingly, the relations between art and death, renunciation and loss. The film, according to Zimmer's description, concerns a writer, Martin Frost, who has, like Mann, decided to retreat from the world; he is vacationing at Tierra del Sueno, Frieda and Hector's ranch (Frost gives a voice-over narrative in the film and mentions Frieda and Hector by name). Frost is, it seems, exhausted: he has just competed a novel and now requires solitude and silence: "*All I wanted was to be there and do nothing, to live the life of a stone*" (245). Unexpectedly, however, Frost is inspired to write and begins work on a story; the next day he awakens to find that he is no longer alone: there is a young woman at the ranch, in fact, in his bed, who claims to be Frieda's niece. Inevitably, Frost and the woman, Claire Martin (her last name immediately signals some uncanny relation between the two), begin a romantic involvement until it is revealed that Frieda has no niece and Claire is some kind of imposter. Frost is unaware of Claire's precise nature until the last movement of the film, when she begins to become ill: she has been pressing Frost to complete his story, in fact, is insistent that he do so; as he writes the story, Claire becomes increasingly ill. Zimmer's description of the film culminates in a numbered list of cross-cut shots of Frost writing and Claire dying; the sequence suggests that Frost, in fact, writes Claire to death. Here it becomes clear to the viewer and to Frost that Claire in some ways is a manifestation of Frost's imagination, is perhaps some kind of muse; it is also clear that Frost has fallen in love with his muse and thus, in the film's final moments, he burns his manuscript page by page: as he does so, Claire returns to life.

The film is an extended meditation on the relation between art and love, between art and renunciation. More, it is a meditation on the relation between narcissism and loss, for surely the film is working to suggest that Frost is, in fact, only in love with an aspect of himself, be it his imagination, his own drive to create, or his own desire for language. The question for readers of *The Book of Illusions*, of course, is this: what is the relation between this film and Auster's larger novel? I think the film—precisely, the *description* of the film—bears a crucial relation to the whole; in fact, the film operates as a kind of spectral mise en abyme of the larger thematic impulses of the novel. First, the film exists as a deeply spectral object: it is seen once and then is destroyed.[6] Moreover, as is true for all the films in the novel, *The Inner Life of Martin Frost* exists only as a narrative description. The film as such thus exists only ekphrastically: ekphrasis functions only to point to the fundamental absence of the art object. And Auster's extensive use of ekphrasis is a particularly brilliant rhetorical turn here, given that the form itself is a sort of renunciation: it points to what is not there.[7] *The Inner Life of Martin Frost*, just as *The Book of Illusions*, is in large part about artistic renunciation and its relation to desire. Frost gives up his work in order to conjure back his desire, the dead. In this way, the film clearly operates for Mann as a kind of wish-fulfillment fantasy: Frost is able to raise the dead, and through this act Mann is perhaps able imaginatively to bring back his own dead. *The Inner Life of Martin Frost*, in other words, is Mann's work of mourning, his consigning of his films to flame, the final, and ultimate, act of penance.[8]

The Inner Life of Martin Frost also completes the psychoanalytical trajectory of the novel as a whole. Recall that Zimmer begins his relation with Mann's films while in the deepest moments of grief; the book he writes clearly is meant to function for Zimmer as a distraction, perhaps even as a form of mourning. It is crucial, as I suggested earlier, to see how Auster traces Zimmer working through his grief through the work of the Other. Zimmer's

The Silent World of Hector Mann fails as an act of mourning—he still feels his loss keenly—but the book does lead him to Mann's secret archive. In my estimation, Zimmer's viewing of *The Inner Life of Martin Frost* is where his melancholy could possibly translate into, turn towards, a kind of mourning (it will not, as I will suggest). And it is crucial to notice the degree to which this process of mourning is purely narcissistic. First, the film itself is a meditation on narcissism and loss; Frost is in effect mourning his own loss in this film, and his renunciation of his art in favor of keeping Claire is a signal, in fact, that his own mourning is a failure. Recall that Freud argues that melancholia, a pathological response to loss, somehow inhibits the subject from letting the lost object go; instead of the normal process by which there is a withdrawal of the libido from this lost "object and a displacement of it on to a new one," (257) the melancholic narcissistically identifies with the lost object:

> But the free libido was not displaced on to another object; it was withdrawn into the ego. There, however, it was not employed in any unspecified way, but served to establish an *identification* of the ego with the abandoned object. Thus the shadow of the object fell upon the ego, and the latter could henceforth be judged by a special agency, as though it were an object, the forsaken object. (Freud 1984, 258)

In other words, Frost has become his own lost object, his own diminished, perpetually melancholic, narcissistic, ego. And Auster does signal that Frost's resurrection of Claire is at best a psychologically ambivalent act (as all acts of resurrection necessarily must be); the film ends with Claire, clearly unhappy—she "seems lost" (268)—asking agonizingly: "What are we going to do? . . . Tell me Martin, what on earth are we going to do?" (268)[9]

Zimmer, too, is enmeshed in a trajectory of almost sublime narcissism; this assertion may seem odd at first blush, because at one level Zimmer is clearly, seemingly, displacing his grief onto external objects, the work of Mann being the primary. He mourns, as I have suggested, through the work of the Other. And if Zimmer's viewing of *The Inner Life of Martin Frost* is the culmination of this externalization of his mourning, we may at first not see any narcissism at work. Zimmer, in fact, seems to be working his way through a "normal" trajectory of mourning. He is withdrawing his libido from the lost object—his wife and sons—and cathecting them elsewhere: to Mann's films, to Alma, with whom he has started a passionately sexual affair. But, and this is crucial, Mann's films, his true secret archive, are only ever traces of a grief that too easily recalls Zimmer's own. When, for instance, Alma narrates how Mann lost his son, Tad, Zimmer immediately makes a connection to his own dead son, Todd: "No mental gymnastics required to understand the situation. Tad and Todd. It can't get any closer than that, can it?" (206)[10] Mann's archive, in other words, is only ever going to recall Zimmer's own loss and place him back within the lethal space of melancholia. And even if this archive has itself been consigned to ashes, to cinders, Zimmer makes it clear, as he meditates on the process of writing this book, that is, *The Book of Illusions* (in itself a testimony of grief's hold on his imagination), that he need only think of *The Inner Life of Martin Frost* for the film to return to and assume a kind of reality. Zimmer, like Frost, is able, in other words, to conjure at will his own desire. *The Inner Life of Martin Frost* is itself, recall, an emblem of failed mourning: surely Zimmer's compulsive recalling of the film is a symptom of his own melancholia, a symptom of his own desire to continually identify with the lost object. Here Zimmer describes how he is able to conjure the film by looking over his notes (he transcribed the film's plot while watching it) and by recalling sessions with a hypnotist:

> Last year, when I began toying with the idea of writing this book, I went in for several consultations with a hypnotist . . . By listening to the tape recordings of those sessions, I have been able to fill in certain blanks, to bring back a number of things that were beginning to vanish. For better or worse, it seems that the philosophers were right. Nothing that happens to us is ever lost. (Auster 2002, 271)

Zimmer credits the philosophers for the idea that nothing is lost, but perhaps he is also thinking of Freud: "In the unconscious nothing can be brought to an end, nothing is past or forgotten" (*Interpretation of Dreams*: 577). Freud's words here are ominous precisely because they indicate the degree to which the unconscious becomes an indelible archive. At once this archive retains events and memories, and perhaps this is a positive thing; but the unconscious, in its ruthless hold on memory, also acts, structurally, precisely as a melancholy archive: that is, the unconscious will hold on to memory, despite the desires of the subject, who may wish to forget in order to move past his trauma. Zimmer here figures his ability to recall—aided by another archival displacement, his tape-recorded sessions with the hypnotist—in a positive light, but surely, as I have been trying to argue, his desire to hold onto this film, this testimony of narcissism and failed mourning, is an index of the claim Zimmer's own past grief has over him. And surely, given events that are to follow, Zimmer's desire to write this book, *The Book of Illusions*, a book written a decade after the events at Tierra del Sueno, is yet more testimony of an attachment both to the manifold losses that initiated his encounter with Hector Mann and to the losses that follow.

The most important loss for Zimmer, after the immolation of the films, is that of Alma. Zimmer returns to Vermont after seeing *The Inner Life of Martin Frost* and Alma stays behind to oversee see the ranch and its operations. As is revealed to us in a letter written by Alma, Alma and Frieda had an accidentally violent encounter: Frieda has burned the biography that Alma is writing of Hector; in a flash of anger, Alma pushes Frieda, who takes an awkward fall and dies. Alma, grief stricken, kills herself. Zimmer recalls his response to her death, and his words are telling: "I was so befuddled, I didn't know how to mourn her except by keeping myself alive. Months later, when I finished the translation [of Chateaubriand] and moved away from Vermont, I understood that Alma had done that for me. In eight short days, she had brought me back from the dead" (315–16). I am fascinated by Zimmer's words here. His mourning takes the form of living and in some sense, this is an orthodox protocol of mourning: he has withdrawn his libidinal attachment from the lost object, Alma, and attached it to his own life. And yet, given the trajectory of what follows, given, that is, his decision to return to *this* narrative of loss and mourning (*The Book of Illusions*), it strikes me that Zimmer's mourning is an incomplete project.[11] Moreover, and this has to be the crucial detail, Zimmer's melancholic return to this narrative, to the narrative of the loss of his family, the loss of the secret film archive, the loss of Alma, is a *secret* return: "It doesn't matter what happened to me after that. This is a book of fragments, a compilation of sorrows and half-remembered dreams . . . It has been eleven years since I returned from New Mexico, and in all that time I have never talked to anyone about what happened to me there. Not a word about Alma, not a word about Hector and Frieda" (316). Zimmer's book, *The Book of Illusions*, is written, moreover, as a direct response to his own failing, as a response, that is, to his own anticipated end: he has had two heart attacks and realizes his death may come at any moment. Dying, he writes his book, his archive, his *compilation of sorrows*, in secret:

> Following Chateaubriand's model, I will make no attempt to publish what I have written now. I have left a letter of instruction for my lawyer, and he will know where to find the manuscript and what to do with it after I am gone. I have every intention of living to a hundred, but on the off chance I don't get that far, all the necessary arrangements have been made. If and when this book is published, dear reader, you can be certain that the man who wrote it is long dead. (Auster 2002, 318)

The Book of Illusions is a book written in secret which works to reveal past secrets, to bring what was lost to light; the book works in secrecy, in other words, to decrypt the secret. And I wonder if Zimmer's not simply conventional nod to the reader—"dear reader"—is a signal of his hope that when that loss is witnessed, when it no longer is consigned to the oblivion of secret memory, it somehow, perhaps, is mourned. Perhaps Zimmer's desire to write is motivated by the idea that a public testimony to loss will allow that loss to be comprehended as such, comprehended and metabolized, if not in the economy of the single subject, then in the public mind. But what *is* the loss of an Other? What is the loss of an Other *to me*? How, in other words, can the loss of the Other ever be comprehended by the subject who never undergoes that grief, that trauma, that loss? It cannot, and thus for the reader, *The Book of Illusions* can only remain a book of translated loss, can only be a book that ekphrastically represents loss: by doing so, by giving words to that loss, by translating loss, Zimmer, in effect, displaces and defers that loss.[12] Surely this *is* a book of illusions because it is attempting to do the impossible: translate loss into comprehensible terms. And like the films at the heart of this book, films that only exist as displaced ekphrastic specters, Zimmer's spectral testimony itself is a displaced loss, an archive of grief—"a book of fragments, a compilation of sorrows"—that can only, and does only, prolong and animate what it hopes to mourn.

1.2 *Oracle Night* (2003)

Writing is always only a game played with ungraspable reality.
—Bataille, *Guilty*

Paul Auster's *Oracle Night* is a novel responding precisely to the issues surrounding the overcoming, the working through, of loss. Indeed, Auster's work has always touched on these issues, has always been about how the individual subject manages, economically or otherwise, the effects of trauma. Sidney Orr, the central character of *Oracle Night*, thus shares a genetic filiation with David Zimmer of *The Book of Illusions*, with Anna Blume of *The Country of Last Things*, with Peter Aaron of *Leviathan*, with Quinn of *City of Glass*, with Blue of *Ghosts*, and with the unnamed narrator of *The Locked Room*. Each of these characters is responding to the loss of family (Zimmer, Blume), of friends (Aaron), or, as in the case of characters in *The New York Trilogy*, of identity itself. At some level, Sidney Orr, who will lose his closest friend and his unborn child and who, crucially, has lost a sense of identity as the novel opens, is a compendium of all these previous characters. *Oracle Night* opens with a description of Sidney Orr, twenty years previous, that makes it clear that he is recovering from the trauma of a near-fatal illness; that he is essentially a specter, a Lazarus come back from the dead; that he is, and this is a central assertion of my analysis, in mourning for his own life.[13] My reading of *Oracle Night*, specifically of the multiple embedded narratives in the novel in which Orr attempts to work through his various traumas, suggests that Auster's novel offers itself as a critique of the idea of overcoming loss, a critique, that is, of the very premise of mourning. If, as one reading of the ambivalent Freudian understanding of mourning has it, narrative is a means towards comprehending loss—and moving beyond it in the process of working through—what happens when the narratives of mourning fail to express that process? What happens economically to the energy and resonance of grief when the means by which that grief is carried across into manageability—and is thus metabolized, in Derrida's terms—reveals itself as only ever capable of reduplicating that grief, of, in fact, entombing that grief in perpetually encrypted stasis?

It is manifestly clear that *Oracle Night*, like the linked narratives of *The New York Trilogy*, is about writing, is, in fact, about the link between narrative and (the experience of) mourning. Its central characters, Orr and John Trause, are writers; the title of the novel refers to a (fictional) novel created by a character, herself created by Orr; Sidney Orr attempts, through his numerous fictions, actually to write himself through his trauma and back to life. As the novel concludes, with its various failed narratives (one of which leaves a character entombed and in perpetual limbo) and as Orr realizes the inadequacy of narrative to accommodate his grief for his life, Auster indicates the general inability of narrative to represent adequately the random absurdity in the order of things. And part of my purpose here is to come to some understanding of the random, chaotic structure of *Oracle Night* as itself reflective of a larger critique of narrative's inability to negotiate the unnamable, unknowable economy of mourning. *Oracle Night* is thus intimately connected to Freud's essay, "Mourning and Melancholia," even functioning as a commentary on Freud's own ambivalence about mourning. If, as I posit, Orr is a subject in mourning, and if his narratives are an attempt to accommodate his mourning *and they fail*, the entire novel can be read as a critique of narrative as a way of working through trauma: narrative as an expression of mourning thus turns toward mourning the loss of effective narrative. Ultimately, it is my suggestion that Orr's narratives and Auster's novel in toto comprise that mysterious *failed* economy of mourning that Freud's cannot anatomize.[14] What Auster reveals, and Freud concedes if only unconsciously, is precisely the failure of the economy of mourning *as* and *in* the economy of narrative: narrative cannot metabolize mourning if the crypt (the story) containing the energy of mourning itself evidences signs of mourning, if, that is, the crypt itself mourns.

The first paragraph of *Oracle Night* makes clear that Sidney Orr is leading a posthumous life. Having recently recovered from a near-fatal illness, Orr finds himself on the gradual road to painful recovery:

> I had been sick for a long time. When the day came for me to leave the hospital, I barely knew how to walk anymore, could barely remember who I was supposed to be . . . They had given me up for dead, and now that I had confounded their predictions and mysteriously failed to die, what choice did I have but to live as though a future life were waiting for me? (Auster 2003, 1)

Orr has essentially been reborn ("I barely knew how to walk"), refashioned in an identity seemingly only tangentially related to him. Orr's memory, barely working, affixes him to a putative subjectivity; Orr's "supposed," in "I could barely remember who I was supposed to be," posits subjectivity as both role and mere supposition of self. Auster makes clear from the outset, thus, that Orr's sense of self—barely grasped—is tenuous, that his mysteriously unnamed illness has almost created a tabula rasa. Orr's final sentence contains and compresses the major tropes the novel will unfold: in words echoing Samuel Beckett's first narrative in *Texts for Nothing* (a series of texts also exploring the idea of posthumous ontology) Orr writes: "They had given me up for dead."[15] Orr is now in the peculiar state of having "confounded their predictions and mysteriously failed to die": the phrase "failed to die," ironic, darkly humorous, also echoes the major Beckettian theme of failure. Orr's failure to die (as opposed, simply, to live) sounds a major theme of failure in the novel: indeed, *Oracle Night* is a novel largely about failure, the failure of the novelist to write, the failure of the subject to mourn. Orr's final clause, "what choice did I have but to live as though a future life were waiting for me," with its echoes of Pascal's wager, makes explicit that Orr is living precisely *as* a "supposition."

Orr's state is one of total removal from familiarity: "I felt like a man who had lost his way in a foreign city" (2); as he drifts "along like a spectator in someone else's dream," (2) it becomes clear that Orr has undergone a process of radical transformation. Indeed, his ontology, like that of Beckett's narrator(s) in *Texts for Nothing,* is difficult to categorize. He clearly is not dead, but has come so close to death as to become a specter in his own life. More precisely, we can say Orr has experienced a virtual death, or that his death was virtual. Having been given up for dead, that is, having symbolically been categorized and configured as dead by, presumably, doctors and family, Orr is in the position of being almost a ghost, almost alive, almost dead, or, perhaps, as *good as* dead. A symbolic death, as Zizek reminds us in *The Sublime Object of Ideology*, is not "the death of the so-called 'real object' in its symbol, but the obliteration of the signifying network itself" (132). In other words, Orr's story—his own sense of self, his family's sense of who he was— has been (prematurely) rewritten. What I wish to establish here at the outset is that all that follows in *Oracle Night* does so from Orr's sense of being, or *having been* (this narrative, of course, functioning as a recollection of the past), in this peculiar existential state. Orr, to put it succinctly, is in mourning for a lost ontology. Indeed, Auster, through Orr, is posing a series of acutely difficult questions: How does one mourn one's own (virtual or symbolic) death? Is a symbolic death more difficult to mourn than a real death?

The beginning of the answer to this first question, for Orr, must be: to write. As the story of *Oracle Night* proper begins, on September 18, 1982 (Orr is explicit about the dates), twenty years prior to the moment of *this* writing (*Oracle Night* being the novel Orr fails to write "in" *Oracle Night*), Orr purchases the mysterious blue notebook from M. R. Chang's Paper Palace and begins to write. And what he writes, of course, is the first embedded narrative in *Oracle Night*, a narrative explicitly modeled on Dashiel Hammett's own embedded story of Flitcraft in *The Maltese Falcon*, and, crucially, a narrative about a man who becomes a ghost to his own life. Orr's story of book editor Nick Bowen begins as an explicit reworking/repeating/working through of Hammett's "curious parable" (13), as Orr calls it, of Flitcraft. Flitcraft, a conventional businessman, one day come close to dying (a plank of wood from a building site falls and narrowly misses him); this close call affects Flitcraft profoundly as it reveals to him the essential randomness of events and precariousness of being. Hammett's Sam Spade narrates: "[Flitcraft] said he knew before he had gone twenty feet from the fallen beam that he would never know peace again until he had adjusted to this new glimpse of life . . . Life could be ended for him at random by a falling beam: he would change his life at random by simply going away" (*Maltese Falcon*: 64). Thus, Flitcraft disappears from his own life, deserting wife and children to start anew in Spokane, Washington.

The Flitcraft episode appeals to Orr for a complex series of reasons, some explicit, some rather more hidden. Orr suggests the episode attracts him because "we have all imagined letting go of our lives . . . because at one moment or another we have all wanted to be someone else" (14).[16] Bowen, however, disappears for reasons slightly more complicated than Hammett's Flitcraft. Orr suggests that Bowen, for reasons to do with suddenly falling in love with another woman (the granddaughter of the author of *Oracle Night*) and being in a general sense of existential ennui, has clearly come to a realization that his life is a failure, that "his life has come to a dead end" (25). A gargoyle falls and narrowly misses killing him, leading to his own epiphany: "if he's managed to escape with his life, it can only mean that a new life has been given to him—that his old life is finished, that every moment of his past now belongs to someone else" (26).

The Flitcraft episode, in both Orr's and Hammett's versions, exposes the radical chaos that, repressed until randomly exposed, threatens the stability of subjectivity itself. Indeed, the idea of randomness is central to each storyteller's reading and interpretation of the set episode. Hammett: "Life could be ended for him at random by a falling beam: he would change his life at random by simply going away" (64). The response to the random beam falling is, of course, anything but random, just as Bowen's choice to leave his life—to die to his old life—is anything but random. What the Flitcraft episode exposes is the fantasy of rewriting one's life, the fantasy inherent, more precisely, in the realization that one's life is merely a story, the setting and plot of which can be changed, can be re-written. Life may be an absurdity, as Flitcraft understands, but it can also become an absurd, but *willed*, fabrication.

Both Flitcraft and Bowen are ghosts, dead to their old lives in the rewriting of new narratives. If, as Derrida notes, "mourning always follows a trauma" (97: *Specters of Marx*), Flitcraft and Bowen are actively mourning their lives by creating new narratives. This refashioning of self is a kind of mourning process by which the realization of the chaotic fact of being is worked through, metabolized into a new acceptance of the loss of surety. What is crucial about both Flitcraft and Bowen is that their processes of mourning fail, Flitcraft's in an ironic fashion, Bowen's in a more complex melancholic manner. Hammett's delight in the story of Flitcraft is in the ironic ending to the story: having abandoned one resolutely typical social context, Flitcraft winds up in precisely the same milieu only in a different part of the country: "I don't think he even knew he had settled back naturally into the same groove he had jumped out of in Tacoma . . . he adjusted himself to beams falling, and then he adjusted himself to them not falling" (64). Flitcraft's act of rewriting—his act of mourning the loss of surety—fails in the sense that he has simply replaced his old life with a simulacrum: the simulacrum, adjusting itself to the not-random, merely represses the previous existential insight into the fundamental arbitrariness and absurdity in the order of things. In other words Flitcraft's mourning is tautological, but because he is able now to successfully repress his own traumatic insight, his mourning is (seemingly) complete. The uncanny effect of

Hammett's parable, of course, is the sense that the randomness of things could—perhaps will—assert themselves again and efface Flitcraft's repression.

Orr's version of the Flitcraft episode is one that offers itself as a critique both of Flitcraft's repression and the idea of successful mourning generally (indeed, his version of things may suggest that mourning is only ever a type of repression). Before examining the psychoanalytical ramifications of Bowen's story I wish to make clear what has been implicit to this point. Bowen/Flitcraft must be seen as a fantasy projection of Orr himself. While it is true that the crucial idea to work through this story of Flitcraft is not Orr's but John Trause's, and while Orr never explicitly comments on his own investment in the story as a version of Flitcraft himself, it is clear that his narrative is, in the true sense of the term, narcissistic. Indeed, as Freud and others make clear, mourning—and the Bowen/Flitcraft story is one of mourning—is entirely a narcissistic process.

Orr, of course, presents a complex case in terms of his specific relation to mourning and melancholia. As I have suggested, Orr sees himself as a kind of ghost in (to) his own life: more precisely, he sees himself *being seen* by others as a ghost in his life ("a spectator in someone else's dream" [2]), an unlikely (uncanny) survivor ("they couldn't believe I was alive, that they hadn't buried me in some graveyard" [117]), a Lazarus. The story he rewrites (or repeats, to put it in Freudian terms) is thus not unexpected: it is his story, with some important alterations. Flitcraft/Bowen have chosen to ghost themselves, while Orr has certainly—indeed as far as we can gather—not chosen to abandon his life in a conscious way, although it is significant that each time Orr sits down to write in his blue notebook, he seems to disappear (27). It is as if the act of writing itself facilitates his absence from a life from which he is already absent: the writing doubles or completes his absence.

Orr's story of Bowen thus must be read as Orr's attempt to work through his own near-death experience: the story becomes a way of controlling, narratively, the experience that was—and still is—completely out of his control. In Freud's terms, Orr is working his way back to the scene of his own trauma. In "Remembering, Repeating, and Working Through," Freud discusses the patient who has no conscious memory of events but seems compelled to repeat the trauma: "the patient does not *remember* anything of what he has forgotten and repressed, but *acts* it out. He reproduces it not as a memory but as an action: he *repeats* it, without, of course, knowing that he is repeating it" (150). Freud's notion that actions occur that are not immediately available to consciousness suggests a link to melancholia. In

"Mourning and Melancholia," Freud suggests that melancholia is essentially a narcissistic process by which the sense of the loss of the object is refracted back onto the ego itself: the "object-loss . . . is withdrawn from consciousness" (254). Melancholia contrasts with mourning in that mourning is always a conscious process (254) in which the subject withdraws his libidinal energy from the lost object and translates it to a more appropriate site (another person, for example). The melancholic, on the other hand, translates that energy to itself and establishes "an *identification* of the ego with the abandoned object' (258). The complex of melancholia "behaves like an open wound" (262) and this trauma ("wound") cannot, will not, be worked through if the subject is consistently working its way back to itself.

Orr is a complex crystallization of Freud's notion of melancholia insofar as his case suggests that the object of loss is always originally the self. As Abraham and Torok put it in their essay "The Lost Object—Me," the sense of loss that results from trauma is essentially unknowable and this unknowability refracts the subject, displaces the subject's sense of self.[17] In other words, the self loses itself; the self is hidden in a "crypt in the ego" (141):

> This segment of an ever so painfully loved Reality [loss]—untellable and therefore inaccessible to the gradual, assimilative work of mourning—causes a genuinely covert shift in the entire psyche . . . This leads to the establishment of a sealed off psychic place, a crypt in the ego. (Abraham and Torok 1994, 141)

Abraham and Torok's notion of the covert shift in the entire psyche recalls Freud's notion that the melancholic "cannot see clearly what it is that has been lost" (254), that the melancholic "knows *whom* he has lost but not *what* he has lost in him" (254). Orr thus becomes a narcissistic melancholic symptomatically searching for an understanding precisely of what he has lost. In my reading, the stories he tells—and ultimately fails to tell (or succeeds in telling their failure)—are ways of entering the crypt to find the hidden, occulted, "untellable" loss, to find the means by which this loss can be made accessible to mourning.

In Abraham and Torok's terms, narrative, specifically in this case, Orr's narrative, is the crypt in the ego, a "sealed off psychic place" that can only be explored through the mediation of a discourse that, crucially in the story of Nick Bowen, *in turn* encrypts the subject. Bowen, we recall, has been hired by Ed Victory to work in Victory's Bureau of Historical Preservation, an underground archive. This bunker contains a vast collection of telephone books:

> Hundreds of telephone books, thousands of telephone books, arranged alphabetically by city and set out in chronological order . . . Ed started the collection in 1946, the year after the end of World War II, which also happens to be the year that Bowen himself was born. Thirty-six years devoted to a vast and apparently meaningless undertaking, which tallies exactly with the span of his own life. (Auster 2003, 90)

This cryptic archive is the product, one might say symptom, of Victory's own trauma. As he tells Bowen, Victory was part of the military force that liberated Dachau in 1945: "That was the end of mankind . . . God turned his eyes away from us and left the world forever. And I was there to witness it" (92). Victory's archive thus is an expression of continual witnessing, a (melancholic) refusal to let the reality of Dachau—of God's disappearance—fade from memory: "I had to keep that place in my head, to go on thinking about it every day for the rest of my life" (93). The archive thus is an expression of the refusal to mourn the loss that occurs in Dachau, a refusal to work through and beyond that trauma. The archive, the melancholy archive, "contains the world . . . or at least a part of it. The names of the living and the dead. The Bureau of Historical Preservation is a house of memory, but it's also a shrine to the present. By bringing those two things together in one place, I prove to myself that mankind isn't finished" (91). Victory's melancholy becomes a positive expression of connection to history: the melancholic impulse—finding its objective correlative in the archive—works to connect the present to the past, refuses, that is, to kill the past.[18] In Victory's terms, melancholia becomes the only proper ethical response to history, to trauma, to loss, a way of proving, in his crucial language, that "mankind isn't finished" (91). The archive, an objective correlative monument to Victory's ethical melancholia, can be seen as a kind of narrative response to trauma. Refusing the transcending (or metabolizing) impulse of mourning, the archive sets itself up as a continual witness to the past, telling the story of the past if only by recalling the names of the dead and the living.

And it is here, in the archive that is both mausoleum and crypt, that Nick Bowen is abandoned. After Victory falls ill (and eventually dies), Bowen mistakenly locks himself into the room that Victory has set up as his living quarters. Encrypted in the crypt, Bowen has only the company of the manuscript of *Oracle Night* and the 1937/38 Warsaw telephone book. Orr's story of Bowen ends here: Orr never returns to his blue notebook to rescue his Eurydice. Given its centrality in *Oracle Night* (it is the longest of Orr's embedded narratives), it is clear that the narrative is crucial for Orr even twenty years after the fact of its writing. The Bowen narrative essentially plays out the fantasy of burial that haunted Orr from the outset of the narrative; that is, Orr projects into his narrative the logical conclusion to his own sense of having died, of having been ghosted. If Orr mysteriously continues to live, the Bowen narrative plays out the phantasmic conclusion to his own story: ghosts need burial. Bowen's story may be an aporetic failure in narrative terms—he calls it an "impasse" (222)—but in psychoanalytical terms, it works towards a kind of logical conclusion.

What is clear from the entirety of *Oracle Night* and the variety of embedded narratives, including the story of Bowen, is that Orr has not moved on from the events surrounding the writing of the failed narratives. We must keep firmly in mind that Orr is writing, rewriting, in fact, these events twenty years after the fact. It is possible thus to read *Oracle Night* as a narrative about the inability to mourn a variety of losses: it is indeed about Orr's own reaction to his near-fatal illness, his transformation into a specter. But the novel is equally about Orr's reaction to the real-world events surrounding the writing of his story of Bowen, namely the loss of his writer friend Trause and the child he (Orr) would have had with his wife, Grace. In other words, *Oracle Night* becomes Orr's own Museum of Historical Preservation, his own archive of memory.

Auster, through various embedded narratives and, indeed, through another failed writing attempt on Orr's part, works to make clear that a central concern of this narrative is the relation between time and memory, between trauma and remembrance, between loss and the *consequences of survival*. If trauma works to displace the "normal" structure of time (or the proper understanding of time), that is, if trauma, as Freud and others note, disrupts the linearity of experience by compelling the victim back into the scene of trauma repeatedly, then any narrative of mourning, any attempt to work through trauma is essentially an attempt to reassert the normal flow of time. In *Beyond the Pleasure Principle*, Freud writes: "Now dreams occurring in traumatic neuroses have the characteristic of repeatedly bringing the patient back into the situation of his accident, a situation from which he wakes up in another fright" (282). The neurotic, through dreams and the acting out of repressed material, finds himself "obliged to *repeat* the repressed material as a contemporary experience instead of . . . *remembering* it as something belonging to the past" (288). The traumatized patient thus is melancholic in the sense that the past is present; the trauma of the past resists the assimilative process crucial to the working of mourning and remains fixed in the self in the present. Derrida's formulation of the melancholic in the *Ear of the Other* situates the crypt at the heart of the traumatized self:

> Not having been taken back inside the self, digested, assimilated as in all "normal" mourning, the dead object remains like a living dead abscessed in a specific spot in the ego. It has its place, just like a crypt in a cemetery or temple, surrounded by walls and all the rest. The dead object is incorporated in this crypt—the term "incorporated" signaling precisely that one has failed to digest or assimilate it totally, so that it remains there, forming a pocket in the mourning body. The incorporated dead, which one has not really managed to take upon oneself, continues to lodge there like something other and to ventrilocate through the "living." (Derrida 1988, 57–8)

Melancholia, precisely because it situates a retroactivity or deferral (*Nachtraglichkeit*)[19] at the heart of experience, thus works to continually facilitate trauma's continual presence in the present: the logic of the archive (as crypt) thus is predicated on a continual lived relation to trauma. Bowen, forever trapped in the archive—interred in the house of memory—becomes an emblem of stasis, of the temporal feedback loop that is the traumatic moment, just as Orr, his real simulacrum, becomes a classic melancholic ventriloquizing the dead past beyond which he cannot move.

Auster proffers several more instantiations of the idea of the traumatic archive, one of the most complex being Trause's story of his bereaved brother-in-law, Richard. Trause's first wife, Tina, sister to Richard, died of cancer in 1974. Tina's death has been massively traumatic for Trause and especially for Richard who, as Trause says, "had suffered the most" (34). Eight years after her death, Richard and Trause meet for dinner during which Richard details his discovery of a 3-D camera and some old photographs of his family. The camera, "a prize relic from the 3-D craze of the early fifties" (36), allows the spectator to take and view three-dimensional pictures of a hyperreal intensity: "Everyone in them looked alive, brimming with energy, present in the moment, a part of some eternal now that had gone on perpetuating itself for close to thirty years" (37–8). As he views an old photograph of a family gathering, Richard encounters the resurrected dead; he sees his father, mother, and Tina, all perfectly preserved. In one picture Richard sees himself standing with his dead family and the image lacerates him: "He was standing on the lawn with three ghosts, he realized, the only survivor from that afternoon thirty years ago" (38). The 3-D camera, as Trause describes it to Orr, is "a magic lantern that allowed [Richard] to travel through time and visit the dead" (39). The camera and pictures are a photographic archive that traumatically collapses temporality itself. Richard finds himself addicted to the archive and falls under the "spell" (39) of the photographs, spending months obsessively returning to 1953. Thus, Richard, a victim of the archive, a victim of his own lethal nostalgia, is a classic melancholic unable to find the appropriate means to work beyond his grief. Richard's pain crystallizes the paradox of the archive: the addiction to the archive, the dark joy that this addiction brings, is one that cannot be maintained unless one is willing to forgo the present moment in favor of the past. Richard's difficulties multiply when—and this occurs at the time of his meeting with Trause—the camera breaks down; without the viewer, there is no access to the melancholic archive: "No image, no more time travel into the past. No more time travel, no more joy. Another round of grief, another round of sorrow—as if, after bringing them back to life, he had to bury the dead all over again" (39). Trause's narrative of Richard ends after Trause succeeds in finding someone to repair the broken camera: Richard, somewhat reluctantly—and under pressure from his wife, who resents Richard's neglect of his family—refuses the offer of repair, arguing that one must live in the present moment. Richard thus is *compelled to mourn*, to reject the past, to finally bury the dead. Trause feels the story has a "disappointing end" (40).

It is clear that Orr offers the story of Richard's 3-D camera as a structural echo—or anticipation; this narrative occurs as Orr has begun writing his story of Bowen, but before Bowen meets Ed Victory—of the Museum of Historical Preservation. Richard's story, ends, perhaps, as disappointingly as Bowen's in strict narrative terms (Trause wishes—as perhaps do we—that Richard would continue time traveling; perhaps Trause realizes that compelled mourning is a kind of dishonesty), but we do notice that Richard escapes the archive while Bowen, not precisely an addict to the past, is perpetually trapped "within" history, compelled into a static melancholy. The two stories, both failures in some sense, shimmer before Orr as possible responses to trauma, to history. Both, perhaps, answer the question: How does the economy of mourning work? According to the logic of Richard's narrative, mourning works, as Freud notices, when the subject responds to the "reality principle," to the realization that the dead are, indeed, dead. Bowen, who I have argued is a fantasy projection of Orr, stands as an emblem of the inability to move beyond loss, the inability, perhaps more precisely, to escape the *claims* of history. Bowen's inadvertent trapping in the archive may stand as an emblem of history's (in this case quite literal) claim to the subject.

There is one further crucial narrative about the relation between trauma and time that I wish to consider. Orr, having interred Bowen in perpetual archival melancholy, receives a commission to write a screen treatment of H. G. Wells' *The Time Machine*. The treatment, not surprisingly described by Orr himself as "pure rubbish, of course, fantasy drek of the lowest order" (127), echoes the fascination with the temporal trajectory of melancholia generally. Orr, feeling that Wells' story is interesting because of the conceit of time travel, nonetheless believes that Wells has made two conceptual errors in his story. First, Wells has misunderstood our desires in relation to time:

> He [Wells] sends his hero into the future, but the more I thought about it, the more certain I became that most of us would prefer to visit the past. Trause's story about his brother-in-law and the 3-D camera was a good example of how powerfully the dead keep their hold on us ... we're hungry to know the dead before they were dead, to acquaint ourselves with the dead as living beings. (Auster 2003, 121)

Second, Orr has a theoretical difficulty with time travel as presented by Wells. If one person is able to invent a time machine, then people in the future would be able to do the same: time itself, he reasons, would change, would be destroyed. Orr's story thus has two time travelers, one from the end of the nineteenth century and one from the mid-twenty-second century when time travel is bureaucratically regulated so as to maintain time's continuous progression. These travelers meet in 1963 at the moment of JFK's assassination, predictably fall in love, and, just as predictably, fail to stop the assassination or alter the course of history: "American history would not be altered by a single comma" (126).

This seemingly inconsequential story—"pure rubbish"—resonates powerfully into the entirety of *Oracle Night* containing as it does an (albeit brief) meditation on the nature of time. Crucially, it contains in miniature, as a kind of mise en abyme, an emblematic statement of the entire novel's traumatic trajectory. *Oracle Night*, as a whole, is precisely about the varieties of time travel that occur in memory, in trauma, in mourning. This novel, written twenty years after the fact and containing a series of interconnected meditations on the nature of time, memory, and ghosts, does collapse the nature of narrative time in much the same manner as time travel (according to Orr at least) would collapse the continuous progression of time into a vast synchronistic blur. Indeed, according to Orr's thinking, the effects of time travel resemble the effects of trauma itself, compelling the subject to inhabit multiple temporalities and collapsing the forward progression of time. Orr's solution to the problem of time travel, to the problem of trauma itself is, in his screen treatment at least, to regulate time: "time has been mastered by then" (123). The bureaucracies of the twenty-second century are able fully to see the trajectory of time, to anticipate its damage, master its outcome. If time travel is a metaphor for traumatic memory in this treatment—and in the variety of stories about memory in *Oracle Night*—if, more precisely, time travel *becomes* traumatic memory, then Orr's story, one of several that fail, is about the failure to master the events of history (JFK's assassination), the inability to control the impulse and effects of trauma.

Orr's dismissal of his treatment as "pure rubbish" is a complex gesture. First, it is difficult to locate "when" the dismissal occurs: is he dismissing it in the now of remembering? Is the dismissal one that occurred twenty years previous? At any rate, it is clear that his memory of the story as rubbish is a retrospective reading. But the dismissal can be read as an anxiety response to the retrospective impulse of memory that itself structures the entirety of *Oracle Night*. That is to say, the anxiety of the dismissal must be seen to resonate into the entirety of the narrative. Certainly the narrative that in some sense is at the heart of *Oracle Night*—the novel-within-the-novel, written by the fictional Sylvia Maxwell, the novel that so affects Nick Bowen—is a narrative all about the devastation that occurs when the linear structure of time is suspended by the blind prophet Lemuel Flagg. The plot of Maxwell's *Oracle Night*, given in précis form by Orr (indeed, Orr gives all his narratives in précis form), concerns the results of Flagg's ability to see into the future (as the result, crucially, of being wounded in the First War).[20] The prophet, who essentially is able to step outside of time and thus live in a kind of double temporality (a temporality that is the moment of trauma), eventually has a vision of the future in which his fiancé will betray him. Orr describes the peculiar agony of Flagg's prediction: "The tragedy is that Bettina is innocent, utterly free of guilt, since she has not yet met the man she will betray her husband with" (62). Flagg's traumatic prophecy so unhinges him that he kills himself. Flagg's prophetic talent is thus quintessentially traumatic, not simply because it leads to "tragedy." Maxwell's narrative makes it clear that prophecy itself—the impulse that brings the prophet into two times—is traumatic in an almost classic Freudian sense. The prophecy can, I think, be compared to the dreamwork as it functions in Freud's discussion of the dreams of trauma victims. We recall Freud's characterization of patients' dreams. In *Beyond the Pleasure Principle* Freud writes: "Now dreams occurring in traumatic neuroses have the characteristic of repeatedly bringing the patient back into the situation of his accident, a situation from which he wakes up in another fright" (282); the traumatized subject is "obliged to repeat the repressed material as a contemporary experience instead of . . . remembering it as something belonging to the past" (288). Flagg's prophecy works in similar way but in the opposite temporal direction: his prophecies are real for him, are contemporary experiences in that that they *will* happen, indeed, are as good as having happened already. Flagg's prophecy is a kind of future dream, a kind of future retroactivity. In both the neurotic and Flagg, temporality is disrupted. The neurotic experiences the past in the present, as the present: Flagg experiences the future in the present, as the present.

Flagg's story about seeing the truth of things has a final crucial resonance in that it prefigures, prophetically, Orr's own experience of betrayal (we must keep firmly in mind that Flagg is Orr's fictional creation). Flagg's story looks forward to the end of *Oracle Night* proper when Orr sits down for the final time to write in his blue notebook. The story he writes, a work of pure imagination—"Imagine this, I said to myself. Imagine this, and then see what comes of it" (212)—places the events of his recent life into a frame of sexual betrayal. Orr imagines—and there is no way for him, or the reader, to confirm the truth or falseness of what he writes—that Trause has long been in love with Orr's wife, Grace, and has carried on a sexual relationship with her even as Orr was thought to be dying. The crux of Orr's narrative is that there is no way to confirm the identity of the father of Grace's child. Immediately after writing out his fantasy of betrayal, Orr destroys the blue notebook. The destruction of the notebook becomes an act that later haunts Orr, as it appears to him that the destruction of the narratives prefigures—indeed may cause—the death of both Trause and Grace's child.

The destruction of the notebook—and the putative effects it causes—recalls to Orr's mind a narrative about a writer who came to believe that his writing actually caused, rather than prophetically predicted, the death of his child; this writer subsequently lapsed into a twenty-one-year silence in which he wrote not a single word. Orr comes to believe that the recent events in his life—the failure to write Nick Bowen's story, the failure to sell his film treatment of *The Time Machine*, his marital difficulties—were somehow a kind of preparation for future trauma: the death of Grace's child, the death of Trause:

> At certain moments during those days, I felt as if my body had become transparent, a porous membrane through which all the invisible forces of

the world could pass—a nexus of airborne electrical charges transmitted by the thoughts and feelings of others. I suspect that condition was what led to the birth of Lemuel Flagg, the blind hero of *Oracle Night*, a man so sensitive to the vibrations around him that he knew what was going to happen before the events themselves took place . . . The future was already inside me, and I was preparing myself for the disasters that were about to come.[21] (Auster 2003, 223)

Orr figures himself as mourning before the fact, before the act: narrative—failed narrative—becomes a way of anticipating, "preparing," for the disasters to come. Orr's narratives thus are a kind of anticipatory mourning. Yet if these narratives are the crypt in which future trauma is contained, in which mourning finds its expression, albeit a kind of "unknowing" expression, what happens to the energy of grief that occurs after the real disaster? When the real disasters occur—Trause dies after an embolism; Grace is physically assaulted and loses her child—Orr finds himself mourning, yet this is a paradoxical mourning, a *repeated* mourning that simply is the fulfillment of Orr's fantasy writings:

I saw John's ashes streaming out of the urn in the park that morning. I saw Grace lying in her bed in the hospital . . . but even as the tears poured out of me, I was happy, happier to be alive than I had ever been before. It was a happiness beyond consolation, beyond misery, beyond all the ugliness and beauty of the world. (Auster 2003, 242–3)

This happiness "beyond" speaks to a kind of transcendence of the present moment of trauma: or, more precisely, it speaks to Orr's peculiar neurotic fixation on having somehow contributed to these events. My suggestion here is that we view Orr as symptomatically displaying the gratified desire of having created *at last* an outcome that speaks to a sense of finality. Having failed successfully to complete Bowen's narrative, having failed successfully to develop Wells' story, Orr finally does manage—in his own mind at least and as an articulation of a kind of magical thinking—to create the finality that a narrative traditionally must have: death. Trause's death, in Orr's mind somehow linked to the now-destroyed, effaced narrative, fulfills the claims of narrative, fulfills the requirements of the story, sanctions, in Benjamin's perfect phrase, "everything that the storyteller can tell" (94).[22]

And yet we, like Orr, must return incessantly to this fact: Orr's happiness is one that occurs twenty years prior to the writing of *Oracle Night*. What are we to make, therefore, of Orr's need to return to this moment, to this scene of narrative success? (We asked a similar question about Zimmer's need to return, narratively, to his past in *The Book of Illusions*). A simple response, of course, would be that Orr is suffering from a kind of lethal guilt precisely over this sense of responsibility for these deaths. The entirety of *Oracle Night* thus—as written twenty years after the fact and thus as a text that tells these stories for a second time—is a studied repetition of the past. In this sense, *Oracle Night* can be seen as an articulation of Freud's *Nachtraglichkeit* in an almost classic sense: Orr is attempting to come to terms, via repetition, with events of the past. He is coming to terms not only with his sense of having caused these deaths but also with having found the ability to write, the ability, precisely, to give voice to the fact that he has caused these deaths. It is in this sense that *Oracle Night*, as a narrative *about* mourning, becomes a narrative *in* mourning: the ability to work through these deaths is the result precisely of having caused them. Auster's narrative thus creates an essential traumatic tautology wherein mourning cannot escape its own cause; and it is here in this tautology that *Oracle Night*, feeding back on its own trauma in order to tell its trauma, precisely demonstrates the impossibility of mourning. Because a process in mourning, endlessly feeding on its own primal scene of (repeatedly) encrypted grief, can only be a narrative of static melancholy.

Orr's case, neurotic, obsessional, magical in its thinking, presents an extreme form of grief as impossible to escape. As I suggested at the outset of this analysis, however, Auster's narrative can, indeed, should, be read as a critique of the idea of successful mourning generally. At a basic level, Auster's narrative suggests that where memory is, mourning cannot be. In other words, mourning—successful mourning in Freud's sense—can only work when the past is killed, metabolized, cannibalized, and worked through. What Auster suggests, through the logic of the varieties of archives of memory, is that memory, history, the past make claims on the subject that cannot be denied, that can never be metabolized. Indeed, in Auster's examination of *Nachtraglichkeit*, we get almost a literal translation of the term: *Nachtraglichkeit* can mean "indebtedness to the past." One is indebted to the past, to history, to memory, to the *specter* of memory. But memory, precisely because it is spectral, precisely because its claims are continually present, precisely because it collapses the temporality of past and present into its traumatic moment, cannot be mourned. The process of memory, moreover, translates and transforms memories into repetitions of themselves: the memory of an event becomes the memory of a memory of the event. In this sense—and Auster literalizes this process by having Orr *write* his memories in the mystic writing pad of his failed narratives—remembering as repetition and thus endless reduplication of event, defers memory, defers and differs mourning. If a working-through is achieved, it can only be a working-through that has attached itself to a version—a specter—of the memory. *Oracle Night* thus is only one of myriad possible versions of events Orr attempts to translate twenty years after the fact. Memory is impossible—or impossibly fractal—and thus mourning is an illusion.

I wish, finally, to return to the beginning of *Oracle Night* and a question I posed at the outset of this analysis: How does one mourn one's own death? Because it is clear to me that despite Orr's claims to the trauma of the deaths of Trause and the child, the novel is fundamentally about his own process of mourning his own death, his own virtual or symbolic death. The "twenty years after" structure of *Oracle Night* sees Orr revisiting the instant of his own death and the consequences of his survival. The end of the narrative, which sees real death supplant the effects of his own virtual death, speaks to a substitutive process where survival is predicated on the deaths of others: Orr's survival as a writer, his ability to achieve this happiness beyond consolation, so indebted as it is to his sense of having killed Trause and the child, speaks perhaps to a desire to translate virtual death into the real. Symbolic death, precisely because it ghosts Orr, translates Orr into a curious state that seems to require expiation. Like all ghosts struggling for release from this state, Orr seeks, through the process he describes throughout *Oracle Night*, a release from his painful ontology.

If death, as Derrida suggests in *The Gift of Death*, is your one single possession, the one thing that gives value to your life, a symbolic death, a virtual death, must represent a (symbolic) loss of value, a loss of singularity. At some level thus, Orr's symbolic death cheats him, robs him of his singularity. And if your death has become merely—but more than merely—symbolic, your death in some sense is no longer yours, because its meaning refracts from you to those around you and back: the virtual death sets up a current of symbolic exchange rather than a closed system where the value of the death cannot circulate, as in real death, where the current is broken. In a symbolic death, the meaning of the death is owned by others who still see you and reflect that meaning back to you. And thus, the question becomes: how does one respond to the devaluing of the only thing that has value for you? Orr's response is to stage another singularity, to create himself anew by first and crucially burying himself properly. Seen from the perspective of the notion of the loss of singularity, Orr's repeated narratives—all of which as I suggest reflect his own state—are attempts to bury himself. Ghosts require burial in order to be stilled; Orr requires a symbolic burial to complete his symbolic death. And we do recall, of course, that one of the effects of writing in the blue notebook is disappearance: Orr quite literally disappears as he writes, effaces himself in burial. And the process of failed narratives, of primarily Bowen, buried yet not effaced in the failure of the narrative, speaks to the failure in Orr's mind of the symbolic burial. This burial of Bowen is the burial of a simulacrum self, and thus, it is only at the final writing in the blue notebook, in the final burial, when Orr writes directly of and about himself and thereby succeeds in producing the desired narrative, death, that expiation is achieved.

1.3   *Travels in the Scriptorium* (2006)

We can bear neither the void nor the secret.
—Baudrillard, *The Perfect Crime*

I have chosen *Travels in the Scriptorium* as the final novel to analyze here because in some ways it perfectly summarizes all of Auster's concerns. It is, like *The Book of Illusions* and *Oracle Night,* a novel about the creative process. And like those previous novels, *Travels in the Scriptorium* is also a profound mediation on the link between the creative act and guilt, guilt over the very act of imagination. *Travels in the Scriptorium* is also typical for Auster in that it is a deeply self-referential novel: it is a novel, one might argue, that could mean dangerously little to a reader not familiar with the entire Auster oeuvre, given that it refers, as we shall see, to the major, and minor, novels that preceded it. In other words, and this is indeed a crucial element of the novel's thematics, *Travels in the Scriptorium,* is a deeply, and intentionally, narcissistic novel: it asks the reader to think about the relation between author and character, between fictional author and character, all the while arguing that the true narrative, the true and perhaps only story, is the story of the author's relation to his own imagination. What I am fascinated to analyze here is the relation between Auster's thematization of the guilty imagination and the figure of the author indebted to his imaginative work: what are the implications of the idea of an author becoming ethically responsible for his imaginative acts? What are the implications of the idea that the very act of imagination is always already marked as guilty? What, precisely, does guilt mean in the context of self-referential, metanarrative textuality? These questions need also to be filtered through the lens of the primary focus of my analysis: the figure of the archive. And what becomes absolutely central here is the figure of the author-as-archive. Mr. Blank, the author-figure in *Travels in the Scriptorium,* is the site of a melancholic attachment to his own acts of creation: he is the ground, the source, of the various characters who haunt him in his enclosed room. But he is, at least initially, an unknowing source: given that he has forgotten his relation—and responsibility—to his creations,

Blank is an archive of unknowing. Blank is thus indebted to a series of authorial acts of which he is unaware and in some ways, unaccountable; in this way Auster raises the stakes of the question of guilt: can the author be guilty for acts of which he is unaware? If the central figure here in *Travels in the Scriptorium* is the author-as-archive, how do we understand an archive that is hidden from itself, obscured and effaced at the moment of its creation? We have, in other words, returned to the idea of the secret.

Travels in the Scriptorium opens upon a simple scene: an old man in a room. The old man (we learn subsequently that his name is Blank) is under surveillance as a camera continually takes pictures of him. The events of the narrative take place in the third person: by placing Blank under the scrutiny of not only the camera but also of the very narrative voice, Auster is able to heighten the sense that Blank is rigorously under the disciplinary gaze of several external forces. But the narrative voice itself is not omniscient and thus poses the critical initial questions:

> It is unclear to him exactly where he is. In the room, yes, but in what building is the room located? In a house? In a hospital? In a prison? He can't remember how long he has been here or the nature of the circumstances that precipitated his removal to this place. Perhaps he has always been here; perhaps this is where he has lived since the day he was born. What he knows is that his heart is filled with an implacable sense of guilt[23].
> (Auster 2006, 2)

Blank cannot articulate the reasons for his guilt and neither, yet, can the reader. To this point, Blank seems almost like an Alzheimer's patient, his mind "elsewhere, adrift in the past as he wanders among the phantom beings that clutter his head" (3); the narrator describes him as lost "in a fogland of ghostlike beings and broken memories" (19). There is a group of thirty-six photographs in Blank's room and he gazes at them, desperate to find some meaning in them; he is able, after some effort, to conjure the name "Anna" while looking at a picture of a young woman. Soon after, Blank meets Anna, a character readers of Auster will recognize as Anna Blume from *The Country of Last Things*; it is here that we begin to understand Blank's guilt, even if he is still ignorant of its full and ultimate cause. Anna's kindness to Blank—she acts something like a very accommodating nurse—seems to free up aspects of Blank's memory:

> I've done something terrible to you. I don't know what it is, but something terrible . . . unspeakable . . . beyond forgiveness. And here you are, taking care of me like a saint.

> It wasn't your fault. You did what you had to do, and I don't hold it against you.
> But you suffered. I made you suffer, didn't I?
> Yes, very badly. I almost didn't make it.
> What did I do?
> You sent me off to a dangerous place, a desperate place, a place of destruction and death.
> What was it? Some kind of mission?
> I guess you could call it that.
> . . .
> I feel so ashamed.
> You mustn't. The fact is, Mr. Blank, without you I wouldn't be anyone.
> Still . . .
> No *still*. You're not like other men. You've sacrificed your life to something bigger than yourself, and whatever you've done or haven't done, it's never been for selfish reasons. (Auster 2006, 24–5)

Travels in the Scriptorium thus begins to offer itself as a complex meditation on writing, on the relation of author to character, on the nature of authorial responsibility. These thirty-six photographs all represent characters from previous novels by Paul Auster: Blank, at this point at any rate, seems to be a projected version of, if not Auster himself, then the idea of the author. But Blank is a curious kind of author in that if he is the source of all these characters—and thus all their misery—he is unaware of his responsibility to them; he is unaware, that is, that he is a writer in the strong sense of the term. It is only after meeting Flood, a character mentioned by another character in an Auster novel—Fanshawe from *The Locked Room*—that Blank begins to accept that he is a writer of sorts, but he still maintains an ignorance of having written anything: "I don't remember Fanshawe. I don't remember reading his novel. I don't remember writing the report" (60).

Blank is, nevertheless, in this room as a form of punishment; he is to receive some kind of "treatment" and, as he discovers as the novel comes to a close, he is to be brought up on criminal charges. Quinn, the main character from Auster's first major work of fiction, *City of Glass*, lays out the charges and the proposed punishment (that he be drawn and quartered), charges and punishment proposed by characters not pleased with having been called into being by Blank:

> Charges? What kind of charges?

The whole gamut, I'm afraid. From criminal indifference to sexual molestation. From conspiracy to commit fraud to negligent homicide. From defamation of character to first-degree murder. Shall I go on?
But I'm innocent. I've never done any of those things.
That's a debatable point. It all depends on how you look at it. (Auster 2006, 135)

At this point of thinking about the relation between writing, criminality, and guilt, I want to turn to a theorist whose work obsessively focuses on the idea of writing as such, a theorist whose work will help, I believe, to unpack and unravel the complexities Auster is presenting to us in *Travels in the Scriptorium*. In *The Space of Literature*, Blanchot begins by meditating on the idea of the art work, the book: he suggests that the work is itself defined by its essential solitude, that once it is finished by the author—but a work is never finished as he tells us—the work enters into an uncanny space of absolute separation from its author; the work enters into its own state of being. Blanchot further suggests that what defines the author's relation to the work at the moment of its completion is the author's radical failure to know the work, to read the work, to interpret the work: "the writer never reads his work. It is for him illegible, a secret. He cannot linger in its presence. It is a secret because he is separated from it" (23). Does this not perfectly characterize Blank's relation to his past work, the work he does not remember (or is disavowing)? These characters who haunt Blank are, initially, unknowable to him because they represent the work that cannot be known, the archive that cannot be read, the imaginative ground to which he cannot return. But if *Blank* cannot return to the work, the work can, indeed it seems *must*, return to him. Auster is careful to figure these characters from previous novels as phantoms, ghosts, as fully spectral: Flood, bemoaning the fact that he has been called into being by Fanshawe (Flood thus becoming a kind of double specter, a specter within a specter's work) characterizes himself thus: "My life is in ruins, Mr. Blank. I walk around the world like a ghost, and sometimes I question whether I even exist. Whether I've ever existed at all" (60).

These revenants are fascinating, of course, not merely because of the guilt they bring, but because of what they represent, literarily. They seem to confirm another of Blanchot's ideas about the infinite nature of the work, its radical incompleteness. These characters, to put it bluntly, do not end, cannot end; they confirm what I would call, following Blanchot, the radical melancholy of the work, the fact that the work cannot end, but maintains itself in a constant, spectral real. Blank's haunting by these figures of his past work is an emblem of this melancholy, of the inability to separate oneself from the work even as one is, ontologically, separate from it. This paradox is what for me perfectly defines Blank's radical agony: the work is secret to him, *his* work is secret to him. It is unknowable to him as its author; the work is unknowable and yet it returns insistently, one might say infinitely (we will return to this point), to hold him accountable for its creation: Blank is haunted, in other words, by the infinite work.

I wish here to quote Blanchot at some length, keeping in mind how perfectly his words describe the author (let us call him Auster for the time being, but we will need correctly to fix his identity as the novel closes), who obsessively returns to core themes, obsessively returns to characters who, like Blank, are haunted by his own work:

> The writer's solitude, that condition which is the risk he runs, seems to come from his belonging, in the work, to what always precedes the work. Through him, the work comes into being; it constitutes the resolute solidity of a beginning. But he himself belongs to a time ruled by the indecisiveness inherent in beginning over again. The obsession which ties him to a privileged theme, which obliges him to say over again what he has already said—sometimes with the strength of an enriched talent, but sometimes with the prolixity of an extraordinarily impoverishing repetitiveness, with ever less force, more monotony—illustrates the necessity, which apparently determines his efforts, that he always come back to the same point, pass again over the same paths, persevere in starting over what for him never starts, and that he belong to the shadow of events, not their reality, to the image, not the object, to what allows words themselves to become images, appearances—not signs, values, the power of truth.[24] (Blanchot 1982, 24)

I want to use this passage as an entry point into considering, if one can invoke the proper author, Auster; for what is Blanchot describing here if not the situation of not only Blank, as author of these previous texts, but also Auster himself? Auster, not Blank, is the proper author of these previous novels; it is Auster who has sent Anna Blume into the dangers of the country of last things; it is Auster who, through his fictional character Fanshawe, has written Flood into painful being. It is, in other words, Auster who, to return to Blanchot, always comes back to the same point, who passes over the same paths; it is Auster who is revisiting the very origins and grounds of his work as an author.[25] *Travels in the Scriptorium* as a whole thus functions as an oddly spectral archive: it is the archive as revenant. The book works to return to that site of commandment and commencement that Derrida suggests characterizes the archive as such. The novel, rather than establishing a point of departure into a spectral futurity, as is proper for the archive as such, returns to its origins, consolidates the past through which this present moment of guilt and responsibility occurs.

But Auster is careful not to allow himself to be figured too clearly as being in the text or being responsible for it; in a neat turn at the novel's conclusion, Auster manipulates the novel into something like a Moebius strip. Blank begins to read a manuscript "of some one hundred and forty pages (140), which is, of course, the same length as *Travels in the Scriptorium*. The manuscript is entitled *Travels in the Scriptorium* and is apparently authored by N. R. Fanshawe, Auster's own character, the fictional author in *The Locked Room*. Fanshawe, like Mann of *The Book of Illusions*, is another of Auster's renunciatory artists: he has written novels and then has disavowed any relation or responsibility for them; perhaps *Travels in the Scriptorium* is Fanshawe's way toward some kind of penance for his renunciation of his art, penning a novel about a man being punished for not recognizing his own work. But the turn is not yet complete; the novel he writes, and the novel Blank reads, is, of course, identical to the novel we have just read. Blank reads the first paragraphs of Fanshawe's novel: they are identical to the first paragraphs of *Travels in the Scriptorium*, Auster's novel, the novel proper. Blank thus is fully encrypted within a fiction, realizes that he is to be fictionalized in perpetuity. After the manuscript ends, the narrator, whom we now know (or can we?) to be Fanshawe, gives us this:

> Mr. Blank might have acted cruelly toward some of his charges over the years, but not one of us thinks he hasn't done everything in his power to serve us well. That is why I plan to keep him where he is. The room is his world now, and the longer the treatment goes on, the more he will come to accept the generosity of what has been done for him. Mr. Blank is old and enfeebled, but as long as he remains in the room with the shuttered window and the locked door, he can never die, never disappear, never be anything but the words I am writing on his page. (Auster 2006, 144)

Blank has essentially been forced to become what Fanshawe is at the end of Auster's *The Locked Room*: the recluse, the renunciatory artist. But he is more: Blank is entombed, encrypted, archived within a fiction preceding and exceeding his own. And he is here, as a fiction perhaps, but surely as a kind of perpetually suspended specter; never to die, never to disappear,

Blank becomes only the trace—"the words I am writing on his page"—of an imagination that has called him into being, an imagination that has displaced his own guilt onto a hapless fiction.

I am fascinated by this ending, not merely for the complexity of Auster's play: indeed, the trope of the fiction within a fiction is, at this point, something of a well-worn conceit. I am more interested in the implications of Blank's encrypting, the fact that he seems aware of the fact that he is being called into being by forces preceding and exceeding him. After reading Fanshawe's manuscript, for instance, he throws it away in disgust and asks "When is this nonsense going to end?" (143). For Blank, this fictionalizing of his own subjectivity is a nonsense, or so he characterizes it in his anger. But surely it is more; surely what Auster is thematizing here is the impulse of the work, the way, to follow Blanchot, the work becomes that force which precedes and exceeds all others. The work, as Blanchot tells us, keeps the writer "in a fundamental passivity where the word, no longer anything but its appearance—the shadow of the word—never can be mastered or grasped" (25). Surely Blank, at the conclusion of Auster's short, enigmatic novel, is a pure thematization of the idea of the radical passivity before the work: Fanshawe in this sense becomes a perfect allegory for the impulse of the work; Fanshawe becomes the work itself and as he places Blank within his own words, within his own pages, Blank is unfolded into what Blanchot calls, beautifully, "the distress of the infinite" (26): "he can never die, never disappear, never be anything but the words I am writing on his page."

And surely this passivity before the impulse of the work explains a feature of Blank's activity that I have to this point not mentioned. It is crucial to keep in mind that Blank, in fact, does take up and write during his residence in the scriptorium: he discovers an unfinished manuscript by Peter Trause (he being the writer in *Oracle Night*, his initials being an obvious anagram of Paul Auster); the manuscript tells the story of an alternate United States and details the efforts of a character, Sigmund Graf, to infiltrate the ranks of a splinter group to locate a traitor, Ernesto Land. Blank is asked by another of Auster's characters, Samuel Farr (he being a character from *The Country of Last Things*) to complete the story; Blank does, in fact, complete the story, narrating it orally to Farr and then, again orally, speaking to his empty room. In my reading of *Travels in the Scriptorium* as a whole, the contents of Trause and Blank's narrative are not crucially important; indeed, the narrative does not function as any critical mise en abyme of the larger containing narrative. What is crucial, however, is that the act of narrating is vital to Blank. The impulse to narrate is clearly shown to come naturally to him and, importantly, he uses the act of narrative to stave off his radical loneliness. What is also crucial, however, is how we read Blank's impulse to narrate retrospectively, that is, after we discover that he is merely a function within a fiction, an impulse of the larger impulse to work. Blank's narrative is fairly substantial and the revelation of Fanshawe's total control over Blank has the effect of cancelling any claims to authority, to power, to control over the very language that animates Blank's narrative. Blank's "when is this nonsense going to end?" now takes on an added resonance, as it begins to sound as if he is calling for an end not merely to these narrative games but also to the very animating principle behind the games, the impulse of the work, the impulse that has imagined Blank into being in the first place. And, of course, as we have suggested, this "nonsense" is never going to end: Blank is encrypted within this archive, never to die, never to disappear.

But notice how the issue of guilt is effaced in this conclusion; notice how Blank's primary emotion has been subtly but radically effaced here. The question for me now becomes: what has happened to the impulse toward guilt here? At some level, the novel argues that the very act of imagination is guilty in that it conjures subjectivities against their wills; what at first seems to be an extended meditation on the relation between imagination—or, perhaps more purely, thinking—and guilt has unfolded into a curiously baroque metafictional shell game. But surely the guilt remains somewhere? It does, of course, remain; it has to remain, if only as a trace, in the sense that *Travels in the Scriptorium*, Auster's novel is, as suggested earlier, a perfect archive of the revenant. It thematizes the return of the past, thematizes, that is, the idea of being indebted to the past. Blank's absorption into the larger fiction, at first blush a way of effacing that theme of guilt, is really an overt gesture of repression, a gesture in fact so overt as to only call attention to what cannot ever be successfully hidden. Blank, and I must keep returning to these words, "can never die, never disappear, never be anything but the words I am writing on his page." But Blank is in place forever. He is an archive of guilt within a larger archive: he, the source and foundation of these returning revenants, is now housed within an archive—call it Fanshawe's story or call it Auster's—which forever keeps his guilt in play even as it claims to reduce him to the status of mere words. But, and this is the crucial point, words are only ever, and have only ever been, the medium for the translation of both subjectivity and guilt. When Fanshawe claims that Blank can never be anything but the words on the page, he really is disavowing the very medium he claims has power to reduce a subject to the status of mere text. In other words, Fanshawe is himself, given that he, too, is inscribed within Auster's own narrative, only ever, always already, drawing attention to the permanence, the *melancholic* permanence, of the guilt that will forever assert itself within the ineradicable archive.

Chapter 2

Burying History: Haruki Murakami

What haunts us are not the dead, but the gaps left within us by the secrets of others.
— Nicholas Abraham, *"Notes on the Phantom"*

I propose here to read several Haruki Murakami texts as a response to a series of questions about the relations between the archive, trauma, guilt, and the secret. At first glance, this line of thinking, one that suggests a link between the archive and secrecy, may appear somewhat counterintuitive, for surely one of the functions of the archive proper is to maintain itself as a public space, a site where, say, records are kept open to public view. This reading, of course, is dependent upon a particular view of the archive, one which sees it, perhaps, in conventional terms: a place of record keeping, a museum, a library, and so on. Murakami's archives are anything but conventional; his novels—and the nonfictional *Underground*—suggest that there are strange homologies between the archive, as conventionally understood, and other more uncanny sites where history is discovered and kept; where trauma maintains itself; where loss secretes itself within the subject (without any subjectivity). Murakami's archives are places of secrecy, sites where the truth of things—the truth of history (*The Wind-Up Bird Chronicle*); the guilty truth of national consciousness (*Underground*); the truth of trauma (*Hard-Boiled Wonderland*; *after the quake*)—is hidden from public view: dry wells, sealed urns, the inaccessible unconscious of the fragmented subject, narratives of obscure histories told to obscure subjects. Murakami's novels become sites where the hidden archive is brought to light, exposed to view, thus revealing the double impulse of his writing: to record the secret archive and to become the archive of the secret.

My questions then are the following: what is the relation between secrecy and the archive? Do the secret and the archive have similar economies, similar logics? How does the secret respond to history, and how is this response related to the archive's response to history? Why is the truth (of history, trauma, loss) always already secret? This last question finds its source in a passage from Heidegger's *Being and Time*, in section six, Heidegger notes that truth, as such, is always hidden. In fact, my question, why is truth always already secret, is not really a question for Heidegger; truth's ontological structure is a priori hidden; truth finds its being in hiddenness. His metaphors here, however, are resonant for a reading of Murakami:

> Truth (uncoveredness) is something that must always first be wrested from entities. Entities get snatched out of their hiddenness. The factical uncoveredness of anything is always, as it were, a kind of *robbery*. Is it accidental that when the Greeks express themselves as to the essence of truth, they use a *privative* expression—ἀ-λήθεια?[1] (Heidegger 1962, 265)

I am fascinated by the violence inherent in the discovery of truth. For Heidegger—and he traces this violence back to the very beginnings of philosophy—truth is only ever violently, aggressively revealed: it is "wrested," "snatched," from its hiddenness; the uncovering of truth is always a form of robbery. I wish to suggest that this central conceit—truth's hiddenness, the requirement that it be violently revealed (if it is to be revealed)—defines Murakami's project perfectly; we must make sense of the sometimes extreme violence that attends Murakami's reading of history; we must make sense of the intimate relation between physical and psychological assault and the revelation of the truth of things. And we must attend carefully to these troubling ideas: if the secret is only ever revealed through violence, within violence, and if the secret has a close connection to the archive, then the archive, too, must be read as a site of violence and horror. And finally, if Murakami's project is to reveal the secret, then his discourse—his novels and nonfiction—must be seen not merely as representations of violence, but as *themselves* works of violence.

2.1 Hard-Boiled Wonderland and the End of the World (1991)

What, then, is it to cross the ultimate border? What is it to pass the term of one's life? Is it possible? Who has ever done it and who can testify to it?
—Derrida, *Aporias*

I wish to begin my analysis of *Hard-Boiled Wonderland and the End of the World* by returning to Abraham and Torok's 1975 essay "The Lost Object—Me." I wish to argue that this essay, an analysis of the relation between trauma and divided, fragmented, subjectivity, is a perfect point of departure for a discussion of Murakami's novel, given that *Hard-Boiled Wonderland and the End of the World* is essentially a precise analysis of the concept—call it the conceit—of split subjectivity. In their essay Abraham and Torok detail how trauma produces a split in the psyche, a split that, in its turn, creates a hidden, secret, crypted aspect of consciousness. The self, in other words, becomes secret to itself, a phantomic presence, precisely as it is secreted away from itself by the force of trauma:

> The image of the phantom does not come to us accidentally as a term for the analyst's torment. This image points to an occasion of torment for patients as well—a memory they buried *without legal burial place*. The memory is of an idyll, experienced with a valued object and yet for some reason unspeakable. It is memory entombed in a fast and secure place, awaiting resurrection. Between the idyllic moment and its subsequent forgetting . . . there was the metapsychological traumatism of loss or, more precisely, the "loss" that resulted from a traumatism. This segment of an ever so painfully lived Reality—untellable and therefore inaccessible to the gradual, assimilative work of mourning—causes a genuinely covert shift in the entire psyche. The shift itself is covert, since both the fact that the idyll was real and that it was later lost must be disguised and denied. This leads to the establishment of a sealed-off psychic place, a crypt in the ego. (Abraham and Torok 1994, 140–1)

This is an enormously resonant passage for our reading of Murakami's novel. The unnamed narrator, for reasons we will see, has a split consciousness: one aspect of his consciousness resides—I am uncertain which metaphors are appropriate to discuss the ontology or topography of the subject, let alone his geographic location—in the here and now, the real world (let us call it that for the moment); the other, hidden aspect finds itself living at (or in) what is called the "end of the world," an uncanny, fantasylike world where the subject spends his time as a Dreamreader. He "reads" the skulls of unicorns, skulls that function as crypts containing the dreams of the dead. It gradually becomes clear over the course of the novel that there is an intimate connection between these two realms, that the subject in the real world is the subject in the fantasy world, but that he does not know how this split in his psyche has occurred. *Hard-Boiled Wonderland and the End of the World* is the record, the testimony, of this split, an etiological narrative detailing how a "crypt in the ego" marks the subject as his own phantom. The narrative, in other words, is an exploration, through fantasy, through science fiction, of the idea of the radically fragmented self, of subjectivity with, perhaps, too many subjects.

But, and this is crucial, we must emphasize that the mechanism of the narrator's trauma and loss—the forces that create his split subjectivity and the crypt in the ego—*are not his own*: unlike Abraham and Torok's subject who has this idyll to lose, who has a memory to bury, who, in other words, has a kind of ownership, if not agency over his own memory, Murakami's narrator is fully at the mercy of forces preceding and exceeding him. The narrator is essentially the subject of an experiment that splits his consciousness in order to most effectively hide valuable data. I wonder, and this notion is one to be explored more fully here, if Murakami's novel—in its explicit figuration of the subject at the mercy of forces (both scientific and economic) preceding and exceeding him—should be read as an allegory of the drives; I wonder if the figure of the scientist who experiments on the narrator and the agency for whom the narrator works as a data handler should be read as allegories of drives over which the subject has no control. I wonder, in other words, if what Murakami offers here is a material exploration of psychoanalytical categories, and if this is so, what we have here in *Hard-Boiled Wonderland and the End of the World* is a material representation of the work of mourning, what Freud calls—in a metaphor itself explicitly materialist—the "economics of pain."

But let us just glance back at Abraham and Torok. It is precisely loss, inaccessible to mourning, that causes the crypt in the ego. It is loss, in other words, that creates the self as hidden to itself; it is loss that creates the self as its own hidden archive/crypt. If Freud was unable, as he admits, to understand how mourning works—if, that is, the economy of pain exceeds its own comprehension—perhaps Murakami's novel, with its explicit materialization of psychoanalytical categories and tropes, is an attempt to understand, materially, how mourning works or fails to work. That is to say, trauma is always a material cause, always has a material cause, but the economy of trauma, its work, takes places at the level of the mental, the psychological, the hidden or secret: Murakami materializes the process of mourning in order to reveal its secret economy.[2]

And so, the question: how did our narrator find himself in this condition of radical separation from himself? Murakami's answer begins with an early revelation that the narrator has always already been able, by virtue of practice and uncanny talent, to separate himself from himself: as he waits to meet the scientist who he thinks is a mere client, the narrator passes the time by counting separate amounts of coins in separate pockets, simultaneously. His left hand counts a certain amount, his right another:

It's hard for those who've never attempted the procedure to grasp what it is to calculate this way, and admittedly it is tricky at first. The right brain and the left brain each keep separate tabs, which are then brought together like two halves of a split watermelon. No easy task until you get the hang of it.

Whether or not I really do put the right and left sides of my brains to separate accounts, I honestly can't say. A specialist in neurophysiology might have insights to offer on the matter. I'm no neurophysiologist, however. All I know is that when I'm actually in the midst of counting, I feel like I'm using the right side and the left side of my brain differently. (Murakami 1993, 3–4)

It is, in fact, this uncanny talent to divide himself that has alerted the scientist to the narrator's particular use value. The scientist, known only as the Professor, though something of a rogue worker (he dislikes having to work for anyone but himself), is employed by the System, a business entity that encrypts valuable data; the narrator also works for the System and is an ideal candidate for hiding—encrypting—data, given his particular talent. The narrator's normal course of work involves being what is called a Calcutec; he has data fed into him and this data is processed and hidden, later to be outputted when conditions are safe: "I input the data-as-given into my right brain, then after converting it via a totally unrelated sign-pattern, I transfer it to my left brain, which I then output as completely recoded numbers and type up on paper" (32). The narrator, as Murakami makes clear early in the novel, is fully enmeshed within an economy of data exchange, an economy, more precisely, that uses him merely as a vessel for its larger monetary needs; it is the System—in a constant battle for data against a rival business entity called the Factory (its operants are called Semiotecs)—that essentially provides the means allowing the scientist to subject the narrator to radical experimentation in subjectivity and consciousness alteration; it is the System, in other words, that will create the subject as archive to himself, as radical Other to himself:

Our organization is generally called the System, theirs the Factory. The System was originally a private conglomerate, but as it grew in importance it took on quasi-governmental status. In the same way as, say, Ma Bell in America. We rank-and-file Calcutecs work as individual independents not unlike tax accountants or attorneys, yet we need licenses from the state and can only take on jobs from the System or through one of the official agents designated by the System. This arrangement is intended to prevent misuse of technologies by the Factory. Any violation thereof, and they revoke your license. (Murakami 1993, 33)

What is critical to notice about the essential premise of the novel—one business entity in competition with another; both using people as vessels for information—is that the economy of information encryption fashions the subject's mind, his consciousness, his identity, as an object for exchange. Moreover, in true cyberpunk fashion—and the half of the novel that takes place in the "real" world is fully cyberpunk—Murakami establishes early that data exchange, even as it uses the mind as its crypt, is a fully material process.

As the narrator learns more about how the System has manipulated his mind, it becomes clear that the alternating chapters—those taking place at the so-called "end of the world"—are a representation of the narrator's core self; more precisely, these chapters represent his lost core self, what the Professor terms "the drama." The scientists in the real world—but this dichotomy between the real and fantasy worlds is one the novel slowly deconstructs—have created the means by which to extract the narrator's "core consciousness" (113)[3]; this core consciousness, to which the narrator has no access, is where the processing of valuable data occurs. The processing of this data—its encryption and decryption (what the novel terms "shuffling")—takes place within the narrator's mind—his crypt—but without his conscious connection to it. The scientists, in other words, have completely alienated the narrator from his own labor; his mind, its core, is hidden from him and has become the perfect secret archive: "'You can call up the drama, because it is your own self, after all. But you can never know its contents'" (114). If it is true that the perfect secret is the secret one has forgotten, the core consciousness becomes a perfect hiding place.[4]

But, of course, there are problems. As the narrator learns, he was not the only Calcutec to undergo this process of archiving the core consciousness. The Professor's granddaughter—who has become the narrator's guide to and from her grandfather's hidden underground laboratory (he has split with the System)—reveals that he was one of twenty-six experimental subjects; of those twenty-six, twenty-five have died, unable to withstand the process of separating self from self. We learn, now from the Professor himself, that the narrator was able to withstand the rigors of archiving the core consciousness because he has always had an innate talent for dividing his own mind, as we have previously seen. But surviving the procedure only leaves the narrator open to experience the true traumatic effects of losing the self: and this loss is a real loss, a material loss of self. The Professor makes clear that his experiments on these subjects—experiments involving extracting the core consciousness—occur materially: "Me, I'm of a more practical bent . . . '*Render unto Caesar what is Caesar's*' and leave the rest alone . . . Metaphysics is never more than semantic pleasantries anyway" (257). This statement prepares the way for the most explicitly materialist aspect of the Professor's work, after explaining that he has managed to extract the narrator's core consciousness, placing it within what he calls a "black box," the Professor is asked (by the narrator) if he has reproduced mind:

> "No, not at all. The mind's beyond reproducin'. All I did was fix your cognitive system on the phenomenological level. Even so, it has temporal limits—a time frame. We have t'throw up our hands when it comes to the brain's flexibility. But that's not all we did. We successfully rendered a computer visualization from your black box . . . A video of your core consciousness. Something nobody'd ever done." (Murakami 1993, 262)

The Professor, confessing that he had served as an "assistant editor in the movies" (263) before the war, now explains that consciousness can be manipulated like film, like video, and transplanted back into the self. The previous twenty-five subjects were unable to sustain this violation of their consciousness, but our narrator, given his ability to separate himself from himself, is able to withstand the process:

> "I thought and thought, now why should that be? And I came to one conclusion: this was something you yourself made. You gave structure to your images . . . "
> "I find that *very* hard to believe," I said.
> "I can think of many possible causes," the Professor assured me. "Childhood trauma, misguided upbringing, over-objectified ego, guilt . . . Whatever it was made you extremely self-protective, made you harden your shell." (Murakami 1993, 268)

It is fascinating to see how explicitly psychoanalytical categories—guilt, trauma, over-objectified ego—are, at once, so easily accepted as being at the origins of the narrator's ability to survive rigidly materialist manipulations of mind. But it is also clear that for the Professor, these origin narratives are largely irrelevant: the narrator has an ability to separate himself to himself, has the ability to lose himself, and it is this talent that allows the System to manipulate its subjects. There is something perverse in the Professor's blithe narrative of his experiments, something almost inhumanly cruel in the way in which his effacement of the importance of childhood trauma (or guilt) mirrors his fundamental lack of understanding of the trauma that is occurring to the narrator *now*. Because the narrator is not merely discovering that his mind has been radically and irreparably altered, he is soon informed that these experiments have resulted in the death of his world in the now. For reasons having to do with a fault in the mechanism by which the Professor has structured the narrator's neural pathways to and from his core consciousness, the narrator will soon lose his being in this world, will forever only exist in the other world of his buried, hidden, self:

"Meanwhile, this world in your mind here is coming to an end. Or t'put it another way, your mind will be living there, in the place called the End of the World. Everythin' that's in this world here and now is missin' from that world. There's no time, no life, no death. No values in any strict sense. No self." (Murakami 1993, 270)

In other words, precisely at the moment when this experiment is explained to him, the narrator is forced, through means external to his own drives, to confront his own loss of self; has, in other words, mourning forced upon him. This is what truly fascinates me about Murakami's complicated, hardnosed materialist examination of his narrator's loss of self: that loss is imposed from without; *mourning is imposed from without and its economies are revealed not to be intrinsic to the suffering subject.* This amounts to what is a kind of radical objectification of mourning: removing its economy from the subject—initiated by the Professor's removal of consciousness from his subject—and then observing how the subject responds to a process that is both his and not his. I wonder, of course, if Murakami's thought-experiment—and this novel really is a large thought-experiment: what would mourning look like if it was external to the subject?—is not really a sly commentary about mourning as it truly is: mourning is always something external to the subject; mourning can, in fact, occur without a subject at all.[5]

But let us take a closer look at how this other world functions; the Professor says that there, at the End of the World, there is no time, no life, no death, no self. He further explains that this world continues forever, or at least, is experienced as a kind of eternity; he theorizes that at the point where consciousness ends, thought continues to subdivide the final moment forever, in a version of Xeno's paradox of motion:

"Think about the koan: *An arrow is stopped in flight.* Well, the death of the body is the flight of the arrow. It's makin' a straight line for the brain. No dodgin' it, not for anyone . . . Time is hurlin' that arrow forward. And yet, like I was sayin', thought goes on subdividin' that time for ever and ever. The paradox becomes real. The arrow never hits."

"In other words," I said, "immortality."

"There you are. Humans are immortal in their thought. Though strictly speakin', not immortal, but endlessly asymptotically close to immortal. That's eternal life." (Murakami 1993, 285)

I am, of course, reminded of Freud here, specifically, his thinking about the human's relation to the idea of his own death. In "Thoughts for the Times on War and Death," Freud muses on how the human refuses to acknowledge that he will die, refuses to acknowledge, that is, the reality of his own death:

> It is indeed impossible to imagine our own death; and whenever we attempt to do so we can perceive that we are in fact still present as spectators. Hence the psychoanalytical school could venture on the assertion that at bottom no one believes in his own death, or, to put the same thing another way, that in the unconscious every one of us is convinced of his own immortality.[6] (Freud 2001, 77)

I would like to place this notion, that the human cannot imagine his own death—that in the unconscious death is not a possibility, but immortality is—alongside one of Freud's most important ideas (previously mentioned in Chapter One) about the archival nature of the unconscious. In Part 7 of *The Interpretation of Dreams*, Freud is discussing the function of the dream and notes that the unconscious, against the best interest of its own suffering subject, always functions as a stubborn archive, refusing to relinquish the past: "Indeed it is a prominent feature of unconscious processes that they are indestructible. In the unconscious nothing can be brought to an end, nothing is past or forgotten" (577). Freud argues that it is precisely the function of psychotherapy to bring these unconscious processes to light in order that they may be forgotten ("to be dealt with finally and be forgotten" [578]): this is, he argues, how mental health is maintained.

It strikes me that Murakami's Professor is offering an analysis of the subject's lost consciousness, which is strangely reminiscent of Freud's thinking on the unconscious; indeed, I want to argue that the Professor's talk of the "core consciousness" works to efface the truly uncanny aspect of his own theory: *he, to this point, has never addressed the idea of the unconscious as such.* He has materialized core consciousness and seems, at least implicitly, to argue that this core is a material reality; but as this core is actualized and then hidden, materialized to be encrypted, does it not become structurally, if not materially, the Freudian unconscious? And if this is the case—as I believe it to be—my questions become more complicated. What happens to the subject who not only cannot forget his unconscious, but *becomes* his unconscious? What happens, more precisely, to the subject who becomes his unconscious—becomes his own lost object—forever? Because this is exactly the position of Murakami's narrator: lost forever to himself in himself. If the unconscious is that archive wherein traumatic occurrences are housed, and if the function of mourning—if not psychoanalysis (but psychoanalysis is only really a kind of mourning[7])—is to bring an end to these traumatic memories, what happens to the subject who cannot be separated from his own unconscious? Murakami offers here an almost unbearably uncanny image (at least from a post-Freudian perspective): the subject without unconscious because *only* unconscious.

And in so doing, in offering an image of a subject who becomes his own lost object, a subject who is made to become his unconscious, to inhabit his unconscious (*to be inhabited by* his unconscious), Murakami also, of course, collapses the logic of both the secret and the archive; effaces the secrecy of the archive by having his subject assume secrecy, by having his subject become his own secret. Before the Professor reveals his complex experiments, before, that is, he reveals precisely how the subject will die to this world in order to live forever in the lost world of the unconscious, the secret remained intact; the archive as such maintained its aura of perfection. Because recall that the Calcutecs were the bearers of the archive, the hidden archive; they themselves had no access to what was hidden within their own core consciousness (which now becomes the unconscious). Prior to the Professor's revelation of his work, it was safe to assert that the economy of the secret was itself a secret economy; that is, no one, save for the Professor—who becomes here the subject supposed to know—knows what the secret is, where it is, or how the secret itself becomes secret. This double process—the secret and the hiding of the origin of the secret—is what defines the perfect secret. The economy of the secret—how it came into being—must, too, be secret. Moreover, and here we begin to track the endlessness of secrecy, a secret is not merely some hidden kernel of knowledge whose origins must be encrypted; *the means by which that hidden kernel of knowledge became hidden must, in turn, become secret, hidden, and archived* (perhaps endlessly, perhaps, to borrow the Professor's word, asymptotically). What Murakami's novel explores is the process by which both the secret and the secret economy of the secret are revealed: *Hard-Boiled Wonderland* becomes something of an allegory of secrecy as such.

But it is, obviously, about more. Or, at least, it is about the terrible consequences of the revelation of the secret's secret economy. Because, the novel seems to ask, what is the price of creating the secret archive? What is the price of actualizing consciousness? The price is mind, a lost mind, a mind now lost to itself within itself forever. We should here pause and recall Heidegger's reading of the relation between (hidden) truth and its revelation. Truth's revelation only occurs within the logic of violence: "entities get snatched out of their hiddenness," he writes. What a perfect way to describe Murakami's narrator: snatched out of his hiddenness to himself, he is compelled, violently, to see and to be his own lost object. And the consequences, from a psychoanalytical point of view, are staggering. Let me focus my final remarks here with one question: what are the consequences of becoming one's own unconscious? From one perspective, a response can only be this: to become one's unconscious means to lose one's unconscious. In other words, if there is only unconscious, the logic of the consciousness/unconsciousness binary is radically dismantled. Murakami is thus exploring a dismantling of Freud's first topology of the subject (conscious, preconscious, unconscious). True to his penchant for the materialization of the immaterial, Murakami plays out this topological dismantling precisely within shifting topographies (we should perhaps begin to speak of Murakami's topography—or psychotopography—of the subject): we move from the real world into a fantasy world, where the subject exists in a permanent twilight of subjectivity. And, of course, when read from the perspective of the mourning/melancholy binary, this loss of the unconscious becomes particularly resonant. If mourning is a response to some lost object or ideal; and if this mourning process, the economy of mourning, takes place within the unconscious (recall that for Freud all loss is housed within the unconscious; all traces of the trauma of loss are housed within the unconscious); and if that unconscious itself is lost (or has become the only aspect of the topology), we are in the position now of speaking of mourning without the unconscious. And this is one of Freud's most important ideas: mourning requires an unconscious, requires an archive, requires secrets. Where there is none, where there is no secret, there is no possibility of mourning. What Murakami offers us, in this final image of the subject who has become his own lost object, is a subject not only in the twilight of subjectivity—for what is the subject without an unconscious? The posthuman? The posthumous?—but in the twilight of mourning, or, to be more precise, in the permanence of melancholy. Melancholy is the refusal to mourn, the inability to mourn, the inability to lose one's identification with the lost object: Murakami's subject, by being forced to become his own lost object, cannot choose mourning or melancholy, but has melancholy thrust upon him. He is compelled not only to exist in a state of impossible mourning—for this is what melancholy truly is: the inability to mourn—but he has *become* melancholy itself. In the final pages of the novel, the narrator, now permanently encrypted within his lost self—but without knowing fully why or how—speaks of his own sense that this world exists only for him, *as* him:

> "I cannot forsake the people and places and things I have created . . . I must see out the consequences of my own doings. This is my world. The Wall is here to hold *me* in, the River flows through *me*, the smoke is *me* burning. I must know why." (Murakami 1993, 399)

To know "why" would mean that the narrator would be able to reflect on his own condition as secret, and secreted, archive; to know "why" would mean the narrator would have to reflect on and comprehend the very grounds of his own precarious being; to know "why" would mean the narrator would have to wrest truth from its hiddenness. But our narrator no longer has any hiddenness. Without an unconscious, without the capacity to hide the truth, the narrator's truth floats free of any restraint but also of any knowing. The desire to know "why" is the impossible, agonized desire to know the end of secrecy itself.

2.2   *The Wind-Up Bird Chronicle* (1994)

We must tell the secret, not reveal it.

—Derrida, *On the Name*

The Wind-Up Bird Chronicle begins with a disappearance. In fact, the entire novel can be read as an enormously complicated analysis of the effects of *disappearance*—understood largely as a type of the hidden; the disappeared as that which has become hidden or secret—not only on its main character, Toru Okada, but on an entire community, if not an entire country. In what follows, I am interested in pursuing this disappearance, much as Toru, clearly a type for Orpheus, pursues his lost Eurydice, Kumiko. The reader of this novel in fact is asked to pursue multiple disappearances, multiple secrets, multiple sites of the hidden. As these disappearances, these secrets, these crypts, are explored the novel gradually unfolds its ethical economy. This is, as I will argue, an economy of the secret, a secret economy, but it is, crucially, an economy that asks to be revealed, that seems to require the idea that secrets—to be understood as such—must always stand in relation to their total revelation, to the risk of their total revelation. *The Wind-Up Bird Chronicle*, in other words, is a novel about secrets, about the bedrock of secrets that underpins all lives at every moment. What is fascinating about the novel, as it tracks back and forth from the past to the present, is the way in which all secrets are shown to be woven into all other secrets: the economy of the novel, its ethical economy, is an economy of connection. All lives are woven into the fabric of all others: but this connection is, at first, a hidden connection, a secret connection, and thus what the novel ultimately wishes to explore are the implications—the risks, the dangers—of exposing the interconnectedness of secrets, of revealing the close presence of the secret lives of others.

The Wind-Up Bird Chronicle is, in terms of pure length, Murakami's most complicated piece of writing to date.[8] In what follows, I will give details of the plotlines I will be tracking, Orpheus-like, but I need to be clear that while the novel seems to unfold in a somewhat haphazard fashion, plot events are crucially connected. I wish to offer an argument, therefore, about the relation between the form of the novel, specifically aspects of its digressive nature, and its content. Ultimately I am interested in pursuing the idea that formally, the digression is the mark and marker of the secret; the digression is, in other words, the trace of the secret, the trace left behind by the secret. To read the novel as emplotting the logic of the crypt—to read the novel as embedding a series of archives, as I will suggest—requires that we think through the relation between the discursive digression and the material archive because both the archive—a crypt, a dry well (the dominant image of the novel)—and the digression—a narrative of events occurring decades before the present day—structurally have similar economies: both are temporal and spatial disruptions; both delay or, more precisely, offer a position from which to step aside from the logics of time and space; both, because secret, ultimately offer themselves as spaces wherein the event of history attempts to maintain itself as separate from the quotidian, the everyday flux of experience.

The central character of *The Wind-Up Bird Chronicle* is Toru Okada. Recently unemployed (he had been studying to be a lawyer), Toru finds himself functioning as a house husband. Toru is married to Kumiko Wataya, the daughter of a well-connected political family: both Toru and Kumiko despise her brother, Noboru, the scion of the Wataya family. *The Wind-Up Bird Chronicle* begins with the disappearance of both the family cat—named after the despised brother Noboru—and Kumiko. What follows in the novel is, as mentioned, essentially a version of the Eurydice myth, with Toru descending into literal and metaphysical depths in his attempt to find his missing wife.[9] Murakami structures the novel around a series of encounters: Toru meets a variety of characters whose stories are revealed in historical flashback; it slowly becomes clear that Kumiko's disappearance is somehow—if seemingly tenuously—related to this series of characters and their respective involvement in events in Japanese history. Toru meets Creta and Malta Kano, sisters who, as mediums, offer their services to Toru in his quest (they, it turns out, also have had violent encounters with Noboru Wataya: he has raped Creta); he meets Nutmeg and Cinnamon, a mother and son team, who also offer their services to Toru; Toru meets, critically, Mamiya, a former lieutenant in the Japanese army who tells what I believe to be the central historical narrative in the novel, a narrative with uncanny connections to present-day events. For my purposes here, it is the narrative digressions offered by Mamiya that I wish to consider at some length, but it is crucial to note, if only at the outset, that all characters and events link up in that they work to set Toru against Noboru in a classic, one might even say archetypal, conflict. That is to say, all events in the novel, those occurring in the present day and those occurring decades earlier, mobilize to bring Toru and Noboru together in ethical opposition: Toru is clearly set against Noboru in the present day (he is, after all, married to his sister); but historical events, as we shall see, work to prefigure and anticipate the conflict. In essence, the disappearance of Toru's wife is only a catalyst, suggesting that all events, major and minor, are loaded with historical purpose: all events, in other words, are *meaningful* in that they bring Toru and Noboru together in violent opposition. In terms thus of both form and content, the novel confirms one of Roland Barthes' most crucial ideas: in the literary work—and especially, I would argue, Murakami's—"everything has a meaning or nothing has" (104).

In what follows I wish to pursue a line of thinking that links the archive, the secret and narrative digression; specifically I am interested in exploring how each of these ideas plays out in the novel in relation to the idea of temporality, to the progression of time. To begin, we should note that Murakami is clear about the fact that the narrative of *The Wind-Up Bird Chronicle* is organized on a linear historical continuum. That is, the novel is divided into three books, each structured around the passing of forward-moving time: Book One, June and July 1984; Book Two, July to October 1984; Book

Three, October 1984 to December 1985. Thus, at one level, the novel is telling a story of the present day and even of a rather limited time span within the present day, roughly a year and a half. But what is also clear is that this forward-moving structure is placed in constant tension with the archival economy of the novel; that is, a critical tension is created when this forward-moving organization of time is displaced by the novel's fascination with the pressures and debts to history. In some profound sense, the novel, with its desire to narrate a story of time moving forward balanced by its fetishization of history, works to offer itself as a massive, *static* edifice, which in some sense ultimately takes place in no singular time at all: the present day, if not placed under erasure by the past, at least loses its claim to priority as it becomes only one of many possible temporalities.[10] *The Wind-Up Bird Chronicle*, in other words, explores the idea that all moments are temporal superimpositions, with the past filtering what we can and cannot know about the present, with the present filtering what we can know of the past. Perhaps the better way of thinking about the novel's theorization of time is to say this: any event only means something in relation to its being echoed in a later or an earlier time. That is, an event—say the Nomonhan Incident of 1939 (the central historical event in the novel)—only means something in as much as its effects are felt in the present day, in Toru, in his relation to his search for his wife. Again, nothing happens in isolation in Murakami's novel; events only signify if they are echoed—that is to say *archived*—in other temporalities.

And thus the question: how does the novel work to blur the present moment? How, in other words, does the novel demonstrate its central thesis, that all events in the present and the past only mean in relation to the echo of that event at a later time and place? The answer, of course, lies in the novel's use of narrative digression.[11] And here we turn to the figure of Lieutenant Mamiya. Mamiya is not the first military figure encountered by Toru in the novel. Indeed, the first, Sergeant Honda, is known to both Toru and his wife Kumiko. Prior to their being given permission to marry, Toru and Kumiko have been compelled by Kumiko's father to consult Honda, who now makes a living as a fortune teller. Both Toru and Kumiko go along with the order, mildly amused by the prospect. And Honda does, in his sybilline fashion, reveal some crucial things to Toru; first, he recites a poem, the importance of which becomes clear during later events: "I am he and/ he is me:/ Spring nightfall" (51). Honda's gloss on this (rather Beatlesque-sounding) poem is this: "Abandon the self, and there you are" (51). Second, Honda gives the couple some initial information about the Nomonhan Incident of 1939, the little-known border war between Japan and the

Soviet Union, a battle in which both he and Mamiya participated. This battle is crucial for a number of reasons, the primary being that, as Toru himself tells us, it is essentially—at least to Toru and Kumiko—a secret war, largely unknown known to the general public: "Until I heard about it from Mr. Honda, I knew almost nothing about the battle of Nomonhan" (53). The battle, resoundingly won by the Soviets, saw the defeat and humiliation of the Japanese army; but for Murakami, these historical facts are not as crucial as the deeply embedded narratives of the players within the battle, namely Mr. Honda and Lieutenant Mamiya, who, after Honda's death contacts Toru to pass along some of Honda's possessions.[12]

The relationship between Toru and Mamiya proves decisive for several reasons. First, in terms of the novel's structure, the relationship is entirely a narrative one; that is to say, it consists entirely of Toru listening, quite passively, to Mamiya's war stories, and particularly the story of Mamiya's encounter with a barbaric Soviet army official. Toru—indeed, like the reader, who assumes a position not unlike Toru—is compelled into a position of a kind of passive relation to time; his relation to the present moment is suspended, in other words, in as much as he gives himself over to Mamiya's narrative. Mamiya's function, thus, is largely a digressive one, a function, I will suggest, related intimately to the central image of his narrative: the well. And it is crucial to notice that Mamiya's story occupies a fairly large amount of space in *The Wind-Up Bird Chronicle*, stretching as it does over two large chapters of reminiscences (134ff; 151ff) and then in three subsequent letters, which supplement the narrative he tells Toru in person (207ff; 345ff; 538, 555ff). And here, briefly, are the details of that story: Captured by the Soviets with the aid of Mongolian soldiers, Mamiya, Honda, and a mysterious Japanese official (most likely some kind of spy) are forced to witness one of the most appalling acts of violence in the novel (and indeed in the entire Murakami oeuvre). The Soviet official orders one of his Mongolian henchmen to stake the Japanese spy to the ground and skin him alive; the scene is almost indescribably painful to read and is clearly intended to traumatize the reader as much as it traumatizes Mamiya. But the torture has a function: the Soviet is attempting to discover where the Japanese spy has hidden some documents; he refuses to tell, as does Mamiya. As punishment for refusing to disclose the whereabouts of the documents, Mamiya is given a choice: be killed immediately or be thrown into an abandoned, dry well. His choice, the well, is momentous, not only for himself, but, as we will see for Toru: this well becomes the central image of the relation between the hidden, the unconscious, the archive, and history.

What is clear about this story is that Mamiya is haunted, purely melancholically in fact, by this experience in the well; he is haunted not only by the extreme violence that attended his experience in Mongolia, but also by what occurs to him in the well and what the well subsequently comes to mean for him. His narrative—as an archive of history and personal trauma—contains within it the image and experience of being utterly isolated with the self; the well, in a sense, opens the self to the self, becomes a kind of gateway to the unconscious. We recall Honda's words to Toru, words that equally apply to Mamiya, "Abandon the self, and there you are," for surely what occurs to Mamiya is a kind of radical loss of self, a loss that continues to haunt him. At some level, Mamiya feels that he should have died in the well but has been denied that opportunity; the utter darkness of the well is broken only briefly by a shaft of sunlight, which comes down once a day; this light, for Mamiya, burns away all life from him:

> Something inside me was already dead. Perhaps, as I felt at the time, I should have died in that light, simply faded away. That was the time for me to die. But, as Mr. Honda predicted, I did not die there. Or perhaps I should say that I *could not* die there . . . After returning to Japan, I lived like an empty shell. Living like an empty shell is not really living, no matter how many years it may go on. The heart and flesh of an empty shell give birth to nothing more than the life of an empty shell.[13] (Murakami 1994, 170-1)

I am fascinated by Mamiya's narrative for reasons to do with the well itself—and we will need to explore its tropological significance at some length—but also with the structural function of the narratives he tells. His story of being cast down the well is only his initial narrative: he later tells Toru of his experiences in a Siberian prisoner-of-war camp where he finally confronts the Soviet official who had his countryman skinned (he is presented with an opportunity to kill the Soviet and fails to do so). These narratives, as I have been suggesting, truly do function to halt the forward movement of *The Wind-Up Bird Chronicle*, or seem to do so: we are placed back into history and are asked to find links between Mamiya's experiences and those of Toru in the present. And this task is, at one level, a difficult one because there seem to be few overt links between these two men, beyond the fact that both have experiences of being encrypted in wells (involuntarily in Mamiya's case, voluntarily in Toru's). But it is clear that both men are linked by a common experience of trauma, trauma that precipitates or articulates their experiences of the world. Mamiya is subjected to the most extreme witnessing of violence and himself undergoes acts of barbarity; Toru, too, in his search for his wife undergoes some acts of violence (he will, for instance, be attacked by an assailant with a baseball bat), but his traumas are ones initiated by experiences of abandonment and loss. And here, indeed, is the precise link between these characters: both undergo radical loss; both experiences of loss are mediated or mitigated by the well, the well which, as I will suggest, comes to function as melancholy archive. But it is fascinating to notice how Murakami sets up this linking of images of wells. Mamiya's narratives, the complex historical digressions, themselves function as the initial archives within the text: Toru, like the reader, is asked to accompany Mamiya into his historical, and in some sense, *secret*, narrative, into his well; as the image of the well is given to us—and as it takes on hugely metaphoric resonance in the novel as a whole—we realize that just as the well itself compels Mamiya into a position of separation and isolation, just as he disappears from history as he descends into his crypt, so, too, the narrative that tells of his experience functions in some sense to suspend the primary narrative impulse of *The Wind-Up Bird Chronicle*. The narrative digression into the well itself becomes a kind of narrative sinkhole in the novel. The central questions for us now must be: what precisely does the well represent in *The Wind-Up Bird Chronicle*? What is the relationship between Mamiya's experience in his well and Toru's own?

Mamiya has in some radical sense been transformed into a phantom in his own life by his experience in the well; there was, as he tells Toru in a letter, something in the light that utterly transformed him; the light, it seems, revealed his own subjectivity to him:

> *Under these special circumstances, I believe, my consciousness had attained such a viscid state of concentration that when the intense beam of light shone down for those few seconds, I was able to descend directly into a place that might be called the very core of my own consciousness.* (Murakami 1994, 208)

In his core consciousness—and surely we are here reminded of *Hard-Boiled Wonderland*—Mamiya sees something begin to emerge, but that thing—Mamiya calls it "the grace"—endlessly fails fully to reveal itself. And it is this loss of total revelation, the denial of total revelation, that haunts Mamiya and will haunt him until his death: "*when the revelation and the grace were lost, my life was lost*" (209).

And it is precisely the economy, or various economies, of loss that are operating within *The Wind-Up Bird Chronicle* for its major characters. For Toru, this loss finds its objective correlative, its archival objective correlative, in the well that he seeks in his own neighborhood. My own reading of the relation between Mamiya's loss of grace and Toru's journey into his own well, his own journey into darkness, is based on the idea that Toru in some fundamental way completes Mamiya: their experiences obviously structurally echo one another in the sense that both have profound experiences within the crypt; but whereas Mamiya experiences only loss, or the failure of revelation, Toru experiences something approaching the discovery of a kind of truth. My language here is, of course, deliberately cautious. It is a central task of what remains here to evaluate precisely Toru's relation to the truth by exploring these questions: what does he discover about his relation to his wife? His relation to Noboru? What kind of truth is uncovered within the crypt that is the well? And perhaps the central question: what does Toru do with what he knows?

Toru enters his well in Chapter Six of Book Two. One of the first things he mentions about his experience suggests that the well has a distinct and crucial relation to memory. The well, in other words, begins to work a kind of archival magic on Toru:

> Here in this darkness, with its strange sense of significance, my memories began to take on a power they had never had before. The fragmentary images they called up inside me were mysteriously vivid in every detail, to the point where I felt I could grasp them in my hands. I closed my eyes and brought back the time eight years earlier when I had first met Kumiko. (Murakami 1994, 222)

Given that Toru's quest is for the disappeared Kumiko, it is not surprising that he uses the well as a catalyst—an archival catalyst—for his memories of their relationship. In a sense thus, he loses himself to the world in order to find another who is also lost to the world: "the best way to think about reality, I had decided, was to get as far away from it as possible—a place like the bottom of a well, for example" (231).[14] Toru notes also that in the well there is a kind of stasis in effect: "Down here there are no seasons. Not even time exists" (392). This is a critical detail in as much as it suggests that time ceases in order for the archival truth of things to be revealed: the well, as a kind of material digression from reality, suspends time in order for what may be called a *cryptological* time to function. By cryptological I mean to suggest that the well begins to reveal a kind of hidden time to Toru, a hidden plane of being, a hidden truth of things. It is while in the well, lost to the world, and lost in some sense to himself, that Toru begins to undergo something resembling an out-of-body experience. He thinks at first that these experiences are dreams but comes to realize that the well, as much as being an archive, functions as a conduit to what appears to be another level of being, a parallel, darker world into which he discovers Kumiko has disappeared. It is fascinating how Murakami mobilizes the various losses in the novel in order to arrive at Toru's melancholy truth: Kumiko is lost; Toru attempts to find her, but cannot until Mamiya reveals his own profound loss. After gaining the knowledge contained within Mamiya's loss—the knowledge of the well as conduit—Toru must himself undergo a radical sense of loss in order to discover the truth of things.[15]

And we may do well to recall Heidegger at this point: "Truth (uncoveredness) is something that must always first be wrested from entities. Entities get snatched out of their hiddenness" (265). In some ways Murakami's novel confirms Heidegger's philosophical position in relation to the truth: the truth is a hidden thing and there is a violence attending its revelation. I am interested in the implications of Heidegger's ideas here, particularly the notion that the truth is always already, in its original state, a kind of secret; further, that when truth is revealed, the truth itself has lost its hiddenness. The truth, when it is known as such, that is, *as* the truth, is itself in a condition of loss, a condition of, according to Heidegger's metaphor, violent loss: it has lost its original hiddenness and is now exposed, *stolen into* revelation. Toru's journey in *The Wind-Up Bird Chronicle* is one that traces the gradual revelation of hidden truth, hidden secrets: Mamiya's revelation of Japan's secret war leads inevitably to Toru discovering the truth about his brother-in-law. This revelation leads to further understandings of Toru's relationship to figures within Japan's historical past: when Toru finally does encounter his lost Kumiko (in the parallel world revealed in the well),[16] he begins to understand that she and her brother, that is, the entire Wataya family, have a tainted "bloodline" (578), that there is a tendency in her family to accumulate power for evil purposes. Kumiko's disappearance, he realizes, was part of her attempt to remove herself from a relationship, her marriage to Toru, that would continue the Wataya bloodline. It is during this final meeting with Kumiko—or, more precisely, her avatar: she is never quite Kumiko in this world; indeed, she is never quite Kumiko again after her disappearance—that Toru is able to see objectively the link between all historical events (his language here is uncannily narratological: he sounds, that is, like a reader):

> "Well, finally, the events I've been through have been tremendously complicated. All kinds of characters have come on the scene, and strange things have happened one after another, to the point where, if I try to think about them in order, I lose track. Viewed at more of a distance though, the thread running through them is perfectly clear. What it all boils down to is that you have gone over from my world to the world of Noboru Wataya." (Murakami 1994, 577–8)

Noboru Wataya, of course, is only the most recent incarnation of the Wataya bloodline, the corrupt and corrupting bloodline. As part of his investigation into the connections between Noboru, Kumiko, and Japan's history, Toru discovers that their uncle, Yishitaka Wataya, had a relationship with Kanji Ishiwara, a Japanese lieutenant-general whose actions essentially brought about Japan's entry into conflict with the Soviet Union. He (Ishiwara) staged what is called the Manchurian Incident, an event that enabled Japan to annex Manchuria and transform it into Manchukuo: it is, therefore, because of Ishiwara that Japan will skirmish with the Soviets in Manchuria, a conflict that leads, inevitably, to Mamiya's entry into this stream, this thread, of history, an entry itself leading, again inevitably, to Toru's entry into his crypt, his well. Yoshitaka Wataya, after the war, and because of his intimate connections to figures of immense power and influence, established himself as a politician, a Diet member in fact: Noboru Wataya has inherited his "political constituency" (497).

In fact, Toru is correct when he says that if one were to try to piece together the connections between all events in this novel, the relationships seem tenuous. Yet, in their own way, these events do link up if, as Toru himself chooses to do, one decides to wrest the truth from its hiddenness, if, that is, one decides to impose a meaning on these seemingly random events. In his interview with Kumiko, Murakami is very clear to suggest that Kumiko is not the one revealing the truth of historical events to Toru: Kumiko's avatar, in fact, communicates like a Delphic oracle, speaking in riddles through a fragmented and displaced subjectivity. It is Toru who decides, in a purely hermeneutic fashion, that this figure is, in fact, his lost wife; it is he who decides, in an act of pure interpretive choice—or power—to read her words as precisely revealing the truth. His interview is a perfect example of truth being wrested from its hiddenness (and again we notice he speaks like a reader attempting to make sense of a complex narrative):

> "Yes, I think you are Kumiko. Because then all kinds of story lines work out. You kept calling me on the phone from here. You were trying to convey some kind of secret to me. A secret of Kumiko's. A secret that the real Kumiko in the real world couldn't bring herself to tell me. So you must have been doing it for her—in words like secret codes." (Murakami 1994, 576)

It is after he decides that his lost wife has been speaking in secret codes that Toru allows himself to read his own truth into the events he has experienced; and he is explicit that his construction of the truth is purely imaginary: " 'This is strictly a product of imagination, but I would guess that there was some kind of inherited tendency in the Wataya family bloodline. What kind of tendency I can't be sure, but it was *some kind of* tendency—something you were afraid of' " (578). He goes on, crucially, to speculate that her brother, Noboru, is accumulating power in order to bring about an apocalyptic event:

> "Now he is trying to bring out something that the great mass of people keep hidden in the darkness of their unconscious. He wants to use it for his own political advantage. It's a tremendously dangerous thing, this thing he is trying to draw out: it's fatally smeared with violence and blood, and it's directly connected to the darkest depths of history, because its final effect is to destroy and obliterate people on a massive scale." (Murakami 1994, 579)

The question now becomes one of how to respond to the threat posed by Noboru. The novel disposes of this problem in a curious way: Toru discovers the truth of Noboru—that is, his plan to eradicate humanity by unleashing its unconscious murderous desires—only after it is reported in the parallel world that Noboru has been attacked with a baseball bat and is lingering on the brink of death. At this point Toru believes himself to be innocent of any involvement in the attack (and as far as he knows in the real world Noboru is perfectly healthy); but, after his imagined insight into Noboru's character, he himself is attacked on the street (he is still in the parallel world) by an unnamed and unknown assailant, and Toru beats this man to death. At this point, in the real world, it is announced that Noboru has suffered a near-fatal stroke. Toru, who clearly believes the events in the real world are what matter, ethically, believes himself to be free of any involvement in Noboru's illness, because he obviously did not beat him in the real world. But he does believe that his beating of a man in the parallel world has had an effect: "There had to be some connection between my having beaten someone to death in the other world and Noboru Wataya's collapse. I clearly killed something inside him or something powerfully linked with him" (598). The problem of Noboru, thus, seems to be resolved, if not permanently (Toru worries that he is still alive in the real world).

But what is, of course, curious about these events is that, in the parallel world at least, effects precede their cause: Noboru's attack is reported before Toru beats his man to death. What are we to make of this temporal anomaly? One response is simply to notice that this attack occurs in the parallel world where the rules of temporal logic do not apply. A more satisfying answer would be to suggest that the event of this attack—effects preceding their cause—is a mise en abyme of the economy of trauma that in some ways is at work in the novel as a whole. Trauma, as we know, is not merely the event of shock, of loss; it is the *effect* of that event of shock which lingers, reappears, haunts the survivor. As Freud and others notice, there is a delay at work in the economy of trauma, a delay effect (Freud calls it *Nachtraglichkeit*), which will, in cases of flashbacks or traumatic dreams, place the victim back in the event of trauma; trauma, in other words, sets up a temporal feedback loop in which the event of trauma returns unbidden repeatedly.[17] Noboru's attack in the parallel world—an attack before an attack, as it were—is a perfect representation of this feedback loop, this temporal distortion that is at work in the logic of trauma.

What is fascinating about this temporal distortion is that it is not commented upon by Toru, by anyone in the novel. Trauma's work seems to be taken for granted; or, more accurately, this distortion is merely one of many at work in the novel. The delay effects set up by Mamiya's (and others') digressive narratives are other examples of temporal distortions; I have already commented on how these digressions work as (and in) a kind of archival logic, but we should also notice how, in Mamiya's narrative especially, the loop back into history works fundamentally to set up a series of echo effects to come. Mamiya's well is echoed in Toru's; Mamiya's sense of being a phantom in his own life is echoed in Toru's sense of utter separation between himself and the world as he enters the trance-effect of the well (230–1). For me, the ultimate suggestion here, as narrative time is displaced and distorted, as the effects of trauma are seen and felt (and we need only mention that Mamiya's narrative is one of *pure* trauma in form and content), is that the logic of trauma is at work at every level in the novel, that this moment in Japanese history, 1984–5, is just that: a moment woven into a larger fabric of trauma. It is in this sense that we may return to something Toru says to Kumiko regarding the "dangerous thing" Noboru plans to unleash on the world: "'it's directly connected to the darkest depths of history, because its final effect is to destroy and obliterate people on a massive scale'" (579); the idea that this "dangerous thing" is linked to the past because its final effects lie in the future seems at first glance rather odd, but if, as Toru has discovered—or believes—all events link up, or perhaps more radically, all events are one (but does this mean there is no such thing as history?), then Noboru's scheme is historical precisely because its effects are present in the future; more precisely, the trauma of the past—the Nomonhan Incident—has laid the groundwork for the trauma to come.

The ultimate suggestion here, as we trace through the temporal illogics of Noboru's attacks in the real and parallel worlds, is that all events are stored archivally, melancholically, in the consciousness not only of the citizens of the real world, but in the consciousness of citizens in the parallel world: trauma's effects are so resonant, in other words, that they have essentially rendered the subjectivity of the world—and I realize this is an uncanny idea—plural. If, in a clinical sense, the traumatized subject essentially lives in two temporalities, two states of being—he is in the present moment; his flashbacks and dreams take him back to the past—is it possible, Murakami seems to be asking, for the subjectivity of the world to be split into two states of being? And if this is the case, what can be said about the link between these two zones? In some senses this uncanny image—the subjectivity of the world split into two—can be more easily understood when placed within traditional psychoanalytical categories: the real world is the conscious mind; the parallel world is the unconscious dream world where things like unmotivated—and atemporal—murderous acts of brutality can take place with impunity: Toru can kill a man, in other words, and get away with it, ethically. But the interpretive comfort of this structure—and I believe Toru sees this split as materially and ethically real—is shaken when we begin to notice that events in the unconscious are felt, if only in a displaced way, in the real world. In the real world Noboru suffers a stroke, and while Toru may wish to disavow any responsibility for his illness, he is ultimately responsible, *if only in his own mind, in his own unconscious.*

We need to keep in mind, by way of conclusion, that Toru's attack on the man in the parallel world takes place only because he is able to move between worlds via the conduit that is the well; there is a complex ethic at work here, I believe, an ethic of the archive, in fact. The well, for Mamiya is a place of failed revelation; in it he was able to approach the truth, the grace, the revelation, but failed fully to see it; because of this, his asymptotic relation to revelation, Mamiya is destroyed, turned into a phantom in his own life. The well, for Mamiya, thus is a place where melancholy is created. Toru, on the other hand, understands the archival logic of the well: his initial experiences in its cryptological depths were essentially historical. He began, as we recall, using the well as a way of remembering—and finding—his lost Kumiko, his Eurydice. But Toru, unlike Mamiya, was vouchsafed his revelation; he was given his grace: he does find the traces of his Eurydice, and while at the end of the novel, Kumiko may have vanished from his life (she, in fact, kills Noboru in the real world), Toru is in a position of knowledge at the end of things. He is not, like Mamiya, condemned to asymptotic agony, forever approaching the truth, knowing it will forever be out of reach. The final questions we need to ask of Toru are these: what does he do with his knowledge? What does he do with his awareness of the links between historical events and his personal trauma? How does he respond to events as the novel concludes with Noboru's death? The answer, and I am not suggesting Murakami is condemning Toru here, is a strange kind of quietism, a calm acceptance of things, an acceptance that is strikingly at odds with, for instance, Mamiya's decision to narrate his experience to Toru. Ultimately we are left—as we contrast Mamiya with Toru; as we read their respective responses to the event of trauma, the event of history— with the difference between the archival and the anarchival impulse. Mamiya tells his story: he is fully melancholic, yet he converts his experiences into the archive of narrative—both oral and written—a narrative that stands as a trace of history, a refusal, ultimately, to give in to the seduction of the secret, to the secret's claims for silence and hiddenness. Toru commits no archival acts in *The Wind-Up Bird Chronicle*: he, as much as his crypt, his well, is merely, it seems, a conduit for historical forces which precede and exceed him: as secretive as a hidden story, Toru remains silent.[18]

2.3. *after the quake* (2002) and *Underground* (2001)

Every work of art is an uncommitted crime.

—Adorno, *Minima Moralia*

In 1995 two traumatic events occurred in Japan. On January 17, an earthquake struck Kobe, killing 5,000 people. On March 20, the Aum Shinrikyo cult released sarin gas into the Tokyo subway system killing 12 and injuring 6,000, some permanently. These events powerfully traumatized Japanese society, exposing as it did hidden—one might say, subterranean— uncertainties and anxieties. As Haruki Muramaki puts it in *Underground*: "Both [events] were nightmarish eruptions beneath our feet—from underground—that threw all the latent contradictions and weak points of our society into frighteningly high relief. Japanese society proved all too defenseless against these sudden onslaughts. We were unable to see them coming and failed to prepare" (237). These events, "two of the greatest tragedies in Japanese postwar history" (237), present serious challenges to Murakami, both as novelist and citizen of Japan. On the one hand, the events demand memorialization, demand, that is, a mourning response; yet on the other these historical events, so cataclysmic, so beyond imagining, resist representation, resist language itself. It is here, in the crucible of history's impossible claims, that an aporetic guilt arises for Murakami and perhaps for Japan: the guilt of failing to imagine the possibility of trauma ("we were unable to see them coming") and the traumatic guilt of being unable to imagine the means to represent the traumatic event in order properly to mourn.

And for Murakami the problem of representation *is* a problem of guilt, a guilty problem: he is faced with the difficulty of attempting to represent trauma and the problem of representing guilt. Both of Murakami's narrative responses to these traumas (*after the quake* and *Underground*) represent Murakami's (guilty) attempt to speak of guilt, to speak through guilt (and thus to mourn), and to speak of the fundamental impossibility of representing guilt within language *itself* a priori incapable of accommodating trauma. Blanchot's words from *The Writing of the Disaster* are thus crucial in what follows: "The disaster, unexperienced. It is what escapes the very possibility of experience—it is the limit of writing [*limite de l'ecriture*]" (7). The disaster defies representation, and in some profound way this defiance—the disaster's resistance to representation—*becomes* the disaster. What Murakami's texts implicitly argue is that authentic trauma—and the guilt arising from that trauma—is not the initial event, but the failure to represent that event: the disaster is both the *limit*ation of writing and that which, as border or boundary, encloses writing's impossibility. What then can be said about guilt, *for* guilt, within this limit-space where writing becomes its own effacement, its own impossibility, its own disastrous immolation?

after the quake and *Underground* stand as testimony, as witness, to Murakami's attempt to find the appropriate narrative means to express the disaster. *after the quake* is a series of six short stories (I will analyze two here); *Undergound*, in its English version, is a series of interviews with victims of the sarin attack (Part One) and with members, past and current, of the Aum Shinrikyo cult (Part Two). In *Underground*, Murakami makes clear that the workings of memory displace historical events, transforming trauma into another narrative:

> To a greater or lesser extent, this is a natural function of memory—a process that novelists consciously utilize as a profession. The truth of "whatever is told" will differ, however slightly, from whatever actually happened. This, however, does not make it a lie; it is unmistakably the truth, albeit in another form. (Murakami 2000, 234)

As we turn to *after the quake* we should note a key rhetorical maneuver here in Murakami's defense of the truth of testimony: the event, according to Murakami, is always troped into another form in the workings of memory.

Moreover, this transformation of the event, "the truth of whatever is told," defines precisely the work of the novelist, which itself becomes the task of the translator. *after the quake* thus offers a series of displacements—call them translations—of the Kobe quake. *after the quake* stands manifestly as an admission that the trauma of the quake, the real "reality" of the quake, cannot be represented as such (hence the temporal designation of the title—"after"—itself an indication that trauma is not only cause but lasting [after] effect). If it is a central tenet of trauma theory that an understanding of the initial event *as* event evades comprehension and that trauma proper must be understood as a doubly inflected temporal event—cause and effect—one way of reading *after the quake* is precisely the expression of the disruptive (after)effects of great shock.[19] The symptoms of the after-effects of trauma, as Freud noted in *Beyond the Pleasure Principle*, are somatic responses that must be *read back* into the originary scene of shock: the victim's body—displaying its hysterical symptoms of paralysis or mutism—is a text through which trauma expresses its (displaced) narrative.[20] *after the quake* must be read as displaced narrative, but—and here we encounter the precise economy of guilt—as a narrative that knows it is a displacement. My task here is to suggest ways of reading this displacement as itself a disaster in Blanchot's sense: the displacement of trauma must carry over a residue, a trace, of the impossible-to-narrate/imagine real. Murakami's six texts, texts at times seemingly only tangentially related to the Kobe quake, carry traces of the traumatic real even as the historical event is subsumed. In this sense the displacement becomes the trauma: the narrative *is* the trauma that cannot be narrated. And thus paradox and aporia attend each narrative as the text both is and is not the originary trauma.

Murakami's texts articulate a kind of traumatized testimony in which the event in a sense is formally traumatized by virtue of its translation into textual and narrative form. *after the quake*, explicitly fictionalized, can be read as Murakami's subjective (impossible) testimony of events beyond the telling. *Underground*, as I will argue, is Murakami's attempt to produce an empirical, call it "objective," historical testimony. Yet as we will see, this attempt to speak objectively, which becomes the attempt to let others—or the *Other* that is the victim—speak objectively, is marked by anxieties about transcending those subjective limitations that mark the explicitly fictional texts as, in some senses, ironized simulacra of the traumatic event. *Underground* thus becomes fictionalized in the way Hayden White reminds us that all histories become fictionalized, and it is here, in Murakami's manipulation of these testimonies, that a fundamental displacement of the event of trauma occurs and a concomitant guilt arises.[21] This guilt resides precisely in the tacit *and* unconscious admission that displacement can only ever be a translation or metaphor of the originary experience. Displacement as representation—representation as displacement—is guilty of an a priori and unavoidable failure. Murakami may wish to maintain that the "truth" of the event survives its transmission, but that very (defensive) statement speaks to an extreme anxiety precisely about the ability to represent and a guilt about the very attempt to represent. In other words, guilt—as manifest in the formal structure of the stories—is itself a displacement of trauma. Here we see precisely the complexity of writing guilt/ writing trauma: if the symptoms of trauma are themselves a displacement of the originary event, then guilt must be understood as a displacement of a displacement, a double deferral of the impossible event of disaster. And because guilt functions to displace trauma (and the narrative of that trauma), mourning, as a kind of narrative return to the originary scene of disaster, is endlessly deferred: guilt makes mourning an economic impossibility. Thus, the initial demand of the event of trauma—that it be memorialized—is impossible to meet and the novelist is left with a remainder, a melancholy debt, which can never be expiated. And certainly the formal arrangement of Murakami's stories bears witness to this uncanny deferral of the disaster. The narratives are not about the quake per se, but all make oblique (or in some cases casually direct) references to the disaster. But the narratives are not set in Kobe; they do not concern characters involved directly in the disaster. The disaster is marginalized in the individual narratives yet paradoxically and uncannily central to the text as a *whole*. Displaced to the center, the representation of the quake reflects formally—en abime—the complex psychoanalytical "rhetoric" of guilt-as-displacement-of-displacement: the texts thus reflect formally the guilt that cannot be expressed as such.

The initial story in *after the quake*, "ufo in kushiro," illustrates the narrative method Murakami will use throughout the collection. The wife of Komuro (she is unnamed throughout the story) is transfixed by news coverage of the Kobe quake. For five days she watches the coverage never saying a word. On the sixth day, she disappears leaving a note: "I am never coming back . . . the problem is that you never give me anything . . . Or to put it more precisely, you have nothing inside you that you can give me. You are good and kind and handsome, but living with you is like living with a chunk of air. It's not entirely your fault, though. There are lots of women who will fall in love with you. But please don't call me. Just get rid of all the stuff I'm leaving behind" (5–6). A possible reading of her disappearance is that the quake brings on a realization of fundamental emptiness; but

Murakami is careful not to make the link between the quake and the disappearance manifest. We only are invited to read this disappearance as a kind of existential aftershock, a transposition of massive trauma onto the all-too-familiar scene of a marriage in crisis.

But this disappearance is only the initial event of the story: the remainder of "ufo in kushiro" concerns Komuro's trip to Hokkaido. Komuro has agreed to transport a small box containing an unknown object, perhaps indeed no object at all, to Hokkaido. This box, which "weighs practically nothing" (8) and which resembles boxes "used for human ashes" (8), becomes a portentous emblem, a physical objective correlative to Komuro's own emptiness. In some ways it is a crypt for what Abraham and Torok, in *The Shell and the Kernel*, would call the "lost object," that element of the ego, unknowable, untellable, displaced by trauma. This box becomes the manifestation of the crypt in the ego, which, as we have seen, Abraham and Torok argue forms in the traumatized subject; the crypt forms as a result of the loss of the valued object, more precisely, the loss and burial of a memory of an "idyll"(141):

> Between the idyllic moment and its subsequent forgetting . . . there was the metapsychological traumatism of a loss, more precisely, the "loss" that resulted from a traumatism. This segment of an ever so painfully lived Reality—untellable and therefore inaccessible to the gradual, assimilative work of mourning—causes a genuinely covert shift in the entire psyche . . . This leads to the establishment of a sealed-off psychic place, a crypt in the ego. (Abraham and Torok 1994, 141)

Murakami's text suggests that the work of mourning required by Komura is work responding not only to the economy of his own loss of his wife, but also the massive loss initiated by the quake. In my reading of "ufo on kushiro," the physically embodied crypt—the box—is a precise symptom of the massive disruption, as if the quake has unearthed, or created an awareness of, the normally sealed-off crypt of loss. And we need to be clear about this: the crypt, physically originating with Komura's colleague Sasaki, incrementally seems to become a part of Komura. There is, therefore, an intimate connection between all who meet in this text and all who are merely phantoms (the disappeared wife, the ghosts of the Kobe dead). Komura speaks to Sasaki's sister Keiko and her friend Shimao, two women he meets in Hokkaido:

> "Do you mind if I ask you about your wife?" Keiko said.
>
> "I don't mind."

"When did she leave?"

"Hmm . . . five days after the earthquake, so that's more than two weeks ago now."

"Did it have something to do with the earthquake?"

Komura shook his head. "Probably not. I don't think so."

"Still, I wonder if things like that aren't connected somehow," Shimao said with a tilt of the head.

"Yeah," Keiko said. "It's just that you can't see how." (Murakami 2002, 15)

The final moment of the story sees Komura begin to think consciously about what the box/crypt contains. Shimao suggests that the box "contains the *something* that was inside you. You didn't know that when you carried it here and gave it to Keiko with your own hands. Now you'll never get it back" (22). The revelation brings Komura to the verge of "committing an act of overwhelming violence" (23) against Shimao until she reveals she was only joking. But what can we make of this moment? Primarily we must notice that Komura's loss of self—a realization initiated ultimately by the chain of events beginning with the quake—is permanent. The event of massive loss finds its echo in the permanent loss of self on a personal level ("you'll never get it back"). Komura has lost the crypt containing his loss (he gives the box to Keiko): this doubled loss, this doubled absence, makes mourning impossible. Murakami has positioned his character in a state beyond mourning: Komura's loss cannot be taken up and metabolized because it is permanently absent; one cannot mourn a loss that one cannot conceptualize as such.

Komura now stands as an almost classic melancholic in Freud's sense of the term. In "Mourning and Melancholia," Freud speaks of the melancholic's loss of the love object:

> Where the exciting causes are different one can recognize that there is a loss of a more ideal kind. The object has not perhaps actually died, but has been lost as an object of love . . . In yet other cases one feels justified in maintaining the belief that a loss of this kind has occurred, but one cannot see clearly what it is that has been lost, and it is all the more reasonable to suppose that the patient cannot consciously perceive what he has lost either. This, indeed, might be so even if the patient is aware of the loss which has given rise to his melancholia, but only in the sense that he knows *whom* he has lost but not *what* he has lost in him. (Freud 1984, 253–4)

The melancholic, failing—or refusing—to metabolize loss, being unable to identify the precise nature of the loss but knowing that some loss has occurred, is thus permanently, painfully, tied to loss, to the unknowable event of loss, to an unknowable, unnamable history. Melancholia, as Eng and Kazanian remind us in *Loss: The Politics of Mourning*, is perhaps the only ethical response to loss precisely because melancholia keeps the memory of loss alive, refuses the comfort of forgetting what should not be forgotten.[22] In some crucial ways, all of Murakami's texts in *after the quake* and *Underground* are exercises in ethical melancholia in this sense. But we must notice the aporia of melancholy—the melancholy aporia—that arises in (at least) the fiction: Komura's loss can never be named; the event—if it is the quake; if it is the event of the quake transposed onto an absent wife—cannot be known and named as such. Melancholia may work to maintain history, but the melancholic, not knowing "what" he has lost, can never name that loss. In this manner Komura is the perfect (melancholic) allegory of the writer who cannot articulate the "unknown loss" that trauma initiates.

"ufo in kushiro" thus allegorizes and thematizes an aporia I wish to suggest is precisely the aporia of guilt: Komura, as suggested, can never name the loss, the "something" that is now absent. And yet he feels compelled *now* to know his loss. Shimao's disavowal of the link between the "something" in the box and Komura—that the something is his loss—only serves to reinforce that desire for what remains unknowable (it is never revealed what is inside the box and it is clear that it is a space into which loss as such is projected and placed under erasure). I suggest this narrative allegorizes guilt because Komura's loss—unknowable, unseen, erased—and his desire to know that loss suggests an indebtedness to loss, an impossible indebtedness. Murakami's guilt as a writer attempting to transcribe, translate, accommodate the loss that is the quake is an indebtedness to an impossible-to-repay debt.[23] The aporia of guilt arises in the inability to pay the debt demanded by history, by the inevitable traumas of history. The disaster, to return to Blanchot, is the limit and end of writing: it conditions writing, it *is* writing's goal, and it brings writing to the ends of what it can do. Guilt thus is expressed formally in the impossible attempt to extend beyond the limits of the disaster into the *disaster of writing's limitations*.

Whereas "ufo in kushiro" instantiates guilt on a personal, subjective level, "all god's children can dance" wishes to transpose (a sense of) guilt into a larger arena. "all god's children can dance" is a text that uses manifest psychoanalytical tropes/narratives to explore the uneasy relation between desire, loss, and national trauma. Yoshiya is the son of Osaki, a member of a religious cult; Osaki believes, as do some members of her cult, that Yoshiya's father is God. Yoshiya has rejected his mother's beliefs and knows rationally that his father is one of his mother's many lovers; specifically, he believes that his father is an obstetrician with a missing earlobe. Yoshiya's early childhood is spent desperately trying to avoid and repress his sexual desires for his mother, and thus Murakami explicitly stages the story according to an Oedipal scenario:

> They slept in separate bedrooms, of course, but whenever she felt lonely at night she would crawl under his covers with almost nothing on. As if hugging a dog or cat, she would sleep with an arm thrown over Yoshiya, who knew she meant nothing by it, but still it made him nervous. He would twist himself into incredible postures to keep his mother unaware of his erection.
>
> Terrified of stumbling into a fatal relationship with his own mother, Yoshiya embarked on a frantic search for an easy lay . . . He should have left his mother's house and begun living on his own, Yoshiya knew, and he had wrestled with the question at critical moments . . . But here he was, twenty five years old, and still unable to tear himself away. (Murakami 2002, 50)

"all god's children can dance" takes place in the immediate aftermath of the Kobe quake. The text, however, contains only one direct reference to the quake: Yoshiya's mother has been staying at her church's Osaka facility (Osaka is close to Kobe) and has been working, offering aid to the survivors. The plot of the narrative concerns Yoshiya as he follows a man (who is missing an earlobe) into the subway and eventually into an abandoned playing field. The man subsequently vanishes, leaving Yoshiya alone to ponder the relation between his desire for his mother, the absent father, and the destruction of cities: "Now that the stranger had disappeared, however, the importance of succeeding acts that had brought him this far turned unclear inside him. Meaning itself broke down and would never be the same again" (63). This is a crucial passage in this story and *after the quake* as a whole. Here Yoshiya—and Murakami—make clear that logical connections between events, whether temporal or causal, at times do not function. The structure of meaning itself, as expressed in narrative terms, or religious-philosophical terms, has collapsed: this collapsing becomes meaningful as itself a kind of meaning: "So what if the man was his father, or God, or some stranger who just happened to have lost his right earlobe? It no longer made any difference to him, and this in itself had been a manifestation, a sacrament: should he be singing words of praise?" (64).

Just as Blanchot reminds us that the true disaster is the failure of writing, the limit of writing, the end of representation, Yoshiya's indifference to the nature of his identity—precisely, his indifference to the *narrative* of his identity—itself becomes a sacrament. And yet, enmeshed in this sacrament, perhaps indeed produced by this sacrament as a kind of uncanny aftereffect, is a feeling of crime committed and punishment deferred. In some ways, the loss of the father, as the strange logic of Murakami's story would have it, can only produce, as a kind of traumatic aftershock, a reminder of a prior guilty desire for the mother. And this desire is intimately linked in Yoshiya's mind to the disaster at Kobe. Murakami's logic of displacement suggests that the trauma at Kobe unearths—displaces in phenomenal and psychoanalytical senses—subterranean and (badly) repressed desires. Yoshiya dances in the field, a dance that works to bring him to this uncanny place of enlightenment:

> And then it struck him what lay buried far down under the earth on which his feet were so firmly planted: the ominous rumbling of the deepest darkness, secret rivers that transport desire, slimy creatures writhing, the lair of earthquakes ready to transform whole cities into mounds of earth . . . He thought of his mother far away in that ruined city. What would happen, he wondered, if he could remain his present self and yet turn time backward so as to meet his mother in her youth when her soul was in its deepest state of darkness? No doubt they would plunge as one into the muck of bedlam and devour each other in acts for which they would be dealt the harshest punishment. And what of it? "Punishment?" I was due for punishment long ago. The city should have crumbled to bits around me long ago. (Murakami 2002, 66–7)

Murakami's analogue of repression—the physical subterranean realm with its rivers that transport desire (a perfect emblem of metaphorical displacement)—suggests that displaced desire, illicit desire, is a foundational element in the formation of the subject and of the city: these subterranean currents of darkness and desire help to "create a rhythm of the earth" (67). And thus, the fantasy that Yoshiya imaginatively plays out—the fantasy of returning to the past to enact these desires—suggests both the inescapability of desire and, perhaps, the inevitable desire for punishment. The phenomenal destruction of Kobe, and by implication Tokyo, thus is the inevitable outcome of a crime repressed and a punishment never inflicted.

Yoshiya thus is indebted: he owes a punishment, a punishment that cannot be paid as such, and therefore a punishment displaced onto the city.

Personal guilt ("I was *due* for punishment long ago" [emphasis mine]) is neatly displaced onto a larger site of trauma ("The city should have crumbled long ago"). By using the manifest Freudian tropes, Murakami, in what is perhaps the most unsettling aspect of this story, evokes a kind of inevitability of trauma: the Oedipal paradigm, the story suggests, is inescapable, erases temporal and physical boundaries, brings us, precisely, to the limits of desire. The resonance of this story lies in the large implication that somehow the guilt we inevitably accumulate, the punishments that are never meted out, *must be* (and will *have been*) expressed: the energy of overdue punishment, punishment for crimes that cannot but occur, produces a guilt that will be expressed as displaced trauma.

Murakami's text suggests, in its analysis of the inevitability of trauma, an essential and ineluctable link between the subject and his trauma (a trauma, in this case, which is transposed onto a larger national scale). It is possible thus to figure this inevitability, this unavoidability, this *desire* to repay the guilty debt of punishment, as a kind of melancholia: because this repayment of guilt, guilt that would only ever reconstitute itself in the Oedipal paradigm, can never be made. The desire for the mother that Murakami suggests brings about trauma on a national scale will always be there. What Murakami has uncannily suggested here in this story is that melancholia—as a process of failed mourning for trauma caused by the individual's illicit desire—is oriented as much to the *future* as it is to the past. And thus the aporetic question: how can we mourn and work through a guilt for crimes that have yet to occur, crimes that will have taken place in a possible future?

Part of Murakami's stated anxiety about both the Kobe quake and the Aum Shinrikyo attack is that no one foresaw the events. In some sense, these inevitable traumas and crimes represent a (guilty) failure of the rational imagination, the failure to imagine the possibility of such future traumas and crime.[24] In some sense, thus, *after the quake* and *Underground* represent archives of failure, guilty (because posthumous) attempts to retrospectively imagine these events.[25] Yet, there is one moment in *Underground*, the text to which I now turn, where Murakami makes an explicit link between his work as a novelist and the Aum Shinrikyo attack. In this passage Murakami speaks not of a failure to imagine the attack (itself a guilty act), but an imaginative responsibility for the attack. Murakami mentions his novel *Hard-Boiled Wonderland and the End of the World* and the fictional race he invented called the INKlings: the INKlings are a subterranean race of eyeless monsters who have created a vast network of tunnels under Tokyo. He imagines a link between the subway attack and his novels, and his words here are crucial:

If I were to give free rein to a very private paranoia, I'd have imagined some crucial link between the evil creatures of my creation and those dark underlings who preyed upon the subway commuters. That link, imaginary or not, provided one rather personal reason for writing this book. (Murakami 2000, 240)

And, of course, it is the words "imaginary *or not*" that contain the maximum compression of responsibility and imagined and imaginary guilt. *Underground*, in one sense, can be read as the attempt by Murakami to exorcise that guilt, to work through the possibility of his imagined guilt (the guilt of his imagination) by painstakingly attempting to understand the real reasons for the traumatic event. *Underground* thus must be read as Murakami's attempt to displace his guilt by uncovering the truth of history.

But this attempt to work through, to mourn the trauma produced by a guilty imagination, can only displace and defer the event. As Baudrillard reminds us in *The Spirit of Terrorism* (in words echoing Blanchot): "there is an absolute difficulty in speaking of an absolute event" (41). Murakami, however, works to maintain the possibility of accurately transposing, translating, transmitting the truth of the event. Testimony, rather than what we may call the "figurative testimony" of fiction, becomes Murakami's way of translating the ineffable real of the traumatic event. And thus, despite the fact that Murakami "edited, reordered, or rephrased where necessary" (4) to make the manuscript of *Underground* more "readable" (4); despite the fact that everyone interviewed "asked for some changes or cuts" (6); what remains in this testamentary archive is "unmistakably the truth" (234). This appeal to the truth, of course, speaks quite explicitly to an anxiety surrounding the nature of testimony, an anxiety that I will link in what follows to Murakami's sense that testimony may only be another form of historical displacement. But it should be emphasized here at the outset that these claims to truth lose something of their authority, their appeal to a kind of historical objectivity, when placed next to these explicit confessions of editing, reordering, and rephrasing, of making the texts more "readable." It is, of course, his term "rephrasing" that speaks most explicitly—and thus ironically—to the fact that *Underground* is as fictionalized as *after the quake*. What we do need to register here, as we pass from one genre (fiction) to another (call it non-"fiction") is the way in which Murakami hides in plain sight the fact that his text is as much a subjective response to trauma as is *after the quake*, subjective both in the sense that each testimony is an individual response and in the sense that Murakami has rewritten each testimony according to specific rhetorical needs. This hiding in plain sight can, of course, be read as another manifestation of guilt about the process of translating what cannot be translated: the attempt to capture the event of trauma in language—and thus to displace it—is a crime to which Murakami, by admitting his fictionalizing, obliquely confesses even as he makes claims to the truth.

And indeed there is a kind of messianic or prophetic impulse at work in this text, a desire to reveal the truth of the Japanese character to the Japanese and a desire to safeguard against future disasters precisely by preserving this trauma in testamentary form. And it is here, in the desire to archive the testimony, that the fundamental aporia of (and desire for) mourning occurs. Because it is clear that one of Murakami's goals here in *Underground* is to force the Japanese to see themselves "in" the trauma (perhaps as in some ways responsible for the trauma) so as to allow a process of mourning-as-healing to occur. And it should be foregrounded here that this attack, originating in human action, perhaps allows itself to be mourned in ways that the Kobe quake cannot: there is no fundamental reason for the quake to have occurred (that is, there is no way to stop earthquakes: there are potentially ways of stopping terrorist attacks). Thus, the stories in *after the quake* must end in a kind of melancholic guilt for the inability to understand and mourn that particular trauma. The Aum Shinrikyo attacks, on the other hand, precisely because they originate in human (and thus potentially comprehensible) action, allow for mourning, demand the process of mourning that narrative—as giving voice to and thus working through—can facilitate.[26] And thus Murakami writes about a "malaise" that lingers after the attacks:

> If only to be rid of this malaise, to cleanse our palates of this aftertaste, most Japanese seem ready to pack up the whole incident in a trunk labeled THINGS OVER AND DONE WITH. We would rather the meaning of the whole ordeal was left to the fixed processes of the court and everything was dealt with on a level of "the system."
>
> Certainly the legal process is valuable and will bring to light many truths. But unless we Japanese absorb these facts into our metabolism and integrate them into our field of vision, all will be lost in a mass of meaningless detail, court-case gossip, an obscure, forgotten, corner of history. (Murakami 2002, 226)

Murakami's language becomes emphatically psychoanalytical as he speaks of the need to absorb the facts of the attack into a collective "metabolism" in order to comprehend the traumatic event. After this absorption, the trauma will be placed into a narrative form that purifies the event: "If we are to learn anything from this event, we must look at what happened all over again, from different angles, in different ways. Something tells me things will only get worse if we don't wash it out of our metabolism . . . what we need, it seems to me, are words coming from another direction, new words for a new narrative. Another narrative to purify this narrative" (226–7). Murakami delineates in almost clinical fashion the Freudian paradigm of mourning: the new narrative—*Underground*; these various testimonials—becomes an archive in which the traumatic event is purified.

Murakami sets *Underground* up as a narrative of mourning and purification, yet the appeal to memory and history (and Murakami's sense of the complicity of the Japanese with Aum Shinrikyo) transforms the mourning archive into a melancholic archive. Because there is something contradictory about Murakami's desires in *Underground*, a contradiction that highlights the aporia at the heart of the work of mourning itself. Murakami desires to integrate the trauma of the attack—to remember in Freud's terms; he then wishes to wash the event "out of our metabolism" (226), to work through, again in Freud's terms. Yet the work itself—*Underground*—like all monuments, all archives working to preserve the past, the memories of the past, stands as the absolute negation of mourning: the text functions thus as a perfect melancholy archive. The individual subjects offering their narratives perhaps have worked through their individual trauma; yet *Underground* functions, to borrow again from Abraham and Torok, as a crypt in which the trauma is preserved.[27] Indeed the first part of *Underground* explicitly functions as a cryptic archive, supplementing the loss that occurred in the victims. One of the central effects of the sarin attack was the loss of memory; some, like Koichi Sakata (86), Noboru Terajima (149), Hiroshige Sugazaki (121), or Shintaro Komada (107), found their short-term memories to be deteriorated (Komada, for instance, could not remember the details of the day-to-day routine of the office); others, like "Shizuko Akashi," a thirty-one-year-old, suffered devastating losses of memory. Shizuko, paralyzed by the attack, has made progress to the point of being able to communicate verbally. Nevertheless, her condition is not promising:

> . . . her memory has almost totally gone. Sadly, she remembers nothing before the attack. The doctor in charge says she's mentally "about grade-school level," but just what that means Tatsuo [Shizuko's brother] doesn't honestly know . . . She remembers most of what's happened to her since the attack, but not everything. (Murakami 2002, 97–8)

The story of Shizuko, one that touched Murakami profoundly, can be seen, indeed should be seen, as a symptom of the trauma that Murakami's archive seeks to preserve, rather than ameliorate and place under erasure through the process of mourning. Murakami's archived story of Shizuko—and indeed the entirety of *Underground*—works to preserve the events and the knowledge of the events prior to the attack that erased her memory. More pointedly, Murakami's retelling of her story works, in fact, to *supplement* the loss of her memory of events prior to the attack by refashioning the narrative of her life. Murakami retells stories of Shizuko's past in order to facilitate an (imaginary) connection to a past that is clearly lost. Murakami describes Shizuko's niece and nephew, who repeat a narrative of visiting Disneyland every time they, in turn, visit their aunt in the hospital: "So Disneyland as a place has become fixed in her mind as something like a symbol of freedom and health" (102). As such Murakami's narrative refuses, or strives to refuse, the comfort of mourning precisely as it maintains and supplements Shizuko's lost memory. Shizuko's narrative, thus archived, thus present to the reader, brings Shizuko back to that event, brings her trauma back to the time of its instantiation; thus, that trauma is maintained in kind of melancholy stasis, a *narrative* stasis brutally reflective of the somatic paralysis of Shizuko herself.

One of the uncanny effects of Murakami's collection of narratives is the (perhaps perverse) connection that is drawn between the victim and the terrorist cult member. Because it is clear from the interviews that loss, deliberately inflicted or welcomed, defines both the victim and the terrorist. The narrative of Shizuko, surely the emotional core of *Underground*, is uncannily refracted, inversely refracted perhaps, into aspects of the narratives of some Aum members. I think here of how Shizuko's loss of her past is echoed by the so-called "renunciate" members of Aum, those members who, on being selected by [the leader Asahara] himself, deliberately—and brutally—sever all ties to the past. As Mitsuharu Inaba, a renunciate puts it, "If there was nothing within me I could rely on, then the only thing to do was to give myself up to Aum. Besides, I always thought that someday I'd renounce the world" (281). Inaba details how a sense of a loss of subjectivity defines the immersion in Aum and how the leader assumes total interpretive control of the world: the leader becomes "the person who would provide the final answer to Buddhist teachings. The one who could interpret it for me" (284). Another renunciate, Hiroyuki Kano, details precisely how the leader compelled a severing of connections to the past, how the leader initiated loss as a central tenet of the Aum faith: " 'You don't fit this transient world,' I was told [*by Asahara*], and I certainly agreed." (258) Thus, what appears to be a voluntary renunciation and loss of the past (for the terrorist) precedes the act of terror that robs the victim of *her* past. And just as Murakami's narrative of Shizuko serves to supplement details of her (lost) past, so, too, do his interviews with Aum members: he forces a kind of nostalgic return to their renounced past. In these interviews Murakami compels the Aum members to revisit the past, to revisit their childhoods, and, in at least two cases (with Miyuki Kanda and Shin'ichi Hosoi), the effects of their renunciation on their families. It is here that Murakami's *Underground* fulfills its purpose as absolute melancholic archive: he compels the Aum member back into the past and he preserves that nostalgic return in the archive that is *Underground*.

Melancholia, as Derrida proposes, prevents the working through that occurs at the site of "normal" mourning. The dead other, the lost object, the event that has caused massive psychic disruption, remains. I quote again from *The Ear of the Other*:

> Now, what is the crypt in this instance? It is that which is constituted as a crypt in the body for the dead object in a case of unsuccessful mourning, mourning that has not been brought to a normal conclusion. The metaphor of the crypt returns insistently. Not having been taken back inside the self, digested, assimilated as in all "normal" mourning, the dead object remains like a living dead abscessed in a specific spot in the ego. It has its place, just like a crypt in a cemetery or temple, surrounded by walls and all the rest. The dead object is incorporated into this crypt—the term "incorporated" signaling precisely that one has failed to digest or assimilate it totally, so that it remains there, forming a pocket in the mourning body. (Derrida 1988, 57)

The event cannot be interiorized and thus "I keep it in me, as a persecutor perhaps, a living dead." (58) It is here, in the sense that the historical event becomes a kind of persecutor, that Murakami's, and by extension the Japanese people's, guilt becomes manifest. Melancholia is a form, as I am characterizing it here, of narrative preservation of trauma: that preservation becomes an objective correlative of the guilt that attends the apprehension of the event of trauma *as such*. Murakami speaks of this guilt implicitly when he refers to the Aum Shinrikyo cult as the distorted image of Japanese culture:

> "[T]hey" are the mirror of "us"!

Now of course a mirror image is always darker and distorted. Convex and concave swap places, falsehood wins over reality, light and shadow play tricks. These subconscious shadows are an "underground" that we carry around within us, and the bitter aftertaste that continues to plague us long after the Tokyo gas attack comes seeping out from below. (Murakami 2002, 229)

Murakami maintains that the Aum Shinrikyo cult cannot be held as the "other" to Japanese culture. The cult, "distorted image of ourselves" (228), must be seen as an integral element of Japanese culture, and thus the actions of the cult are in some ways the responsibility of all of Japan. Murakami's reading of the relation between Aum and Japanese society, therefore, also transposes the guilt for the crimes. *Underground* becomes a mirror reflecting the totality of Japanese culture, not merely the faces of victims and a few perpetrators: as a melancholy archive, *Underground* strives to maintain the truth of the historical events of the attack present for all and for all time.

Yet the links between Japanese culture, Aum Shinrikyo, and Murakami himself are perhaps more complex than Murakami tacitly would admit. In the Preface to Part Two of *Underground*, Murakami makes a cryptic statement that stands alone without commentary or further elaboration. He has mentioned his interviews with members of Aum and then he writes: "still, talking to them so intimately made me realize how their religious quest and the process of novel writing, though not identical, are similar" (250). There is much hidden, encrypted, perhaps in a guilty fashion, in this statement. And it should be clear that Murakami sees a link not merely between the religious quest of Aum and the novelist, but between the inevitable outcomes of that quest—terrorism—and the work of the novelist. Perhaps, at some level, terrorism and art are works of imaginative transformation; perhaps terrorism and art work to shock the complacent imagination with new perceptions of the real (indeed, this may be what *after the quake* in toto is "about"). Yet at work in Murakami's cryptic statement, and at work in both *after the quake* and *Underground*, is a perception, perhaps too difficult to bring fully to light, a perception that must remain present in its guilty repression, of the relation between terrorism and testimony (both *after the quake* and *Underground* function as testimony). In *The Illusion of the End* Baudrillard suggests that the end or goal of terrorism is the end of history: Terrorism, as an expression of a kind of messianic apocalypticism, works to bring about an ecstatic end to the narrative of history: "And what, indeed, is terrorism, if not this effort to conjure up, in its own way, the end of history?" (8) The link between terrorism and testimony may seem a perverse one, an impossible one, and an absurd one. But the logic of both *after the quake* and *Underground* suggests, even as the texts struggle to grasp and understand the nature of terror and terrorism, that testimony is itself only ever a displacement of history, of historical events. Murakami's desperate assertion of the truth of his accounts—that are *his* after all—can only be seen as an expression of anxiety about the way the testamentary narrative serves to displace even as it supplements history. And Murakami's strange sentence about the relation between the religious quest and writing begins to take on an added resonance, offering, perhaps, a commentary both on his own work and, we might add, on Adorno's comment: "Every work of art is an uncommitted crime" (*Minima Moralia* 111). Precisely as Murakami's texts become the guilt they wish to express; precisely as the texts archive trauma (even in and especially as its supplemental displacement) and thus become that trauma; precisely as history is effaced by the logic of testamentary melancholy, the work of art becomes a *committed* crime in every sense of the word. Committed to the preservation of trauma, to a continual melancholic return to the scene of the crime, the criminal narrative act *is* guilty even and especially as it acknowledges its failure, tacitly or otherwise, to mourn that trauma.

Murakami has created a narrative crypt in an effort to keep memory alive as a constant reminder to the Japanese of the failure to have seen clearly the true lineaments of their own culture, their own faces. *Underground*, as both testimony and persecutor, becomes the guilt of which it wishes to speak: it speaks of guilt as it becomes that guilt. More precisely, *Underground* reminds us of the peculiar nature of guilt; guilt is the remainder of the past and a reminder of the future to come. It is clear that a testamentary narrative like *Underground*—and by extension *after the quake*—works to remind of the past and to warn against potential blindness to come. Murakami wishes the Japanese to take responsibility for the failure to have recognized themselves "in" Aum; the inevitable corollary of this guilt is the idea that the potential for this misrecognition to repeat itself, a misrecognition that perhaps allows the Japanese to define themselves against the other, is always present. It is in this sense that we can say that testimony—as a discourse of memory and a discourse oriented to the future—is always conditioned by twin absences or displacements: the past can never be rendered as such; the future, cannot, will not, take place as such.[28] Texts like *Underground* and *after the quake*, precisely as they attempt to speak of guilt and responsibility, to speak past and thus to mourn this guilty responsibility, inevitably fail, fail in fact a priori to carry out the business of testimony. The writing of disaster becomes the disaster of writing, the failure, the guilty failure, to translate the event, the disaster, the narrative that must contain the past in order to work through. As the logic of the melancholy archive demonstrates, the past will always make claims on the present and the future, rendering any attempt to mourn impossible: the testament—as archive, as monument to loss, of loss—will only and ever render history melancholic. What remains then of the text, in the text, what indeed can only *be* remains, are the traces, the cinders of the trauma: the writing that immolates as it speaks its failure to speak.

Chapter 3

Humanizing History: David Mitchell

The act of memory is an act of ghostwriting.
—Mitchell, *Ghostwritten*

Memory does not only bear on time: it requires time—a time of mourning.
—Ricoeur, *Memory, History, Forgetting*

I would like to begin this chapter by turning briefly to Michel Foucault and *The Order of Things*. Here Foucault unravels an analysis of the genealogy of the modern subject, a genealogy that begins, he argues, as a response to loss, a loss of history. In the final moments of *The Order of Things* he traces a radical epistemic shift back to the beginning of the nineteenth century. Prior to this shift humankind could conceive of a natural relation to history and historical events, what Foucault calls "historicity"; that is, the human could easily believe that the unfolding of world events, even the natural historical unfolding of the earth's own evolution (this is what Foucault calls "natural time" [368]), was occurring for him, for his contemplation, according to his constructed religious, scientific, and philosophical logics. A fundamental sense that things—the world—worked according to its own constituted logics, however, made it clear to the modern subject that he was cast out of the paradise of history:

> Things first of all received a historicity proper to them, which freed them from the continuous space that imposed the same chronology upon them as upon men. So that man found himself dispossessed of what constituted the most manifest contents of his history: nature no longer speaks to him of the creation or the end of the world, of his dependency or his approaching judgement; it no longer speaks of anything but a natural time; its wealth no longer indicates to him the antiquity or the immediate return of the Golden Age . . . The human being no longer has any history. (Foucault 1973, 368)

What then happens to the subject dispossessed of history? What happens to the subject when the world no longer reflects his fundamental fantasies of meaning? For this is truly the radical anxiety at the heart of the epistemic shift Foucault traces. Foucault himself argues that one response, indeed a concomitant response to the loss of the intimate connection to the world (it no longer reflecting back fantasies of *arche* or *telos*), is the construction of the human subject—indeed subjectivity—itself. Foucault suggests that the human subject discovers its proper historicity, "a history that now concerns man's own very being" (370), by retroactively tracing the very genealogy of that primal scene of traumatic loss: "It was just this primary erosion [the loss of the connection to the historicity of the world] that the nineteenth century sought in its concern to historicize everything, to write a general history of everything, to go back ceaselessly through time, and to place the most stable of things in the liberating stream of time" (370). And if through this process of reconstructing a traumatic loss the human fashions itself as a subject, we can argue—and this truly is the radical thought behind Foucault's *The Order of Things*—that subjectivity itself is a form of mourning, a precise, economic response to loss.

I wish to argue in what follows that David Mitchell's texts begin by unraveling the implications of Foucault's analysis of the human subject and its relation to history. Specifically I am interested in exploring how the relation between loss and subjectivity is inflected as a historical process, or unfolds within a specific conception of history. I wish to explore how Mitchell's various texts fetishize the image and idea of the human dispossessed of and by history: what happens, I will ask, when the human discovers that she is preceded and exceeded by history, by historical forces beyond her (*Ghostwritten*)? How does the subject negotiate an identity fashioned in relation to loss (*number9dream*)? What place is there for the archive of individual memory within larger historical processes (*Cloud Atlas*)? How precisely does loss constitute subjectivity; that is, how can a response to historical loss—or fantasies of loss—become productive? Just what *does* subjectivity mean for Mitchell, for Mitchell's characters?

3.1   *Ghostwritten* (1999)

The unconscious abides.

—Bachelard, *The Poetics of Space*

Ghostwritten, Mitchell's first novel, sets out the experimental narrative ground for all of his subsequent work. The novel is divided into ten chapters, each of which unfolds in a specific geographic location. We move, for instance, from Okinawa in the opening chapter, to Tokyo, Mongolia, London, Ireland, and elsewhere. Each narrative is self-contained, but Mitchell carefully alludes to previous narratives, weaving in verbal echoes and character references as the novel progresses. It becomes quite clear, therefore, that the novel wishes to plot a sense of connection between subjects over time, history, and geography. In some crucial way, *Ghostwritten* offers itself as an ethical meditation on the possibilities of connection, suggesting ultimately that no action takes place in historical or geographic isolation: ultimately, the novel seems to imagine the human species within a kind of connected ecology. And yet, there is a crucial existential threat to this delicate ecology, a threat that comes into being in the central—perhaps perverse—fantasy of the novel: the fantasy of total isolation as a precursor to total oblivion. That is, while structurally the novel makes connections between characters and times, individual narratives seem to fetishize the idea of absolute isolation and oblivion as a dark, and desired, fantasy: the radical effacement of the terrorist's subjectivity in the "Okinawa"; the death of the banker in "Hong Kong"; the clear exuberant celebration of noncorporeal and multiple subjectivities in the central chapter "Mongolia," all speak of an attraction to the idea that subjective oblivion is the inevitable end of the human.[1]

The question for me thus becomes: what fantasy is the strongest here? The fantasy of the individual as always already obliterated by the forces of history, or the fantasy of connection, which would seem to ameliorate the existential threat of total oblivion? In some sense the answer has to be that these fantasies play out as a precise dialectic; that is, they are connected and interdependent. This connection, in fact, becomes the site where the archive as such begins its work: each individual—the central or even peripheral characters in individual stories—is remembered and reconfigured in subsequent texts. These stories—these lives—become the place where the lost individual continues to *be* in some sense; the story thus becomes the archive inasmuch as it effaces the loss of the individual even as that loss as such is celebrated. I say "celebrated" here to indicate my sense that this novel is, in fact, working out the fantasy of the loss of self, staging repeatedly, almost fetishistically, the idea of a radically annihilated subjectivity. We have thus in *Ghostwritten* a resonantly aporetic text that celebrates loss while simultaneously effacing that loss: in this way, obviously, the novel becomes the perfect text of melancholy.

The narrative(s) that bracket(s) *Ghostwritten*—that of the terrorist cult member Quasar who releases poison gas into the Tokyo subway system—in many ways perfectly exemplifies this complex economy of melancholy. It is clear on the one hand that by giving over his life to the Fellowship cult, Quasar (his real name is Keisuke Tanaka) has willingly effaced his own subjectivity. In this obvious sense, by taking the name Quasar he has attempted to erase a critical connection to his own history; by dedicating his life—and actions—to His Serendipity (the Leader of the Fellowship) Quasar has, as one character puts it apropos of all cult members, abdicated his "inner self" (22).[2] Quasar examines his face in a mirror and fantasizes about how the Fellowship will cleanse the earth, leaving only righteous survivors: "Quasar, the harbinger. His Serendipity had chosen my name prophetically. My role was to pulse at the edge of the universe of the faithful, alone in the darkness" (5). Closely following this description of subjective abdication, Quasar recalls an incident from his childhood where, bullied at school, his classmates (and, perversely, his teacher) all pretended he was dead; plainly, this is a terrifying memory—and being that it is the first of many memories Quasar presents, it is perhaps the crucial one—and Quasar places it in context to his life as a cult member now: "Before His Serendipity lit my life I was defenceless. I sobbed and screamed at them to stop, but nobody saw me. I was dead" (5). This juxtaposition of a memory of imaginary death with the fantasy of the total effacement of interiority does suggest that Quasar has worked back to a central trauma and has now merely structurally repeated that perverse economy: one imaginary death in childhood has prophetically led to another death, which Quasar perversely embraces.

It is not my purpose merely to read Quasar as an individual, psychoanalytically. Rather, I am interested in the structure of repetition compulsion that seems, to an extent, to have worked its way into his life. Perhaps, more crucially, we should consider what being a cult member means, psychoanalytically, that is to say, subjectively. Because it is clear that His Serendipity at least knows that joining his cult means entering into that process of familial rejection Freud termed the Family Romance: "'You have freed yourself from the asylum of the unclean. Little brother. Today you have joined a new family. You have transcended your old family of the skin, and you have joined a new family of the spirit . . . Our family will grow until the world without is the world within'" (9). The deep irony of Quasar's membership in this cult—the *Fellowship*—is that he, true to the meaning of his new name, is radically isolated from the outset: he has rejected his earthly family for a spiritual family, which in its turn places him on the radical margins, isolated and alone, as a participant in a terrorist attack must be.[3] And so, who then is Quasar, as a subject? Who is he?

One way into this question is again through Blanchot's notion of subjectivity without any subject, an idea that, in my estimation, perfectly summarizes the ontology, the subjective ontology, of the cult member. Recall that for Blanchot the modern subject is defined by a relation to trauma, precisely to a historical trauma that forever recedes from any intellectual grasp. Blanchot does not use the term trauma, preferring the idea of the disaster (a key term for Mitchell as we will see): "The disaster, unexperienced. It is what escapes the very possibility of experience" (7). The experience of the disaster takes place at the limit of understanding, the limit of intellectual power, but its presence is inevitably, disastrously, felt. The disaster, like Freud's notion of an originary but unknowable trauma that can only be glimpsed in retrospect, can be approached only through repetitions that would stage approximations of that originary experience. Blanchot, like Freud, ultimately is interested in knowing what happens to subjectivity—the subject's sense of itself as a being within ontologically verifiable experience—when the disaster occurs. Thus, Blanchot asks if it is any longer possible to use this word, "subjectivity," after the disaster:

> If one wishes to use this word—why? but why not?—one ought perhaps to speak of a *subjectivity without any subject*: the wounded space, the hurt of the dying, the already dead body which no one could ever own, or ever say of it, *I, my body*. This is the body animated solely by mortal desire: the desire of dying—desire that dies and does not thereby subside. (Blanchot 1995, 30)

Let me return to Quasar's memory of being imagined dead before considering Blanchot:

> I remembered the day when the bullies had got everyone in the class to pretend that I was dead. By afternoon it had spread through the whole school. Everyone pretended they couldn't see me. When I spoke they pretended they couldn't hear me. Mr. Ikeda got to hear about it, and as a society-appointed guardian of young minds what did he take it upon himself to do? The bastard conducted a funeral service for me during the final home-room hour. (Mitchell 1999, 5)

In some senses this strange, perverse, and ultimately uncanny ritual of imagined death—of performed death; of *authority* performing the rituals of death—creates Quasar, fashions him as Blanchot's "already dead body"; and if, as I do, we follow Freud on the economy of repetition compulsion, we can understand Quasar's joining the Fellowship as one way—unconsciously—he comprehends his originary trauma of being imagined dead. The Fellowship becomes thus the confirmation of his fantasy of annihilation, of disappearance; his original trauma, now repeated, becomes prophetic. And is there a better description of a cult member—one who has abdicated his interiority, his will, his very self—than Blanchot's "subjectivity without any subject"?[4] For surely this is what Quasar now is: he carries the markings of a subject, he bears the traces of subjectivity (he is recognized as a subject by others, for instance), but existentially, perhaps even ontologically, he is a void, a cipher, the subject-as-quasar: distant, removed, radically marginalized.

And yet, for all this, Quasar still is unable, perhaps unwilling, to efface all traces of his past. It is enough to recall his original scene of trauma to confirm this idea, but there are other instances where memory intrudes, critically, to reanimate Quasar, to return him, perhaps inevitably, nostalgically, to his previous existence, his previous familial community. If we inflect this idea of the persistence of memory through Blanchot, perhaps we could say that the archive never is fully effaced by the disaster. Scattered throughout Quasar's narrative—a narrative in which he attempts to valorize his present relation to The Fellowship—are intrusive memories of his childhood: he remembers his "biological uncle" (12) taking him to the harbor in Yokohama; juxtaposed with a memory of his releasing the poison on the subway (and looking into the eyes of a child soon to be dead), he thinks "Mom. Dad" (29); crucially, as his narrative winds down and he begins to think that he will be discovered by the authorities, he thinks of Mr. Ikeda, the perverse homeroom teacher, with something approaching compassion: "What happened, I wonder, to Mr. Ikeda? Where do people who drop off the edge of your world end up?" (30). In some ways this persistence of memory indicates that a complete effacement of the subject is an impossibility (and, indeed, Quasar's curiously gentle recalling of Ikeda indicates, again, a nostalgic desire to maintain some connection to a past, a past experience perversely that threatened his own sense of self). Another way of putting this is to say that despite having given himself up for dead, having attempted to efface himself as a subject (through his joining of the cult and his act of terrorism), memory in its turn effaces that effacement, insists on maintaining the subject despite itself, perhaps *to* spite itself.

As we move into a consideration of other narratives in *Ghostwritten* we need to recall how Mitchell weaves connections between these stories. This is more than simply a device offering a sense of continuity between what may appear to be disparate narratives. This linking, in my mind, has at least two critical functions: first, it obviates the apocalyptic economy of both the individual narratives and the total containing structure of *Ghostwritten*; second, the linking weaves the subject into a larger ethical community, maintaining him—as memory does in Quasar's narrative—as a subject for others. By apocalyptic economy I mean to suggest that *Ghostwritten* presents narratives of various ends. We have catastrophic acts of violence ("Okinawa," "Holy Mountain," "Petersburg"); we have a threat of a cosmological event ending all of humanity ("Night Train"); we have narratives of individual ends: the end of one man's life ("Hong Kong"), the seismic alteration of the narrative of individual lives, as such ("Tokyo," "Clear Island"). Despite these ends, threatened or actual, the narrative linking of subject to subject, which in some ways simply means that the narrative persists and continues, indicates that the end of one character or event is never at an end. At the end of Quasar's narrative, for instance, he makes a phone call he believes is to his cult facility (he's hoping for instruction and rescue): there is no response at the other end of the line (as he believes should be the case). In the next chapter, "Tokyo," Satoru, a character having no connection to Quasar, receives the phone call. For Satoru, the event is random; for the reader, who perceives the link back to Quasar, the event of the phone call speaks to larger issues of connection, the desire for connection, the possibility of connection through randomness. And, of course, examples of these events of connection abound in *Ghostwritten*: Quasar's terrorist act is mentioned in several subsequent narratives; the consequences of Neal Brose's death at the site of the monument to Buddha in "Hong Kong" reverberates into a later narrative ("London") where we meet his widow; a murderer in one narrative ("Mongolia") appears in a subsequent narrative ("Petersburg"[5]); a woman, hit by a taxi but playing no substantial role in "London," appears as the central character in a subsequent chapter, "Clear Island"; the meteor mentioned in passing in the first narrative of the book appears again as the central catastrophic focus of the penultimate chapter ("Night Island"). Thus, an event—or even subjectivity, as we will see—reverberates beyond its seeming end in *Ghostwritten*. Mitchell seems to suggest that a subject or event persists if the subject is remembered, recalled, or connected to another subject: if the subject or event exists for the other, the novel suggests, the end never comes, never can come. As Neal Brose expires at the conclusion of "Hong Kong," he looks about him and thinks briefly about causality: "Or is it not a question of cause and effect, but a question of wholeness? I'm this person, I'm this person, I'm that person, I'm that person too" (105). Brose's thoughts recall Quasar's moment of hesitation in the Tokyo subway system as he is about to release his poison: "The baby in the woolly cap, strapped to her mother's back, opened her eyes. They were my eyes . . . And reflected in my eyes was her face" (24–5). In both Brose's and Quasar's thoughts we have a fairly acute sense of intersubjectivity, the idea that the self is not entire on its own, but cathects to and is completed by the Other. I am fascinated by how neatly Mitchell arranges the structure of his narratives to reflect this essentially ethical theme: just as the narratives connect structurally, so, too, do subjects connect ethically.

And it is in "Mongolia," the central narrative of *Ghostwritten*, where the question of the relation between subjectivity and the Other is most acutely examined. "Mongolia" is essentially a quest narrative; the speaker of the story is a "noncorpum," a bodiless mind seeking its own origin and identity. This noncorpum has come to consciousness in 1950s China with no sense of its origin, save for a memory of a narrative, a legend, about "three who think of the fate of the world" (151). These three, the crane, the locust, and the bat, each anticipate the end of the world; thus, the crane treads lightly, believing a heavy step will collapse mountains; the locust keeps "a watchful eye on the high peaks, and the rain clouds that might be gathering there" (151); the bat believes the sky may collapse at any time and thus "dangles from a high place, fluttering up to the sky, and down to the ground, and up to the sky again, checking that all is well" (151–2). This legend is etiological in two important senses: in the most obvious sense, the legend accounts for the behavior of these animals; more importantly, however, this story forms part of the identity and origins of the noncorpum, who believes that finding the source of the legend will explain its own origins.

The noncorpum is thus the perfect emblem of Blanchot's subjectivity without any subject: having no body, the noncorpum can transmigrate into the body of any human it encounters, travelling with it, inhabiting its mind, incorporating its memories, its knowledge. The noncorpum thus becomes an archive of sorts: "I am apparently immune to age and forgetfulness" (165): as in Freud's conception of the unconscious, in which, "nothing can be brought to an end, nothing is past or forgotten," (*Interpretation of Dreams*: 577) the noncorpum-as-archive has a curious agency because it supersedes any physicality, any subject as such.[6] Indeed, over the course of this narrative, the noncorpum transmigrates from a Danish tourist in Mongolia (Caspar) to Gunga, a Mongolian woman (159); to Jargal Chinzoreg, a truck driver (170); to Punsalmaagiyn Suhbataar, a senior agent with the Mongolian KGB (174) (who knows where to locate a folklorist of Mongolian oral history); to Baljin, the folklorist's daughter (177); and finally to the folklorist's brother (178), who is shot dead by Suhbataar. After this death, three months pass and the noncorpum is reborn into the body of an ailing baby whose grandmother knows the origin legend story: she knows this story, it is revealed, because she was present at the noncorpum's original death in 1937. The noncorpum was a monk's apprentice put to death during the social engineering purges in Mongolia. At the moment of his death, his master attempted to transmigrate him into the body of a young girl (revealed now to be the grandmother); the transmigration only partially worked, and the grandmother has, since 1937, been a carrier of this young boy's memories, including the original story of the three who think of the fate of the world, a story the monk told the noncorpum just before his death and failed transmigration.

This elaborate narrative neatly serves, of course, as a mise en abyme of Mitchell's larger narrative practice: what is an author but a sort of noncorpum inhabiting, directing, for a time, the mind of a character, only to move on to another? What is *Ghostwritten* as a whole if not a version of this noncorpum's journey, its quest? But beyond this metanarrative reflection, the story as such is a careful meditation on the nature of memory and identity. In fact, the logic of "Mongolia" as a whole suggests that memory *is* identity: "My own infancy was spent at the foot of the Holy Mountain. There was a dimness, which I later learned lasted many years. It took me that long to learn how to remember" (152). Memory, as such, is a skill conferring upon the subject precisely a sense of itself as a subject. Mitchell radicalizes this notion, estranges it, by asking us to think about what memory is, what agency is, stripped of the subject-as-body.

We should note, first, that both the noncorpum and Quasar—not to speak yet of at least two later characters—both have their origins as displaced, disinterred, nonlocatable subjects in trauma. Quasar's symbolic death at the hands of his schoolmates produces a displacement radicalized in his membership in the cult, a radicalization that involves, recall, a symbolic giving up of the body ("your old family of the skin"); the noncorpum's displacement takes place at his body's violent death. The noncorpum's search thus ultimately is for the way to die properly (by entering the body of the baby at the story's close, he chooses to be human and ultimately, thus, to die). Both Quasar and the noncorpum are reconstituted, however, by memory: the function of the archive of personal memory in Quasar's narrative is to threaten to reconstitute him into precisely the family he has rejected; the noncorpum, having rediscovered, uncovered, a lost and densely archived memory, chooses to reconstitute itself by rejoining the community of humanity. Having claimed previously to be a "non-human humanist" (165) the noncorpum now becomes fully human again. But are we not suspicious of these (re-)integrations? Is not one of the uncanny, and unsettling, fantasies of Mitchell's narratives the suggestion that the subject, despite being tied melancholically to memory, is ultimately willing—and in the case of the noncorpum, able—to float freely from subjectivity, is able to become, as it were, ontologically nonlocatable? Certainly the readiness with which the noncorpum assumes a body at the end of his narrative only highlights the arbitrariness of subjectivity as such. Surely the fantasy of "nonlocality" and nonsubjectivity is the prevailing fantasy in this novel.

I am, of course, using this term "nonlocality" because of its centrality in the "Clear Island" chapter of *Ghostwritten*. "Clear Island" is the story of Mo Muntervary, a physicist on the run from the CIA: she had been working for an agency contracted out to the CIA, and Muntervary has discovered that her research, which has entered a crucial phase, is now being used for military purposes.[7] Muntervary has fled her research institution and has made her way back to her childhood home on a remote island in Ireland. Muntervary's research into "quantum cognition"—something she acknowledges that laypeople will have never heard of—is fascinatingly vague. That is to say, Mitchell does not set out any explanation of her work and at times seems deliberately, and humorously, to baffle his reader. Take this moment when Muntervary, hiding out in Hong Kong, details her work: "There were wrong turnings. I had to jettison matrix mechanics in favor of virtual numbers, and my doomed attempt to amalgamate the Einstein-Podolsky-Rosen paradox with Cadwalladr's behavioral model set me back weeks" (335). All the reader is vouchsafed in terms of information about her work is that if quantum cognition is "'spliced with artificial intelligence and satellite technology . . . [it] would render existing nuclear technology as lethal as a shower of tennis balls'" (323): this, indeed, is how her pursuer from the CIA puts it. The reader also knows that her research has progressed to the point where she is on the verge of solving what her CIA nemesis calls the problem of "nonlocality," an idea left undefined but one Muntervary thinks of as being, perhaps, not a problem at all: "Strip quantum cognition down to first principles, and rebuild it incorporating nonlocality, instead of trying to lock nonlocality out" (334).

And, of course, the prevailing theme, even economy, of this story is the idea of nonlocality: Muntervary has left her childhood home (and family, including her son), has worked in Switzerland, has fled to Hong Kong, and has now made her way back home (this trajectory is, of course, not unlike that of the noncorpum in "Mongolia" who eventually finds his origin story). Becoming unlocatable is what allows Muntervary to escape the CIA and allows her time enough to archive her theoretical knowledge in her little black book. When the CIA does eventually find her, Muntervary has fed the book to a goat: Muntervary's knowledge itself has become nonlocatable in some profound sense. She now is the only archive of her work and can effectively dictate terms of continued employment by the CIA (she will be "'accountable to nobody'" [370]) in matters pertaining to her research; John, her husband, will accompany her back to the States; her son will be able to visit). Scattered throughout her narrative are theoretical musings on the nature of the self, of time, of subjectivity: and it is clear that Muntervary is working through the implications of the idea that the self, too, is a nonlocatable thing, as seemingly random as quantum particles:

> Why am I who I am? Because of the double helix of atoms coiled along my DNA. What is DNA's engine of change? Subatomic particles colliding with its molecules. These particles are raining onto the Earth now, resulting in mutations that have evolved the oldest single-celled life-forms through jellyfish to gorillas and us, Chairman Mao, Jesus, Nelson Mandela, His Serendipity, Hitler, you and me. Evolution and history are the bagatelle of particle waves. (Mitchell 1999, 359–60)

As she later muses: "Quantum physics speaks in chance, with the syntax of uncertainty" (364). I am fascinated by the implications of Muntervary's musings. To imagine history as a bagatelle is to invoke a fairly complex metaphor: a bagatelle is a game involving hitting small balls into holes in a board; these holes have pins obstructing them so there is clearly an element of chance, luck, and randomness in the outcome. A bagatelle is also a short, light piece of music and thus is an organized thing with rules and logic. And if, as the logic of Muntervary's thoughts indicate, the subject is the outcome of a random—yet also organized—historical process, the subject is *subject to* forces beyond his or her control. Our question thus must be: what precisely is Muntervary's disposition toward the idea of randomness? What is her attitude toward the discourse of a historical process preceding and exceeding the subject (she speaks of the language and syntax of quantum physics and uncertainty)?

To answer this question, a question that implicitly suggests that for Muntervary, the subject has a random relationship to the real, an arbitrary, negotiated, relationship with the nature of things, requires that we observe how Mitchell characterizes the subject as *subject to* in this story. What is fascinating about this narrative, especially when placed in conversation with those of the noncorpum and Quasar, is that Mitchell here attempts to offer a rational, scientific view of the idea of the subject under erasure; that is to say, where before we spoke of the subject undergoing a symbolic death or series of symbolic deaths; where before we encountered what appears to be a metaphysical or science-fictional version of Blanchot's idea of subjectivity without any subject, here in "Clear Island," Mitchell offers a scientific vision of these philosophical ideas. He attempts, in other words, to materialize, *even reify*, a philosophical, perhaps psychoanalytical, conception. And yet even here, even at this point where philosophy is concretized—yet perhaps ironically in a language beyond the understanding of most—the idea of a process of connection binding disparate subjects (can we now call them quantum subjects?) is in play. We have, perhaps, a quantum version of Freudian melancholy in the following, a sense that despite distance, despite the severance between subjects that Freud would conceive of as being the grounds of loss, an inevitable connection asserts itself. Muntervary posits the subject as a kind of particle linked to other particles; ineluctably, melancholically, *quantum mechanically*, subject is bound to subject: "Phenomena are interconnected regardless of distance, in a holistic ocean more voodoo than Newton" (366). This line neatly conflates the metaphysical (voodoo) and the scientific (Newton) to offer a view of the universe where distance becomes meaningless; where objects inevitably harmonize with other objects; where narrative meets narrative, conflating and neutralizing space and time; where, in other words, nothing can be lost. Muntervary's "holistic ocean" is really a cosmological model of the universe as interconnected archive, a version of the Freudian unconscious where, to quote once again, "nothing can be brought to an end, nothing is past or forgotten."

As her story concludes, as Muntervary asserts a delicate power over her CIA captors; that is, as she dictates terms that practically collapse the distance between herself and her loved ones (John is with her; Liam, her son, will be with her), Muntervary thinks: "Finally, I understand how the electrons, protons, neutrons, photons, neutrinos, positrons, muons, pions, gluons, and quarks that make up the universe, and the forces that hold them together, are one" (371). At first glance this line would seem merely to confirm her holistic view of the universe as an interconnected web; but is there not more than a hint of anxiety in this deliberate, almost ritualistic, litany of terms? Is there not more than a hint of anxiety arising from the ambiguity of the phrase "the forces that hold them together"? Are these forces the elemental, naturally occurring laws of the universe, or are they the forces of human-asserted agency, desire, and power? If human agency is a randomly generated outcome—as she has learned—are we not to read into this final moment a radical sense of contingency and thus the possibility, the inevitability, of the tragic?

In curious ways, this last question reverberates into the final extended narrative of *Ghostwritten* (the novel proper ends with a coda from the first narrative of Quasar). "Night Train" presents what is essentially the extended monologue of a late-night radio DJ, Bat Segundo. His radio phone-in show has begun receiving transmissions from what turns out to be the quantum cognition—operating on its own volition—created by Mo Muntervary. The quantum cognition, yet another version of subjectivity without any subject (another noncorpum, in fact), has decided to bring the world to the brink of a nuclear Armageddon, and over the course of approximately one year we follow the progress of the inevitable apocalypse. The quantum cognition—it calls itself the Zookeeper—conflates the two fantasies of *Ghostwritten* perfectly: subjectivity without any subject and apocalypse. More precisely, by linking the Zookeeper's origin back to a prior narrative, Mitchell invites us to see how Muntervary's first principle—that the substance of the universe and the forces that hold them together are one—has apocalyptic implications despite her best intentions of creating a cognition that can act according to ethical principles. The Zookeeper's first conversation with Bat Segundo concerns ethics: "'By what law do you interpret laws?'" (379); the Zookeeper, evidently programmed to follow what it calls a series of ethical principles, has come up against the aporia of the law: in order to preserve humanity, it must act unethically (destroying a military base, for instance). The Zookeeper's ethical quest brings the world's superpowers to the brink of paranoid annihilation, each thinking that the other controls the Zookeeper. And Mitchell does allow the fantasy of total annihilation to play out as far as possible: we learn, for instance, that the United States actually does fire its thermonuclear weapons. The Zookeeper, happily, prevents the missiles from reaching their destination and ultimately the conflict between powers dissolves, but the idea of apocalypse looms as a distinct possibility and fantasy here. The United States is clearly shown to desire the end. But Mitchell draws back from the brink, refuses to allow the end to occur (we will see a variation of this theme in the central narrative of *Cloud Atlas*). And the question must become: why? What is the effect of refusing to allow the end to come?

I need to refine my sense of what apocalyptic ends mean here. Mitchell presents the end as the possibility of the complete eradication of human life from the planet; that is to say, apocalypse means here, practically, the end of subjectivity—human or otherwise—as such.[8] But is there not something curious about this fantasy? Because has not the narrative of *Ghostwritten* as a whole already presented the end of subjectivity as always already having taken place? That is, from Quasar, to the noncorpum, to Muntervary's sense of the randomness of the subject, to the quantum cognition, we have already seen the end of subjectivity, at least as traditionally conceived in humanist thought. In some sense thus, a practical end of the human would simply be a redundancy: the posthuman already predates (and anticipates the end of) the human in *Ghostwritten*. The posthuman—and what are Quasar, the noncorpum, and the quantum cognition entity if not versions of the posthuman?—*is* the apocalypse. But, of course, Mitchell's posthuman fantasies have a curiously humanistic quality to them. Radical forms of subjectivity—the symbolically dead human, the fluid transhuman that is the noncorpum—inevitably show themselves as being more human than human: Quasar still persists under the aegis of an all-too-human melancholy; the noncorpum allows itself to be welcomed back into the human family, reborn from the posthuman to the human; the quantum cognition—surely merely a noncorporeal site of Muntervary's ethics—acts according to human-implemented law.[9] This is to say that even as posthuman fantasies inscribe a kind of apocalypse of subjectivity, a curious reentry into law, ethics, and human emotion acts to countervail the radicality of the idea of the human under erasure. And, of course, we cannot forget the structural—narrative—law of *Ghostwritten*: the principle of connection as such overrides the idea of a disappearing subject. Quasar's voice is heard—that is, continues to *be*—in the narrative immediately following his own ("Tokyo"); his voice also is heard, crucially, in "Night Train" (he believes the Zookeeper is His Serendipity and phones into the talk show [406]) as if to remind us that all events link up—and back—to a holistic vision of a universe existing as and for others. And this leads me to the final answer to my question about Mitchell's refusal to allow the end as such: the apocalypse, as the removal of all consciousness from the universe, is an impossibility *as a representation*.[10] Consciousness persists, even, perhaps especially, at the level of narration. The only end to the universe is the end that is in place in all narrative representations: the end of the novel, the space after the final page. As long as consciousness is there to record the end, in other words, an end cannot be represented.

This is all perhaps to say that for Mitchell, consciousness itself—be it the consciousness of a fractured subjectivity (Quasar, Muntervary); the consciousness of a free-floating subjectivity (the noncorpum); the consciousness that is, essentially, ethics reified (the quantum cognition)—because it radically resists any full, final, apocalyptic effacement, operates as the perfect site of archived memory, history, and futurity. We recall Derrida's notion that the archive fundamentally operates as a call to the future:

> [T]he question of the archive is not, we repeat, a question of the past. It is not the question of a concept dealing with the past that might *already* be at our disposal or not at our disposal, *an archivable concept of the archive.*

It is a question of the future, the question of the future itself, the question of a response, of a promise and of a responsibility for tomorrow. The archive: if we want to know what that will have meant, we will only know in times to come. (Derrida 1995, 36)

The archive, in other words, works to bind temporalities and subjectivities into a specific economy of ethics: the human subject now is subject to what Nietzsche would call the "full weight" of future history, given that the archive now works in anticipation of what may come, works to bind the subject into a relationship with the spectral. I am fascinated by how Mitchell's novel presents consciousness operating at both local and general levels in a manner similar to Derrida's notion of the archive. At a general level, *Ghostwritten*, in its weaving of subjectivities that perhaps have no business together, offers itself as an archive wherein past, present, and future are bound together into what essentially is an ethical ecology. At a local level, individual consciousness finds itself unable to move past history—Quasar is haunted by his past actions, his (badly) repudiated past; Muntervary literally is pursued by the implications of her past (research); the noncorpum, at some profound level, is victim to what Derrida elsewhere calls the "nostalgia for origins"[11]; the quantum cognition is haunted by an ethics it perhaps cannot understand, yet which drives its actions (ethics here operates as a parasite, reminding us, perhaps, of the noncorpum's parasitical relationship to its hosts). All these subjectivities, these consciousnesses, in various ways link up to future narratives and thus serve as entry points into a kind of responsibility to the future. But it is the final sustained narrative of *Ghostwritten* that is perhaps most important here: because this final narrative of the apocalypse averted continues to speak to a potential (call it spectral) apocalypse always to occur again. An apocalypse averted is always just that: the logic of this narrative suggests that bringing about the end—the end of history, the end of subjectivity—is always going to remain the final, dominant, fantasy.

And thus perhaps we can make sense of what is really the final narrative of *Ghostwritten*, this curious, brief coda that returns us to Quasar, returns us back into history to the moment of the novel's opening. By returning us to this initiatory action—an action both violent and apocalyptic—to the narrative that structurally leads into and anticipates teleologically all subsequent narratives, Mitchell again reminds us of the essential connectedness of all subjects. But is there not something more uncanny operating here? Is there not also a sense that by returning to this initiatory action Mitchell has not merely reminded us of the beginning but indicated a kind of inevitability of return, the *inescapability* of return? I wonder about Mitchell's shift from "Who was blowing at the nape of my neck" (3) to "Who is blowing at the nape of my neck?" (426); for surely the penultimate line of the novel, with its near identical repetition of the first (save for the shift to the present tense) signals both a continuity of action and a sense that the present tense, the present moment itself, gathers now the full weight of importance. I wonder at the significance of this final narrative taking place in the present tense; I wonder at the significance of Quasar's metaphor as he imagines the timer in his bag, soon to release the poison: "Stowed away in the sports bag at my feet the device has begun expelling dead seconds" (423). This is a crucial metaphor in a number of ways; primarily it signals that time has stopped, will stop for these passengers; but the metaphor also sets up a sense of return, which will play out in this brief narrative. As Quasar rises to exit the train, he catches sight of a variety of objects, advertisements, books, pamphlets, which recall the previous set of narratives: he sees an advertisement for Nippon Air and a beach in Okinawa; from the earphones of a passenger he hears the saxophone music so beloved by Satoru in "Tokyo"; he sees a booklet advertising St. Petersburg, "*City of Masterworks*" (425); he imagines the plains of Mongolia, sees the label of Kilmagoon whiskey and Muntervary's Irish island. Quasar thus anticipates, in terms of narrative time, what stories will unfold (this moment taking place before the other narratives occur); but for the reader his last narrative *recapitulates* narratives we have read, narratives containing traumas that now are returning in a sense. This final narrative, in other words, is a perfect representation of the logic of traumatic return, what Freud calls *Nachtraglichkeit*; this final narrative becomes an uncanny archive of *trauma past and yet to come*. And, of course, the full implication of Quasar's final narrative of traumatic return is that these actions—Quasar's act of terrorism, the noncorpum's rebirth, Muntervary's escape and capture, the quantum cognition's potential apocalypse—are not complete, can never be complete, may return, will return. No event is final in Mitchell; all action continues.

3.2   *number9dream* (2001)

Nothing is more illegible than a wound.

—Derrida, *On the Name*

In *Memory, History, Forgetting,* Paul Ricoeur writes: "Memory does not only bear on time: it requires time—a time of mourning" (74). Ricoeur makes this statement at the conclusion of his analysis of Freud's "Mourning and Melancholia." He comments that, for Freud, melancholy can dissipate after a time—in Freud's words, melancholy "passes off after a certain time has elapsed" (252)—and thus that the movement from a pathological state (melancholia) to a normal state (mourning) requires the time to translate a present state of loss—a present unshakeable effect of loss—into the memory of loss. As soon as trauma can be put into memory; that is, as soon as trauma can be seen as being only a memory of trauma rather than a present state of being inhabiting the subject, the subject can effect a break from that loss, severing the narcissistic identification from the event of loss. Ricoeur puts it thus: "the time of mourning is not unrelated to the patience required by analysis in the passage from repetition to memory" (74). Ricoeur means here that instead of the subject repeating and returning to the event of loss—in unconscious actions such as dreaming or flashbacks—the subject is able to consign the event of trauma to memory, thus remembering the event of loss as such—an event in the past—rather than repeating it. At one level here Ricoeur seems simply to be commenting on the economy of mourning as working through. But his phrase "Memory does not only bear on time: it also requires time—a time of mourning," needs careful attention because of the implication that memory itself (can we say not simply the memory of trauma but all memory?) is fully dependent on the economy of mourning; memory requires the process of mourning to function; memory is defined as a kind of mourning. I am fascinated by the implications of this conflation of memory and mourning here. First, a successful negotiation of trauma—and let us for the moment simply remind ourselves that Freud himself does not know how this process works—sets the subject up as a kind of archive. The subject moves from inhabiting, or being inhabited by, the effect of loss, to being able to distance that loss, to memorize that loss, to turn loss into a memory. Mourning creates the subject as archive; to be a subject, in other words, is to be not only the subject of mourning, subject to mourning, but, perhaps, *is to be mourning itself.* Ricoeur's ideas allow another critique of Freud's perhaps too easy dichotomy of melancholia and mourning to emerge; Ricoeur seems to be suggesting that a full break from loss is not a possibility (perhaps even a desirability). If memory is continually defined by mourning, and the subject in its turn requires memory to be a subject as such—and this is what I mean by the subject becoming the archive—then we do not have a successful working through into the process of mourning, but we have instead another instance of the subject as melancholy archive: "Memory does not only bear on time: it also requires time—a time of mourning." What, I have been asking here, is the archive if not a materialization, perhaps a reification, of the idea of a continual relation to memory? The subject, as he becomes the subject-as-archive, in other words, is not merely defined by his relation to loss, but is in some crucial ways *loss* itself. We need thus to begin asking about what the subject-as-archive looks like. And this question, of course, leads us directly in to Mitchell's *number9dream*.

Because Eiji Miyake, the central character of *number9dream*, is a subject completely defined by his relation to loss. The entire novel, verging at times into a parody of the Oedipus story, is about Miyake's quest to find his father, but it also traces his responses to the loss of both his mother (she has abandoned him and succumbed to alcoholism) and, crucially, his twin sister Anju (who died when Miyake was eleven). *number9dream* thus is a novel about nostalgia, in the sense that nostalgia is a mode of being that places the subject in continual relation to the past; in Miyake's case, his nostalgia is what Derrida calls the nostalgia for origins, a desire to return (nostalgia means "return") to the source of being, the Father. But this return, the novel argues, is always an illusory one, always one defined by fantasy. That is to say, *number9dream* offers the Father quest merely as a pretext for exploring the idea of haunting, of being haunted, more generally. It comes as no real surprise, ultimately, to discover that Miyake's father is not some grand, totemic figure of power and authority, but is merely a common, rather petty lawyer, more concerned with gratifying sensual appetite than anything else.

Mitchell signals from the outset that Miyake's quest for the Father is a phantasmic one. The opening chapter of the novel, blurring at times into a kind of surrealistic cyberpunk, sees Miyake figuring himself as an antihero straight out of William Gibson. And it is crucial that he is shown to be doing precisely that: *figuring himself as*. As Miyake imagines himself into a heroic role, his fantasy acts as a commentary on the logic and economy of fantasy as such. Consider this moment: Miyake has, in his imagination, penetrated his father's offices to confront his secretary, Akiko Kato. A gorgonlike protector of the father, Kato derides Miyake: "Not Luke Skywalker? Not Zax Omega? Do you seriously expect to reduce me to a state of awed obedience by your pathetic spiel? 'One island boy embarks on a perilous mission to discover the father he has never met.' Do you know what happens to island boys once they leave their fantasies?" (10) Miyake's own reduction of his desire to cliché—he is imagining this, after all—signals how the official narrative of *number9dream* can only be serving as a pretext, a screen, for larger concerns. And, crucially, Miyake himself has revealed the true impulse behind the narrative: to reveal the end of fantasy, to explore what happens when fantasy is left behind.

The question, of course, must now follow: how does one leave one's fantasies? More precisely, how can a subject as defined by loss as Miyake—that is, by memory and melancholy—ever hope to leave behind his fantasies, fantasies that, quite clearly, articulate his memory as such? Miyake, to return to Ricoeur, is defined as a subject-who-mourns: to remove the phantasmic element—that is, the fantasies that have grown up in place of memory; the memories that have become fantasies—would be to reduce his subjectivity altogether. *number9dream* is not exploring this apocalyptic reduction of the subject—that is, we are not here in the realm of *Ghostwritten*'s noncorpum or quantum cognition—but it is concerned with tracing the lineaments of Miyake's desire, is concerned with tracking the subject to the brink of a shattered interiority. As I will suggest in what follows, the novel places Miyake in a variety of sites—lost property offices, libraries—or in contact with various historical documents—letters from the living and the dead—which function to manage and negotiate his relation to loss. These sites and documents thus function as archives within which Miyake is offered the opportunity to work through his loss. As one character puts it to Miyake, "'All we are is our memories'" (62): Mitchell will reveal that this "all," this reduction of subjectivity to the traces of history, traces that have elements of the phantasmic about them, has potentially lethal consequences. In crucial ways, thus, *number9dream* explores the particular economy of memory and interiority and offers a critique of the very idea that subjectivity is *only* a function of memory: that is to say, *number9dream* can be read as a trenchant critique of the very idea of Freudian melancholy, of the idea that the past is purely, ineluctably, inescapable.

The second chapter of *number9dream* sees Miyake employed in a lost property office of the Tokyo railway system. The office, like the General Registry in Saramago's *All the Names* (or even Melville's Dead Letter Office in "Bartleby the Scrivener") functions, clearly, as an archive, a repository of loss. For Miyake, however, isolated and alone, the office seems only to compel a kind of specular response: that is, Miyake himself begins to remember his losses, begins, that is, to become an archive. In this office, he thinks, "My memory is the most regular visitor" (51). Mitchell thus fashions this chapter on a careful dialectic between the present moment and memories of a specific past event: the loss of his sister. We move here from Miyake's encounters with various figures, also trapped by their agonized relation to memory and the past, to a careful tracing of the primal scene of trauma in Miyake's life. We see, for instance, Miyake befriend Suga, the quintessential computer geek, himself seemingly a victim of some horrendous primal memory; one day during lunch, Miyake overhears Suga (in the office toilet) talking to himself:

> "I don't *wanna* remember, I don't *wanna* remember, I don't *wanna* remember. Don't make me. Can't make me. Won't make me. *Forget* it! *Forget* it! *Forget* it!!" His voice reverts to its bland, nasal calm. "It wasn't my fault. Could have happened to anyone. To anyone. Don't listen to them." (Mitchell 2001, 54–5)

This uncanny moment—and surely the uncanniness stems from Suga being inhabited, cryptically, by the voice of (perhaps) his past self at the moment of some transgression—signals to Miyake the dangers of being what he terms "memory-whipped," (55) a metaphor not merely suggestive of the pain of being in thrall to the past, but, perhaps, of the threat posed to one's very masculinity by such a victimization (for surely we are meant to hear the phrase "pussy-whipped" echoing in Miyake's words).

The lost property station is a site not only of a painful, melancholic relation to memories one wishes to move past or repress (*Forget* it! *Forget* it! *Forget* it!). Miyake also encounters figures who represent, again as a kind of objective correlative, the idea that some memories are required but have become lost. The so-called Picture Lady is a case in point; this homeless women, a "regular customer," (62) repeatedly comes to the office in search of what Miyake and others assume are actual lost pictures, perhaps some sort of "family album" (62) as Miyake guesses. The Picture Lady has retained, she herself says, her old pictures—"'I got the old ones back'" (61)—but cannot find her new ones, pictures that she needs to "'cover up the clocks'" (62). Miyake's employer, Mrs. Sasaki explains: "'I took her literally at first, too . . . But I think she's talking about her memories . . . All we are is our memories'" (62). And perhaps Sasaki is correct about the Picture Lady and her memories: perhaps the old woman retains, as the elderly do, older memories but lose connection to the recent past. I am interested in how the Picture Lady represents her need for these present memories, her need to use them to cover the clocks; surely this is a trope for the use of the present moment to cancel the progression of time; surely the Picture Lady requires the present in order to halt time's forward progress. And surely she stands, for Miyake, again, as an emblem of how one can find oneself bound irrevocably to the past, willingly bound to a past that blinds one to the present moment. The Picture Lady, in some ways similarly to Suga, has become a kind of crypt for the past, a repository wherein only the past is allowed to retain any resonance, any authority.

And if these figures represent warnings about how not to stand in relation to the past—in painful, perhaps voluntary, thrall—Miyake is shown not yet to have found the means to step past his own past. Clearly, given that his desire to find his father is still his primary compulsion, Miyake is still in thrall to a phantasmic past, to a *phantasmic idea* of the past. But Mitchell is careful to show that other historical forces compel Miyake, other melancholic presences threaten to transform him into precisely the crypt he sees in Suga and The Picture Lady. The first of these enthralling forces comes in a letter Miyake receives from his mother, now confined in an institution for recovering alcoholics. This letter sounds as if it were written as part of a twelve-step program, a deliberate confessing of her past transgressions. And this confession is particularly ghastly: she outlines how, as Miyake's father's mistress, she had been left to care for two infant children; the disgrace, the boredom, the crushed aspirations, all took a toll on her health, physical and mental. This leads to a critical event:

> I'd been working all night so I washed down some pills with vodka and left you to it [Miyake is crying loudly]. Next thing I knew you were rattling my door—you were walking by this time, of course. My migraine wouldn't let me sleep. I lost it. I screamed at you to go away. So of course you bawled some more. I screamed. Then silence. Then I heard you say the word. You must have got it from kindergarten.
>
> "Daddy."
>
> Something broke in me.
>
> Quite calmly, I decided to throw you over the balcony. (Mitchell 2001, 73)

Obviously his mother did not follow through on this desire, but she did throw Miyake across the floor and down the stairs; the subsequent injury precipitates her desertion of Miyake and Anju (she leaves them with her own mother). What is crucial about this confession is not merely the admission of the desire to kill one's own child, surely a traumatizing enough event, but the trigger for that desire: Miyake's "Daddy." His desire for the father, announced early in his infancy, is what precipitates his desertion by the mother as well; this confession, coming now when Miyake is nineteen, only serves further to bind Miyake to that desire.

But, as becomes clear as this chapter progresses, and as Mitchell moves the narrative from present to past memory, there is a homology between the desertion of the parents and Miyake's primal memory of guilt and loss: the death of his sister. This chapter's central memory is of Miyake having travelled by boat to play in a soccer tournament: Anju has had to stay behind and, as we discover, subsequently dies by falling into the ocean. It is never clear if Anju has died accidentally or if her death is a (narcissistic) act of suicidal revenge on Miyake for deserting her, but what is clear is that this chapter—"Lost Property"—is all about the economies of desertion and loss. And what heightens the loss for Miyake is his sense, a childish sense but one perhaps still continuing into his young adulthood, of responsibility for his sister's death. Prior to departing for the tournament, Miyake has come to the shrine of the thunder god and asked for the god's intercession in the games he will play (he desires to become the greatest football player in Japan). In exchange for the win, Miyake promises to rebuild the god's shrine; he also, fatally, promises the god "anything" (70) else he desires. Anju's subsequent death is read by the young Miyake as the god's doing and thus ultimately his own responsibility: he subsequently returns to the shrine and decapitates the god's image. This act, clearly a displacement of his own guilt, is crucial because it resonates throughout the novel. Miyake will return to the god at the very end of the narrative (after seeing his father and being disillusioned by his banality) and notice that his shrine is neglected: "I see the forest has nearly smothered the step path. Every winter his believers become fewer. So gods do die, just like pop stars and sisters" (415); and he might as well have added, just like ideas of fathers. Because surely Miyake's desecration of the thunder god's shrine is an act not only of narcissistic guilt but also of rage against the absent father, a totemic assertion of power over absent power. And as in all killings—all totemic killings especially—the traces of the death are hard to eradicate. Because in a crucial way this desecration sets out Miyake's goal, if only unconsciously: we are asked here to view this act of rage as only the initial act, which will culminate in the ultimate act of desecration against the father, against the name of the father. Clearly Miyake's desire is to kill the *memory* of the father—the (phantasmic) memory of his desertion; the memory of a life without him—as much as it is to encounter him: and consigning the father to oblivion, the oblivion of history or of indifference, is, of course, the ultimate form of killing.

But this desire is not easily realized, as Miyake himself understands: "once you try to forget something you already remember it" (69). Here Miyake acknowledges the role consciousness and agency play in the act of consigning the past to oblivion; he understands that the conscious will to forget can only reinscribe, by that act, the thing to be forgotten. Mitchell's narrative plays against this idea of agency and will begin by setting Miyake's quest within a quintessentially picaresque narrative mode: that is to say, while there is a primary quest in play here (the search for the father), the narrative is composed carefully as a series of digressions, diversions, and distractions from the major narrative impulse. Chapters like "Video Games" and "Reclaimed Land," for instance, see Miyake's increasing entanglement in the world of Tokyo's yakuza underworld; and while within these digressions we see Oedipal themes at play (various father figures come and go), they ultimately serve only as deferrals of the major plot. That is to say, Miyake is not represented as a full agent within his own narrative: his quest is delayed, deferred, by social, economic, and historical forces, which precede and exceed him. It seems indeed at times that as soon as Miyake deliberately attempts to find his father, asserts himself willfully in his primary quest, that quest is diverted; it is only by chance, by a kind of *amor fati*, in fact, that Miyake is able eventually to meet up with his father.

Subsequent chapters like "Study of Tales" and "Kai Ten" may seem also to serve only as digressions, but they are, as I see them, really quite trenchant dilations upon the theme of archived, historical connections to the past and thus serve as meditations on what it would mean to negotiate a relation to the past, to a lost past, to a traumatized past. If, in some ways, Miyake's desire—unconscious or not—is to consign the father to the oblivion of history, he will perhaps discover here that such a desire is impossible. "Study of Tales" sees Miyake taking refuge in the house of the sister of his former employer, Mrs. Sasaki; he has, in the previous chapter, become increasingly, and dangerously, linked to the yakuza, to the point where he is now marked for death. Sasaki's sister is a writer, and the chapter alternates between the text of one of her stories and Miyake's further attempts to find his father. Miyake discovers this story in an upper-floor library:

> Book walls, book towers, book avenues, book side streets. Book spillages, book rubble. Paperback books, hardback books, atlases, manuals, almanacs. Nine lifetimes of books. Enough books to build an igloo to hide in . . . Enough books to make me wonder if I am a book too . . . Apart from the bookcases and sagging shelves, the only item of furniture is an old-fashioned writing bureau . . . On the writing bureau are two piles of paper—one white and blank as starched shirts, the other a manuscript laid in a special lacquer tray. I cannot help myself. I sit down and begin reading page one. (Mitchell 2001, 210)

I have spoken about how Miyake's quest for the Father is inscribed within the economy of fantasy: his early imagined encounter with the dread secretary, Ms. Kato, speaks of his sense that his quest is bordering on the archetypal, if not the clichéd: "'One island boy embarks on a perilous mission to discover the father he has never met'" (10). Miyake's description of this archive of books—it is more than a mere archive; it is a city, with towers, streets, avenues—makes it clear that he sees this library as a refuge ("Enough books to build an igloo to hide in"), a refuge within the larger refuge which is the house proper. But we must attend carefully to this line: "Enough books to make me wonder if I am a book too." Miyake's musing leaves open the possibility that the entire narrative of *number9dream* is an elaborate fantasy. Surely the manner in which Mitchell wrong-foots the reader with Miyake's fantasy imaginings in the early going of the novel is intended to suggest the possibility of an entire narrative of fantasy. But even if *number9dream* is not a large fabrication of fantasy or dream, surely this chapter, a meditation on narrative and confabulation, indicates that another level of displacement between Miyake and the idea of the Father is in place. That is to say, one of the functions of this chapter is to highlight the specifically *constructed* nature of Miyake's narrative. He may not engage directly with meditations on his own writing of this story—it is, after all, a first-person narrative—but this chapter does function to make the reader aware of the fragility, the constructedness of his narrative, and thus perhaps his desire, his quest. And thus, we can perhaps makes some sense of the narratives he reads as mise en abymes of his own desires. And I use the phrase mise en abyme here not merely because the narratives of Goatwriter, Mrs. Comb, and Pithecanthropus reflect the larger containing narrative, but also because of the specific abyssal nature of this mise en abyme (French: to place within the abyss), the way in which these small narratives figure the writer—in this case, Goatwriter—as desiring oblivion, the absolute end.

Let us consider two of these abyssal tales. The first, "Margins," concerns Goatwriter's anxiety about one of his missing stories (we have, thus, stories within stories about stories going missing). This initial narrative follows Goatwriter's attempts to track down his missing manuscript; believing a rat has stolen the story, he, Mrs. Comb, and Pithecanthropus, track the rat down but discover that he is not in fact the thief. It turns out that, unconsciously, Goatwriter has been consuming his own stories, literally eating his own words. If this small narrative is functioning en abyme, we can clearly see that the quest for the missing narrative mirrors Miyake's own quest for his missing father (and what is a missing father but the absent source of the narrative of one's own life?); the conceit, that Goatwriter eats his own narratives, perhaps indicates that the writer/Miyake is both producer and consumer of his own fantasies, that inevitably the fantasist unconsciously consigns—or wishes to consign?—his quest, his fantasy of a quest, to oblivion. And oblivion is, as I have said, precisely what Goatwriter desires. The final tale, entitled, like the chapter itself, "Study of Tales," concerns Goatwriter's desire to locate a "truly untold tale" (251); he subsequently disappears into the forest, leaving Mrs. Comb and Pithecanthropus to track him down. Goatwriter, having been told that the source of the truly untold tale lies in a sacred pool, dives into the pool and subsequently is drowned. The pool is oblivion, is the space of death, as Blanchot would say, where writing begins, because, as we discover, Goatwriter, after death (and now truly the *ghost*writer we hear in his name), comes to the source of writing itself, the very attic, the same writing bureau upon which the manuscript of this story, "Study of Tales," rests. That is to say, Sasaki's sister brings her writer/character to the source, the site, of his own creation, the archive within which he is written.

And so, what are we to make of this marked relation between death/oblivion and writing? Between death and discovering the source of being? We notice, crucially, that as Miyake reads the story of Goatwriter, his own activities during his nonreading time mirror in some ways those activities of his abyssal, specular doubles. That is to say, as Goatwriter seeks the source of all writing—as he engages his own nostalgia for origins—so, too, is Miyake actively pursuing further information about his father: thus, he contacts a private detective (whom he has hired before to track down one of the yakuza) to see if she can find his father. Although not providing information about Miyake's father, the detective does bring a letter from Miyake's grandfather, who requests a meeting. The chapter concludes before any meeting takes place, but certainly we are invited to see the conflation of these narratives as operating as a kind of warning to Miyake: surely Goatwriter's death upon discovering the source of all writing stands as an emblem of the dangers of obtaining one's desires? Or, at least, Goatwriter's death should suggest the radical debt one enters into at the point of obtaining knowledge of one's origins. We will perhaps see if this warning unfolds as such in the subsequent chapter, but before we move on we should note that Miyake's quest has not precisely mirrored that of Goatwriter: if Goatwriter has discovered, and paid the price for, the source of all narrative, the source of all writing, the source of being itself, Miyake has not. He has a letter from someone claiming to be, not his father, but his grandfather: that is to say, he has only a displacement (a letter) of a deferral (grandfather) of the father; even as Miyake seems to close in on his goal, that goal recedes.

I am fascinated by how Miyake's desires are continually deferred in this narrative; I am especially fascinated to note how these desires are deferred in this chapter and the next, both of which unfold within or in response to some kind of archive. Chapter Five, "Study of Tales," thematizes the idea that a return to the archive—Goatwriter's return to the writing bureau—is necessary in order to find the source of all untold tales, the source of being and knowledge; Chapter 6, "Kai Ten," unfolds largely as a reading of a decades-old diary of the Second World War. Having hoped to meet his grandfather, Miyake instead is met by a friend of his grandfather, Admiral Raizo (it will turn out that this figure is indeed his grandfather pretending to be Raizo); Raizo gives him the journal of his grandfather's brother explaining that "'Flesh and blood matter, Miyake! Blood-lines are the stuff of life. Of identity! Knowing who you are from is a requisite of self-knowledge'" (274). Miyake, asking after his grandfather's desires, is told his grandfather wants what Miyake himself wants: "'Meaning'" (275).

The diary is figured as a possible entry into history and thus as the source of self-knowledge. But again, Miyake's own primary desire to know his father is displaced; indeed Raizo/grandfather so despises Miyake's father—the father has, it seems, sold a precious sword long held in his family—as to effectively deny his very being. Raizo, in other words, makes it clear that Miyake's quest for the father is not the proper quest; true knowledge resides, he suggests, within the archived memories of his great-uncle. And the description of the journal is crucial. Raizo speaks:

> "A loan, not a gift. This journal is his most treasured possession. Guard it with your life . . . Questions?"
>
> "We never met—is it wise to trust me with something so—"
>
> "Brazen folly, I say. Make a copy, I told the stubborn old fool. Don't entrust some boy with the original. But he insisted. A copy would dilute its soul, its uniqueness. His words, not mine." (Mitchell 2001, 274)

It is obvious that the grandfather believes that the (fetishized) original words of his brother will transmit meaning; that the resonance, the aura, of the original archived memory will make clear Miyake's relation to a larger historical economy, a larger pattern of meaning. In this sense the grandfather becomes something like Derrida's conception of what he terms the "first archivist" (*Archive Fever.* 55) who "institutes the archive as it should be, that is to say, not only in exhibiting the document but in *establishing* it" (55). In transmitting the document—the original—to his grandson, skipping over his son, Miyake's father, the grandfather creates his grandson as a kind of double of himself: Miyake now has the responsibility for the document and the responsibility, again to borrow from Derrida, to respond to the *promise* of the archive, the archive which here moves into the space of the ghostly past. The words of the journal, the voice of one now long dead, give the document its ghostly quality, the quality of spectrality that Derrida notes is essential to the archive as such: "A spectral messianicity is at work in the concept of the archive and ties it, like religion, like history, like science itself, to a very singular experience of the promise" (36). Of course, our questions now become: What kind of promise does this archive offer? What kind of responsibility to that promise will this archive claim on Miyake?

And indeed the question of the promise is sounded early in Subaru Tsukiyama's journal. Subaru sees himself bound by two promises, the first, to his brother, to tell him every detail of his training in the Imperial Navy; the second, to his emperor, is to keep his training a secret. His journal, as he writes, resolves his dilemma, presumably because his suicide mission will compel his silence even as the journal will speak his archived secret. Subaru's account of his training covers four months, from August to November 1944; Japan, at this point deeply entrenched in its losing struggle with the United States, is desperate to find new means to attack its enemy. Hence, the kaiten, essentially a torpedo outfitted with a pilot. Subaru's journal traces details of his training; gives accounts of his fellow trainees, those who are fanatically dedicated to dying for country, to those who are more ambivalent; tracks Subaru up until the moment of his (failed) suicide run: Subaru's torpedo strikes his target ship but fails to explode, leaving him stranded, yet able to record his final thoughts (on paper he eventually puts into a bottle).

At first glance this journal seems, like a great number of the narratives in *number9dream*, not to have anything directly to do with Miyake's story; this diversion back into history serves mainly to highlight the (perhaps dubious) heroism of his great-uncle and dedication to his brother. But there are crucial moments in the journal, and in Miyake's reflections on the journal, which make it clear that this distant historical event contains real meaning for Miyake:

What would Subaru Tsukiyama say about Japan today? Was it worth dying for? Maybe he would reply that *this* Japan is not the Japan he did die for. The Japan he died for never came into being. It was a possible future, auditioned by the present but rejected with other dreams . . . I wonder how I would have fared in the war. Could I have calmly stayed in an iron whale cruising towards my death? I am the same age as my great-uncle was when he died. I guess I would not have been "I." I would have been another "I." A weird thought, that—I am not made by me, or my parents, but by the Japan that did not come into being. (Mitchell 2001, 310)

This, discursively, is a complex passage, perhaps the most complex—and crucial passage—in *number9dream*, for it is here that Miyake begins to realize that his single-minded dedication to finding the father—the father as source of meaning—is perhaps off the mark. The process of his thoughts is important: he, first, imagines himself to be something of a double of his great-uncle (he having already, as I have mentioned, been figured as a double for his grandfather in taking possession of the journal/archive): "I am the same age as my great-uncle was when he died"; he thus imagines himself as not being who he is, but an optional version of another self; this thought, in terms of its phantasmic temporality, imagines Miyake into the past. But we notice the shift in the next sentence to the present: "I am not made by me, or my parents, but by the Japan that did not come into being." That is to say, he imagines himself the product of a country. Miyake's disavowal of the generative power of the father (and mother) signals a crucial shift in his self-understanding, and does explain perhaps, the importance of the diversions and digressions in this narrative: his adventures with the yakuza and his jobs in the lost property office or in the video store (he is working in the store while this chapter unfolds) are experiences of the Japan that has come into being after the end of the war. These experiences are what form him as a subject; he is, like Tennyson's Ulysses, a part of all that he has met. And yet, it is vital to notice that it is through this archived document, this encounter with the spectral voice of a dead relative, that Miyake is able to come to this understanding: without this archive, Miyake's understanding of himself as subject would not have occurred. Without the encounter with the ghost of Subaru, Miyake would himself remain a ghostly subject, doomed forever to maintain an unreal connection to the absent—and phantasmic—father.

And so what then of his responsibility to the promise of this archive? At the conclusion of the narrative Miyake has a meeting with his step-mother and step-sister, vile creatures both who desire nothing but Miyake's disappearance from their lives (they believe he will make financial claims on his father). Part of their demand is the return of all property belonging to the "proper" family. He, in a crucial moment, refuses to return the journal, and therefore quite literally takes responsibility not only for the material archive, but also for the history and future promise it contains, the future promise of his severed attachment to the phantasmic father. As he walks away from the meeting with his step-mother, Miyake, having been informed that his father does not wish to see him—and having arrived at the idea that perhaps he no longer needs to see him—wonders: "Do I mean it? My father never wants to meet me . . . So my search for him is . . . not valid? Finished? My meaning is cancelled? I guess, yes, I do mean it" (322). And while the novel has two brief chapters remaining, Miyake has essentially come to the end of his quest. But what remains is the critical realization that his "meaning" does not reside in—and thus can be cancelled by—his father: it remains for him to meet the father and realize that the meaninglessness resides within this externalized fantasy. And here we can recall the now crucially prophetic words from the beginning of *number9dream* when Miyake imagines his father's secretary mocking him: "Do you know what happens to island boys once they leave their fantasies?"

Mitchell's answer to this question, to the central question of *number9dream*, is a curious one. After finally encountering his father—in a scene that lasts a mere page of text—and realizing his father's utter and banal conventionality (he is a rather petty man working as a mid-level lawyer)—Miyake thinks, "I want to smash your skull with your golfing trophy. I want to shout and I think I want to cry. I want to know. Your consequences, your damage, your dead. I want to drag you down to the seabed between foot rock and the whalestone" (374). Clearly connecting his father's absence to the death of his sister, Miyake is unable, or unwilling, to speak, realizing, as he says, that this encounter is not really what he wished: "I feel sad that I found what I searched for, but no longer want what I found" (375). Later he thinks: "I met my father this morning. I feel loss, I feel victory, but most of all I feel free" (382); this sense of freedom is crucial, signifying as it does the end of the phantasmic idea of the father. And as this sense of freedom develops, he realizes his true responsibility is to meet up with his mother and attempt a reconciliation. The final chapter of *number9dream* sees Miyake returning to his childhood home to effect this meeting and, as previously mentioned, to return to the shrine of the now-defunct thunder god. This chapter clearly represents Miyake coming to some kind of reconciliation with his past, both through these ritualized encounters—the mother, the god—but also through the surreal dreams he experiences during this journey (he dreams of dead acquaintances and his sister). But Mitchell chooses not to end the novel in this state of reconciliation; he chooses instead to end the novel with a disaster, a massive earthquake which strikes Tokyo. The quake, measuring 7.3 on the Richter scale, has possibly killed all his friends and his girlfriend, Ai, (the quake has, at the very least, cut off their phone lines, thus all possibility of immediate communication). The novel ends with Miyake now imagining the disaster:

> The radio man announces that a state of emergency has been declared. I imagine a pane of glass exploding next to Ai's face, or a steel girder crashing through her piano. I imagine a thousand things. I grab my bag, slide down the hallway, scrunch my feet into my trainers, and scrape open the stubborn door. And I begin running. (Mitchell 2001, 418)

Mitchell's ending reminds me of Blanchot on the disaster: "*When all is said, what remains to be said is the disaster. Ruin of words, demise writing, faintness faintly murmuring: what remains without remains*" (*The Writing of the Disaster.* 33). Miyake, having freed himself from the fantasy of the father, now, it seems, must pay for that freedom with the potential loss of lovers and friends. The disaster, as Blanchot says, is unexperienced by the subject because it is beyond understanding, and here beyond Miyake's immediate experience; the disaster leaves remains, traces that cannot be accommodated as such. We notice the disastrous slippage into fantasy that is occurring as the novel ends: he imagines the disaster, fantasizes about its extent, "I would give anything to be dreaming right now" (418). And surely the blank Chapter Nine of the novel—the number nine dream of the title— signifies Blanchot's remains without remains: the pure space of uninscribed, unwritten experience that nevertheless asserts phantasmic claims upon the briefly free, now once again disastrously indebted, Miyake.

3.3   *Cloud Atlas* (2004)

Who can swear that our unconscious is not expecting this?
—Derrida "*No Apocalypse, Not Now*"

Any consideration of *Cloud Atlas* must begin with the novel's structure; indeed in this chapter I am primarily concerned with a meditation on the implications of the novel's structure and not immediately with an analysis of the contents of the six stories contained within the larger whole. *Cloud Atlas* is composed of six individual narratives, each set in a different historical period: "The Pacific Journal of Adam Ewing" takes place in 1841; "Letters from Zedelgheim" in 1931; "Half-Lives: The First Luisa Rey Mystery" in 1975; "The Ghastly Ordeal of Timothy Cavendish" at a point not long after September 2001; "An Orison of Sonmi-451" in approximately 2100;

"Sloosha's Crossin' An' Ev'rythin' After" in a distant post-nuclear war future. With the exception of "Sloosha's Crossin' An' Ev'rythin' After," each of these narratives is split into two parts, interrupted by the first half of the next narrative: thus, we read the first half of each of the first five narratives until we reach "Sloosha's Crossin' An' Ev'rythin' After," which is presented in its entirety. After this central narrative we read the second half of each narrative starting with "An Orison of Sonmi-451" until we finally reach the second half of "The Pacific Journal of Adam Ewing." That is to say, Mitchell has presented a nested series of historical narratives which moves us from the past into the future and back into the past:

1841→1931→1975→ca. post-2001→2100→distant future ←2100←ca. post-2001←1975← 1931← 1841

It is clear that this structure is intended to suggest a connection between narratives. More precisely, there is a (curious) teleology set up here, a repeating trajectory from one point of origin (1841) to the end of history and back again. But what are we to make of the first half of the novel's teleology? What are we to make of the fact that *Cloud Atlas* does in fact quite literally have a center, a central narrative, "Sloosha's Crossin," entirely on its own? What are we to make, in other words, of *Cloud Atlas'* fetishization of this central narrative of the post-apocalypse? This, indeed, will be the question guiding my various considerations of this most complex, most troubling novel, and to begin, I wish to suggest that this center structurally, symbolically, functions as a sepulcher, the sepulcher of history.

Let us return to Paul Ricoeur's *Memory, History, Forgetting* and his discussion of the writing of history. Ricoeur is discussing Michel de Certeau's conception of the historical text as a monument to loss, as, that is, a sepulcher; we will turn to de Certeau himself in a moment, but Ricoeur is eloquent here:

> Sepulcher, indeed, is not only a place set apart in our cities, the place we call a cemetery and in which we depose the remains of the living who return to dust. It is an act, the act of burying. This gesture is not punctual; it is not limited to the moment of burial. The sepulcher remains because the gesture of burying remains; its path is the very path of mourning that transforms the physical absence of the lost object into an inner presence. The sepulcher as the material place thus becomes the enduring mark of mourning, the memory-aid of the act of sepulcher. (Ricoeur 2004, 366)

I am fascinated by Ricoeur's sense of how the materiality of the sepulcher—the act of burial; the place of burial—transforms, or is transformed into, what he calls an "inner presence." Certainly this notion of absence and loss (of mourning) transforming into this "presence"—that is, something that continues to haunt—is one way of thinking about the sepulcher as the place of melancholy (a trope we will see again in Saramago). An "enduring mark of mourning" is precisely the site of melancholy and surely this is how we should be thinking about Mitchell's novel: it sets itself up as a very material act of sepulcher that works to anticipate loss (in the future) and the return to origins (1841), which in a way creates the conditions of that loss. Mitchell is careful to remind us that what we are reading is not transparently appearing narrative but real, material, historical documents: we have, thus, journal entries ("The Pacific Journal of Adam Ewing"), letters ("Letters from Zedelgheim"), and archived interviews ("An Orison of Sonmi-451"). We have, in other words, a series of archived texts, texts archived within the larger sepulchral archive that is *Cloud Atlas*.[12]

In "Psychoanalysis and Its History," Michel de Certeau offers a way of thinking about the relation between historiography and psychoanalysis which may help us to think about the complex implications of the structure of *Cloud Atlas*. I draw on de Certeau here, like Ricoeur, because he is interested in the materiality of the act of memory; that is, he is interested in the spaces of psychoanalysis and historiography in ways that speak to the very architectural—even psychogeographical—logics of Mitchell's narrative design, a design that, to my mind, conflates the impulses of both psychoanalysis and historiography:

> Psychoanalysis and historiography thus have two different ways of distributing the *space of memory*. They conceive of the relation between the past and present differently. Psychoanalysis recognizes the past *in* the present; historiography places them one *beside* the other. Psychoanalysis treats the relation as one of imbrication (one in the place of the other), of repetition (one reproduces the other in another form), of the equivocal and of the *quipropquo* . . . Historiography conceives the relation as one of succession (one after the other), correlation (greater or lesser proximities), cause and effect (one follows from the other), and disjunction (either one or the other, but not at the same time). Two strategies of *time* thus confront one another. (de Certeau 1986, 4)

It is my sense that this confrontation between repetition and cause and effect, between seeing the past in the present and seeing the past beside the present is what characterizes Mitchell's narrative impulse here in *Cloud Atlas*; moreover, it is precisely this confrontation—succession as a kind of working through, repetition as a kind of melancholic return—which creates this novel as a perfect archive. Because surely the impulse toward working past a scene of history, *being able to see cause and effect as such,* and the impulse to stage a return to or repetition of that historical moment (and this is the precise logic of Mitchell's narrative structure), surely these impulses, if they do not cancel each other out, place the narrative in a kind of suspension where loss is maintained *and* worked through; where loss is preserved because it is repeated, but always with the possibility of its moving toward an anticipation of the future.[13] In *The Writing of History* de Certeau notes that "Writing speaks of the past only in order to inter it" (101); writing functions to inter, that is encrypt, history within what I have called the melancholy archive. But what of Mitchell's (albeit fictional) writing of the future? How can we conceive of his anticipation of loss—thus the anticipation of the sepulcher—without thinking about spectral, archived memories, that is, without Derrida?

This is to say, to return to my central question, what is the function of the future in Mitchell's novel? How can we begin to think about what we have now to call "future melancholy," being tied, indebted, to a loss that has yet to occur? To answer these questions, I wish to consider the relation between the three main narratives in *Cloud Atlas*: "The Pacific Journal of Adam Ewing," "An Orison of Sonmi-451," and "Sloosha's Crossin' An' Ev'rythin' After" because these narratives do concern various scenes of historical and futural traumas: "The Pacific Journal" takes place during and at the site of the Moriori genocide in New Zealand; "An Orison" is a meditation on the ideas of slavery, freedom, and consciousness; "Sloosha's Crossin'" concerns the near obliteration of the entire human species. My own sense of the relation between these narratives is that Mitchell is offering a kind of teleology here: we move from historical New Zealand, to a near-future Korea, and finally to post-apocalyptic Hawaii. These three distinct and distant geographic sites are linked by structural and symbolic echoes: one character in each narrative will bear either a tattoo or a birthmark that is identical to the mark born by a major character in a different story (in fact, all narratives in *Cloud Atlas* are linked this way, implying, perhaps, a kind of reincarnation). But there is a relentless, and despairing, logic at work here which suggests that the desire to annihilate a people (the Moriori), to enslave the Other (the clones of "An Orison"), leads logically to the annihilation of an entire species. If, in *Ghostwritten*, Mitchell drew back from the apocalypse, here we see him embrace the end as fully as possible and still retain what Beckett would call the "mere minimum" of humanity required for narrative to exist as such.[14]

In some ways, thus, the apocalypse at the center of the novel in "Sloosha's Crossin'" is merely a repetition of the apocalypse writ on a smaller scale in the previous narratives. That is to say, and this is one of the truly uncanny and unsettling effects of the narrative structure, this apocalypse is set up as a *kind of nostalgia for what has yet to happen*. I am reminded of Benjamin's description of humankind's pleasure at witnessing—perhaps anticipating—its own destruction in those final, apocalyptic words in "The Work of Art in the Age of Mechanical Reproduction": "[Mankind's] self-alienation has reached such a degree that it can experience its own destruction as an aesthetic pleasure of the first order" (242).[15] Anticipating the disaster becomes the desire of this novel; representing the disaster, that which, as Blanchot says, cannot be represented, as a pleasurable, aesthetic act, becomes the task of this novel. Having set up the central narrative as the logical, teleological outcome of known and imagined disasters (genocide and slavery), Mitchell sets up his disaster as both entirely spectral *and* real, hence its radical uncanniness. And yet, if the novel is read in succession, with each narrative laid out in a series of historiographical correlations, Mitchell deepens the uncanniness as we trace from the ultimate, apocalyptic disaster, back to that disaster's very roots in the Moriori genocide of the nineteenth century (a disaster that takes on the shape of all genocides to follow in the twentieth century and stands as a *type* of genocide, as such). The novel thus is simultaneously teleological and about repetition and return: history moves to its disaster, yet moves back to itself. As the novel closes with the return to 1841, the memory of the disaster yet to come but *having already occurred* is in place.[16] This sense of the apocalypse forever suspended is echoed, structurally, in the obvious fact that there is no ending proper to *Cloud Atlas*: the final chapter in the novel is also its first. If all narrative, as Steven Connor and Frank Kermode have argued, works toward the end, habituates us to what Connor calls "living-towards-ending" (200)[17]; if, that is, an ending works as a kind of revelation (and this is, of course, what apocalypse means), then Mitchell suspends the revelatory aspects of the narrative just as he suspends the historical (im)possibility of apocalypse as the absolute end.[18]

Thus, Autua, the Moriori runaway slave in "The Pacific Journal"—and in some sense the last traces of his people—becomes a type of the runaway clone slave in "An Orison": both Autua and Sonmi-451 manage to leave archived traces of themselves, their narratives. Autua's story is recorded as an embedded narrative within the journal of Adam Ewing: Ewing, thus, becomes responsible, becomes the secret sharer and archivist, of Autua's narrative of extermination at the hands of the Maori. Sonmi-451's slave narrative, of course, forms the content of "An Orison," a story taking the form of an interview between Sonmi-451, a cloned subject created to serve the Corprocracy, and an Archivist interviewer; Sonmi's narrative, a recounting of her coming to awareness of her status as clone and her subsequent attempts to attain rights for the cloned—for all repressed subjects, in fact—takes place soon before she is to be executed as an enemy of the State. "An Orison" thus takes the form of a last testament, a discursive form of resistance and a statement of a general ethical system. Moreover, her narrative is explicitly a document to be preserved by the Archivist interviewer; her interviewer has asserted *"Rule 54.iii—the right to archivism"* (189) to obtain her story despite the fact that, as a runaway—as a "heretic" to the "Corprocracy" (189) she serves—Sonmi's story represents a potent threat to the very culture that created her. And, of course, there is a deep irony in the fact that precisely because this Corprocracy does archive Sonmi's story, she, her life, her thoughts, persists in the spectral afterlife of a religious icon. That is to say, we must attend carefully to the fact that Sonmi's presence as deity to the primitives in "Sloosha's Crossin' An' Ev'rythin' After" is testament to the uncanny persistence of the force of her ideas.[19] And despite the fact that her materiality is shown to the narrator of this central narrative; despite the fact that she is shown to be merely human and not a deity, Sonmi's charisma continues, preserved by the technologies of the superior group that has arrived on Hawaii to study these primitives. Sonmi's narrative is preserved within what is called here an orison, a recording device that holographically archives data. Meronym, the representative of the last group of technologically advanced peoples on earth, describes the orison thus:

> *An orison is a brain an' a window an' it's a mem'ry. Its brain lets you do things like unlock observ'tree doors what yo jus' seen. Its window lets you speak to other orisons in the far-far. Its mem'ry lets you see what orisons in the past seen'n' heard, an' keep what my orison sees'n'hears safe from f'getting'.* (Mitchell 2004, 276)

The orison, in other words, is an archive, an archive that has preserved the aura of Sonmi from hundreds of years ago and is working in the post-apocalyptic now to preserve and record this present state of devastation. But we need to attend to the word "orison" because it does have a specific meaning that resonates nicely with the metaphysical tenor of this narrative. "Orison" is an archaic word meaning prayer: Sonmi's testimony—"An Orison of Sonmi-451"—thus functions as a prayer to the future, an appeal—and is this not what prayer actually is?—to a future hearing, a future acknowledgment of her life and word. The orison in the now, the technological device that records the present and archives the past, is thus similarly functioning as an appeal to what will come: as prayer, this orison, this archive, again recalls the Derridean notion of an appeal to futurity. Derrida's words now take on another level of significance: "a spectral messianicity is at work in the archive." The orison contains the appeal to and from a long-dead, spectrally preserved Sonmi, an appeal that has placed a burden of responsibility on both this primitive tribe, which worships her, and this advanced group, which sees her not as a deity, but a figure of ethical action, a figure, more precisely, of the ethical life.

I wish to conclude my consideration of *Cloud Atlas* by turning to the final moment of this central text; that is to say, the central event—both structurally and, I will argue, philosophically—in the novel. Let me approach this moment—when the narrator's son passes on the orison to his listeners—through a diversion into Derrida. In *Specters of Marx*, Derrida, in a crucial passage reflecting essentially on his life's work as a philosopher, is meditating on the work of deconstruction, its burdens, its debts. His thoughts here resonate forward into *Archive Fever* insofar as he is thinking about the responsibility for and of ideas: in some ways this passage makes clear that the work of deconstruction, the work of radical interrogation, of radical reimagining, is always already the work of the archive insofar as deconstruction must always attend to the burdens of past thought and assume a responsibility for thought to come. And certainly Derrida's thoughts here about the debt to ideas are a theme around which Mitchell's narrative has revolved and, indeed, will conclude. For is not the very structure of *Cloud Atlas* one that confers a great burden of history to and on the present moment? Does this structure not place what Nietzsche calls the greatest stress, the greatest responsibility, upon the present moment? I need to quote at some length:

> A deconstructive thinking . . . has always pointed out the irreducibility of affirmation and therefore of the promise, as well as the undeconstructibility of certain ideas of justice (dissociated here from law). Such a thinking cannot operate without justifying the principle of a radical and interminable, infinite (both theoretical and practical, as one used to say) critique. This critique belongs to the movement of an experience open to the absolute future of what is coming, that is to say, a necessarily indeterminate, abstract, desert-like experience that is confided, exposed, given up to its waiting for the other and for the event. In its pure formality, in the indetermination that it requires, one may find yet another essential affinity between it and a certain messianic spirit. (Derrida 1994, 90)

This passage strikes me as an uncannily apposite commentary on Mitchell's narrative, a precise commentary on the central moment in the central narrative. For we must read the continuity, the spectral continuity of Sonmi-451, as a pure example of the irreducibility of an "idea" of justice; for surely the continuity of her narrative of freedom, of rights for the cloned, speaks to the idea that these ideas have a persistent claim on the real. And if I am correct to suggest a genealogy of (in)justice being traced in *Cloud Atlas*, a genealogy traced back to an event of nineteenth-century genocide, the novel begins, in Derrida's words, to take on the shape of a critique. And so, let us attend carefully to the final moment of this central narrative, at last. Zachary's son has, as is shown, inherited the orison given to Zachary, Sonmi-451's orison: that is, Zachary's son has inherited the archive that contains the origin of this remaindered culture's sense of religion and justice, both. Zachary's son has inherited an enormous gift and uncanny debt: the gift of the archive becomes a debt to the past and the future. This orison telescopes all the previous narratives into one concentrated site, and this moment thus, this moment where the son speaks of the orison, is one in which we are clearly shown his debt to all the dead who have proceeded this moment, all the dead who have, in their ways, created the conditions of this *event of inheritance*. Here are the son's words:

> See, after Pa died my sis'n'me sivvied up his gear, an' I finded his silv'ry egg what he named *orison* in his yarns. Like Pa yarned, if you warm the egg in your hands, a beautsome ghost-girl appears in the air an' speaks in an Old-Un tongue what no un alive und'stands nor never will, nay. It ain't Smart you can use 'cos it don't kill Kona pirates nor fill empty guts, but some dusks my kin'n'bros'll wake up the ghost-girl jus' to watch her hov'rin'n'shimm'rin. She's beautsome and she 'mazes the littl'uns an' her murmin's babbybie our babbits.
>
> Sit down a beat or two.
>
> Hold out your hands.
>
> Look. (Mitchell 2004, 309)

Let us just recall Derrida: "This critique belongs to the movement of an experience open to the absolute future of what is coming, that is to say, a necessarily indeterminate, abstract, desert-like experience that is confided, exposed, given up to its waiting for the other and for the event." Mitchell ends his narrative, his "terminal art," with a clear appeal to the listener/reader to attend, to view, the orison[20]: it is an ending that confers upon the listener/reader a burden, the burden of responsibility for what we know is the story of Sonmi-451. If these remnants of humanity will never understand her "old-Un tongue," *we* have, we shall continue to do so. Surely his ending is an appeal for Sonmi-451's critique of power, her critique of injustice, to continue beyond her. But is there not something desperate about this end? This appeal to the desertlike experience of futurity, this appeal to an event that will never come—but for us has already come—in the context of the narrative proper is a despairing appeal precisely because of the disruptive linguistic divide that separates Sonmi-451 from her followers. In some ways the crucial question this narrative asks is this: if death, as Paul Virilio tells us, is the "interruption of knowledge,"[21] can a critique continue *as* critique across a linguistic divide? Will the decay of language—and surely one of the most obvious effects of the apocalypse on this remaindered tribe is the decay of language—prevent the critique from working? In some ways, from a Derridean perspective, this question is not a real one: the event, the appeal to the Other, is always one of waiting, of expectation, of a messianic spectrality. Moreover, this linguistic divide is effaced by the very weight of the inherited responsibility for what is contained within the archived orison; as Derrida writes: "There is no inheritance without a call to responsibility" (91). And, as I have said, if the appeal cannot be linguistically communicated to this tribe, this "Hold out your hands. Look" is an appeal to us, to the reader holding the archive, *Cloud Atlas*, which in its own crucial way has become its own orison.

And yet we cannot quite simply pass this ending on to the reader; that is, we cannot quite ignore the appeal being made here in this central narrative, this final moment, which, in historical terms, is the final moment of *Cloud Atlas*. I wonder if Mitchell is not signaling to us that Sonmi's critique, despite linguistic barriers, despite the barriers of translation and interpretation—despite the radical problematics of hermeneutics as such—continues but at a level beyond merely the intellectual. Notice how Mitchell is careful to signal to us the appeal to sight and touch, not hearing. This "Hold out your hands" signals an appeal to the materiality of the archival object. History here is materialized as a thing to be handled, to be known through the logic of touch; history's inevitable spectrality—be it a tragic spectrality or a promissory, messianic one—is effaced by the material sepulcher. Again I am reminded of Benjamin and his *Theses on the Philosophy of History*: "To articulate the past historically does not mean to recognize it 'the way it really was' . . . It means to seize hold of a memory as it flashes up at a moment of danger. Historical materialism wishes to retain that image of the past which unexpectedly appears to man singled out by history at a moment of danger" (255). I am fascinated by how Mitchell's ending here literalizes Benjamin's desire to seize hold of history, actually, as if both history and the ability to grasp it were indeed material things. But Mitchell's ending is more than a mere allegory of Benjamin's fantasy, because his narrative ends, authoritatively, with an appeal not merely to tactility, but to vision: Look. And it is with this word that Mitchell returns to a kind of spectrality, returns, that is, to an appeal to the spectrality of the historical. These spectators will not understand what they hear: Sonmi's language is beyond them, but her image remains and retains within it a lasting appeal. I referred earlier to Sonmi's charisma, and I do so again with an eye to its etymology: charisma means "grace of God." If the orison is a prayer, but in this case a prayer whose words cannot be comprehended, Sonmi's grace, her charisma, archived now and forever, will continue but only at the level of vision, only insofar as she remains, in the narrator's words, "a beautsome *ghost-girl.*" Mitchell's ending thus attains the true, ambivalent, and tragic condition of the apocalyptic: Sonmi's prayer, her grace, *are* revealed, but only to those who do not have ears to hear; having eyes to see only the grace, the beauty, of history, these remaindered humans will forever and always fail to comprehend its critical, but secret, wisdom.[22]

Chapter 4

Archiving Melancholy: José Saramago

So I write in order to keep.

—Derrida, *"Dialanguages"*

In this chapter I wish to explore the relation between history and spectrality in José Saramago's novels. Perhaps the simplest way to begin would be to suggest that in Saramago, history is a spectral presence: it haunts the subject, binding him or her to an unavoidable past. And while it is too easy to suggest that because history is precisely that, the past, it is a priori spectral, surely this notion is at work centrally in *The History of the Siege of Lisbon* and, in a complicated way, *All the Names*. But I wish to refine the idea of the spectrality of history by linking it to a conception of the archive. I have suggested in my readings of Mitchell through Derrida that the archive is spectral because, as Derrida says, it is always a structure oriented to what is to come. Derrida, in this maneuver, tends to discount the weight of history, what Nietzsche calls the "greatest stress": Derrida, that is, tends to overwrite the promise of the past in favor of the promise and responsibility to the future. In some ways I am wondering here if Saramago's novels pose a problem to a Derridean reading of the archive precisely because they wish, at least at one level, to negotiate an understanding of how the past works on the present, how, in Freudian terms, the past continues to work itself out through the subject in the present. My real beginning point here is the idea that we must, in our reading of Saramago, attend to how he posits the subject itself as always already a potential archive and thus as spectral: the subject in Saramago is always a kind of remainder, a trace, a spectral revenant of the past forever attempting to orient itself in the present moment. My interest thus will be to attempt to demonstrate Saramago's concern with what we might call the responsibility of the specter, the ethics of spectrality, for surely each of Saramago's novels is about the individual's awareness of his place within the historical continuum, the necessity, that is, of the subject responding to the claims of history even as he or she is effaced precisely by history's inexorable momentum.

It will become clear as we trace through the novels under scrutiny here that Saramago is centrally concerned with questions of origin, trace, and voice. In some ways his novels all display what Derrida, somewhat disparagingly, calls the "nostalgia for origins." Major characters are haunted by the desire to trace sites of originary historical events (*The History of the Siege of Lisbon*); they are haunted by events of the past which have shaped them in ways beyond their control (*The Year of the Death of Ricardo Reis*); they desire to track and trace the voices of real or imaginary objects of desire (*The History of the Siege of Lisbon*, *The Year of the Death of Ricardo Reis*, *All the Names*). We could say, in fact, that each major character in these novels displays a version of a kind of archive fever; this here, for me, means an addiction to the past, to history, an addiction to past events which transforms the subject into a crypt containing what they believe to be, or desire to be, a version of the past. But I use the term archive fever with obvious attention to how Derrida employs the term. He is clear that at the heart of the drive to archive is a kind of violence; at the heart of the archive lies, in fact, the death drive, which, as part of its essential economy, leaves no trace of itself; the death drive, as Derrida reads Freud, is a destructive compulsion—a repeating destructive compulsion—which effaces its *work*. In this sense the death drive obliterates any attempt to record its passage, any archive that could stand as testimony to its destructive economy. Thus, Derrida describes the death drive as *anarchivic* and *archiviolithic*: it effaces all traces of itself. In my reading of Saramago through Derrida's reading of Freud, I mean to suggest that Saramago quite brilliantly represents the archiviolithic aspect of the death drive, not necessarily as it itself appears—Freud would say this is impossible—but in its effects. We are concerned here thus with an analysis of the effects of various traumas that cannot simply, without problem, be linked back to clearly definable causes. Moreover, we are concerned with analyzing how Saramago negotiates a relationship between the event of memory and its representation in narrative, in the subject of the narrative, in the interiority of the writing subject. My sense, to offer a glimpse of my thesis here, is that the subject—Reis, Silva, Senhor José—becomes the site of this archival violence, this site of the effects of a drive toward destruction and effacement. Saramago's novels thus, in one reading, stand as fairly acute warnings about the effects of one's nostalgia for history, for origins: the trace will always damage, but the trace is unbearably, inexorably, demanding.

4.1 The Year of the Death of Ricardo Reis (1984)

Loss is impossible.

—Blanchot, *The Step Not Beyond*

Perhaps the crucial question for a reading of *The Year of the Death of Ricardo Reis* is that of Ricardo Reis's status as subject. Indeed, the term "subject" may not be an appropriate term for one as complex, ontologically, as Reis. Ricardo Reis is, first, a heteronym of Fernando Pessoa.[1] Reis, in Pessoa's imaginary, was physician and poet: he composed a series of odes, a number of lines from which are cited over the course of Saramago's novel. Reis was also conceived of as being politically conservative, a Royalist forced into a fourteen-year exile in Brazil after 1919. Thus, Reis is a fully fleshed fictional subject who in turn is reimagined by another writer, Saramago. Reis is, second, a simulacrum of a heteronym, twice removed from his point of origin and therefore ontologically of an extremely tenuous status. I am fascinated by what has occurred to Reis in this novel: Reis, as heteronym, is always already a spectral creation, a ghostly creation. He both is and is not Pessoa in the sense that a character (or the constructed personality or subjectivity, which is the heteronym) always finds its source in an author's imaginary and yet stands absolutely at a remove. But Reis is, obviously, more than a character (both in Pessoa's imaginary and Saramago's); Reis, as imagined by Pessoa, is a writer, and if the problem of the ontology of Reis himself arises, so, too, must the question of the status of his writing, both in Pessoa and in Saramago. It is my purpose here, thus, to think carefully about the relation between writing—as itself an activity of the trace—and the specter, writing spectrally doubled by Saramago as he transposes a subject from the imaginary of another into his own. In some crucial way the central question of Saramago's novel—and this, too, must be the question of Pessoa's oeuvre—is always: Who speaks? Whose voice are we attending to as we read Saramago's novel?

The Year of the Death of Ricardo Reis is a novel clearly about the economy of haunting and thus a novel about the economy of traces, voices, effaced yet insistent remainders. Perhaps most obviously Reis himself is haunted by the presence of the dead Pessoa: this structure—one writer communing with another (dead) writer—surely stands as a mise en abyme of the larger economy of influence in Saramago's novel: for if Pessoa is haunting Reis, he is also haunting—or is made to haunt—Saramago himself. It is crucial that we keep in mind how Reis functions in this doubled way (in a novel all about doubles, this is a complicated one): Reis, as Pessoa's heteronym, functions as a double for Pessoa; as a figure of the author haunted by a precursor—and Pessoa is quite literally (and literarily) Reis's precursor—Reis stands in, as it were, doubles for Saramago himself. *The Year of the Death of Ricardo Reis* thus becomes more than simply an analysis of a subject out of step in changing political times; it is more than simply an analysis of personal and political apathy and passivity. The novel becomes a quite acute meditation on the idea of literary influence as historical, thus spectral, process and in this way becomes a fascinating analysis of the idea of literary melancholy.

Ricardo Reis has returned to Lisbon after a sixteen-year absence; he offers various reasons to various people for his return (nostalgia, political instability in Brazil [65]), but it is clear that he is back in his homeland because Fernando Pessoa has died. His return does thus operate as a kind of mourning, but, of course, the question must be: for whom? Pessoa, as precursor, origin, source of Reis stands as the obvious object of mourning, but Reis and Pessoa, arguably, are the same: Reis's return and mourning here takes on the unmistakable economy of narcissism. But Saramago makes this diagnosis of Reis playfully difficult by staging Pessoa's repeated return: Pessoa has, according to a logic at work for the dead, been given a few months to haunt the living. Pessoa, therefore, appears to Reis several times over the course of the novel, and these returns, already spectral, already fantastic, simply highlight another impossibility: that Pessoa and Reis have distinct subjectivities. In some ways the novel operates as a kind of elaborate thought experiment, exploring the idea of the invented subjectivity and asking: what would happen if a constructed, fictional self took on a life of its own? What is the status—ethical, ontological—of the imagination? We must inflect this question in a specific way in order to answer it: what is the status of the spectral imagination? The imagination as trace?

Reis feels, to put it simply, that he is not complete, entire, on his own; he feels as if he functions as a marker or site for the working through of other subjectivities. One way of thinking about Reis is that he senses his own haunting, his own function as a crypt for the subjectivity of another, or others. If we return to Blanchot, we may suggest that Reis is a subjectivity without a *single* subject. In a crucial moment early in the text Reis muses on the status of his own thoughts; he has been composing poetry:

Innumerable people live within us. If I think and feel, I know not who is thinking and feeling, I am only the place where there is thinking and feeling, and, though they do not end here, it is as if everything ends, for beyond thinking and feeling there is nothing. If I am this, muses Ricardo Reis as he stops reading, who will be thinking at this moment what I am thinking, or think that I am thinking in the place where I am, because of thinking. Who will be feeling what I am feeling, or feel that I am feeling in the place where I am, because of feeling. Who is using me in order to think and feel . . . Who am I that others are not nor have been nor will come to be. (Saramago 1984, 13)

This passage must, first, be read self-reflexively, for surely Reis's sense that he is being used in order for someone to think and feel is a clear reference to the economy of the heteronym: Pessoa's creation of various personae functioned in one way to allow him to think and feel as other subjectivities. But the passage also indicates Reis's sense that, as a site of innumerable subjectivities, his own proper self—whatever that may be—has no more claim to the world than the subjectivity of the Other. He becomes here a perfect reflection of the cryptological economy of Lacan's idea of desire: desire is always the desire of the Other. Reis merely becomes the desire of Others and if on a first reading this idea resonates into Pessoa's practice of creating heteronyms, surely we must now see Saramago's desire in Reis, Saramago's desire to be as if he were Reis, as well. Because ultimately this novel is about staging various encounters between Reis and Pessoa, and if Saramago's desire animates Reis—and I use the word deliberately—it is a desire that speaks to a further desire to commune—as a companion to Orpheus (25)—with Pessoa himself. Thus Reis's question, Who is using me in order to think and feel?, has another answer: Saramago will always be interested in pursuing what is lost. As Derrida tells us, we pursue what is lost in order to keep it, to house it, to encrypt it. *The Year of the Death of Ricardo Reis* thus becomes that crypt, that site wherein one author animates another in order to preserve the dead precursor.

But this writing, this text that is the crypt of *The Year of the Death of Ricardo Reis*, is more than merely the melancholy archive preserving Pessoa as precursor. For surely one of the trajectories of the novel is to stage the return and final disappearance of both Pessoa and Reis. Reis's time back in Lisbon—with his languid, apathetic affairs with the chambermaid, Lydia, and Marcenda, the disabled hotel guest—is merely that, time, a passage from one state of disappearance (Brazil) to another (death). It is not accidental that the novel opens and closes with a repeated image of a kind of no-man's land, the liminal state between sea and land: "here the sea ends and the earth begins" (1); "Here, where the sea ends and the earth awaits." (358) Lisbon is a kind of limbo, a place of waiting: Reis occupies that curious place between areas and ideas of disappearance; like Pessoa, given nine months to wander the earth before finally disappearing completely into death, Reis is merely—but what a word!—what Heidegger calls a "'stand-in' [*Platzhalter*] for Nothing" (*Existence and Being*: 343), a site where Nothingness awaits its return.

The economy of the novel thus writes the return of the dead, the disappeared, and the effacement of the traces of that return. The novel therefore speaks appositely to Blanchot's meditation on the status of writing in *The Step Not Beyond*:

> Writing is not destined to leave traces, but to erase, by traces, all traces, to disappear in the fragmentary space of writing, more definitively than one disappears in the tomb, or again, to destroy, to destroy invisibly, without the uproar of destruction. (Blanchot 1992, 50)

Blanchot's paradoxical ideas—writing as trace that eliminates the trace; writing as the proper tomb for subjectivity—surely does speak to the paradox of melancholy's economy, and thus to the total economy of Saramago's novel: writing tracing the elimination of what, or who, are always already traces of writing: Pessoa and Reis. In one way, what I am suggesting here is that Saramago's novel—as tomb, as crypt—becomes the proper space for both Pessoa and Reis precisely because it both cancels and preserves their traces. It is in this sense—subjectivity preserved even as it is effaced—that I understand Blanchot's unsettling idea: "loss is impossible" (68).

I have suggested that the key rhythm of this novel is established by the meetings between Pessoa and Reis. It is here, during these meetings, where the central conceits of the novel play out: memory, forgetting, oblivion, melancholy. Pessoa himself is keenly aware that his very presence is dictated by the logic of memory: he has nine months left before total oblivion because it takes nine months for people to forget the dead (64). In a later meeting, Pessoa speaks of his weariness with this rhythm of return and withdrawal (he presumably spends some of his time in his crypt):

> what has annoyed me and left me feeling weary is all this going back and forth, this tug of war between memory that pulls and oblivion that pushes, a useless contest, for oblivion and forgetting always win in the end. I haven't forgotten you. Let me tell you something, on this scale you do not weigh much. Then what is this memory that continues to summon you, The memory I retain of the world, I thought you were summoned by the memory the world retains of you, What a foolish idea, my dear Reis, the world forgets, as I've already told you, the world forgets everything. Do

you think you've been forgotten. The world is so forgetful that it even fails to notice the absence of what has been forgotten. (Saramago 1984, 235)

It is clear thus, that for Pessoa fully to die he, too, must forget himself, lose himself to himself. And in some ways, what is being suggested here is that because Reis and Pessoa essentially are the same, Pessoa is asking Reis to forget himself to the world, in the world. Pessoa is asking, in other words, that Reis complete his process of dying. As Pessoa rises to leave, this exchange occurs:

> What time is it, Almost midnight, How time passes, Are you going, I am, Would you like me to accompany you, For you it is still too early, Precisely, You misunderstand, what I meant is that it is too early for you to accompany me where I am going. I am only one year older than you, by the natural order of things. What is the natural order of things. That is how one usually expresses it, by the natural order of things I should have died first. As you can see, things have no natural order. (Saramago 1984, 242)

In this curious time of waiting, this liminal space, Reis, as placeholder of nothingness, simply *attends* to the world. He, as mentioned, carries out two love affairs, affairs dominated by his own radical ambivalence about the women, about his relationship and responsibility to them. It is here, in this curious half-life of waiting, that Reis observes the passing of world events: his regular reading of the newspaper is ominous given that this is 1936, that Hitler is coming to full power, that Mussolini is flexing his military might in Ethiopia, that revolution is underway in Spain. World events unfold before Reis merely as events to attend to, neutrally, as if they have no real concern for him.[2] As he takes up residence at a hotel, the narrator writes: "But for the moment the hotel will do nicely, a neutral place requiring no commitment. He is in transit, his life is suspended." (11) In this life of suspension, in this place Lacan might have called the "zone between two deaths,"[3] Reis exists, if this is the word, according to the maxim that he himself inscribes in his own poetry: "Wise is the man who contents himself with the spectacle of the world" (259).

This line, of course, has a complex resonance in Saramago's novel; Saramago quotes it as an epigraph to his novel, along with a line from Bernardo Soares, another of Pessoa's heteronyms: "To choose ways of not acting was ever the concern and scruple of my life." It is a line speaking, obviously, to Reis's sense of detachment, or desire for detachment, from the world; and it does occur at least two other times in the novel, both moments of which see Reis confronted by the reality of world events (the first when he reads of the aftermath of the Italian campaign in Ethiopia; the second after the Portuguese bomb a ship in Lisbon's harbor manned by a supposedly rebellious faction in the navy). But we must keep in mind what is even more obvious, so obvious that we may miss it: this is a line of poetry, one of many inscribed over the course of the novel. We need to think carefully about the tropological significance of this poetry even as we think about its overt content. That is to say, I wish to spend some time looking at specific moments where Saramago's Reis quotes "himself," rewrites "himself," speaks Pessoa's language. Because at one level these lines form a kind of crypt of and for Pessoa: they continue to speak of and for him after his death, in the novel, and in the real. Blanchot may argue that in writing one disappears more perfectly than in a tomb (and this idea at one level holds true here), but surely also this writing—as quotation, as re-citation—marks itself as a doubled ground from which the past speaks, continues to speak.

Saramago signals the idea of writing as a ground of being by having his Reis cite the first line of the real Reis's poem (that is, Pessoa's Reis) "Securely I sit on the steadfast column/of the verses in which I'll remain" (104)[4]; the poem continues:

Not fearing the endless future influx

Of times and of oblivion,

For when the mind contentedly studies

In itself the world's reflections,

It becomes their plasma, and the world is what

Creates art, not the mind. Thus

On the plaque the outer moment engraves

Its being, and there endures. (Saramago 1984, 104)

The poem is consistent with a certain order of passivity we find in Reis: he allows the world to inscribe itself on him and he in turn becomes its monument. But it is crucial that Reis here asserts that he, as subject and as text, will remain to defy oblivion, will endure despite the flux of the world, of history. But this is, again, only to read the lines in terms of semantics; that is, at the level of meaning. There is a crucial moment in the later portion of the novel where lines from previous poems occur with great rapidity and without obvious meaning (258–9). Reis has just read about, as mentioned earlier, the ravaging of Ethiopia by the Italians and his mind, the mind of a poet, muses over this historical event. The narration here stretches over two pages in a tour de force of interior poetic monologue and precludes full citation, but a line repeats itself in Reis's mind (I use the passive voice here purposefully) as a leitmotif: "Addis Ababa is in flames, her streets covered with dead bodies, marauders are destroying homes, committing rape, looting and beheading women, as Badoglio's troops approach" (258). After the third repetition of this line Reis is startled to hear other words intrude "Addis Ababa was in flames [we note the shift in tense], homes burned, castles were sacked, bishops stripped, women raped by knights, their children pawns skewered with swords, and blood flowed in the streets. A shadow crosses the mind of Ricardo Reis. What is this, where do these words come from?" (258–9). As it turns out, Reis is conflating the content of a book he is reading (*The God of the Labyrinth*) with a poem the real Reis has written about an ancient Persian war, "The Chess Players." This is a complex moment: *The God of the Labyrinth* is a fictional, that is, nonexistent, detective novel written by Herbert Quain, a character in a short story by Borges ("An Examination of the Works of Herbert Quain"); Saramago here thus conflates in Reis's mind the content of an invented novel written by a fictional novelist with the contents of a real poem written by a fictional poet. Reis, in attempting to understand this conflation of news events with poetic invention, leafs through his poetic jottings to find the opening line of "his" old poem (published, we note, in 1916): "I heard how once upon a time when Persia" (259). When Reis discovers the line and recalls his own poem, he successfully deflects the reality of the event of trauma by transposing it into a poem that already anticipates and represents the event of trauma in Ethiopia: in other words, Reis retrospectively aestheticizes the moment of great trauma, diffuses its reality. In fact, after this remembrance, we read that "the doctor is in good spirits" (260).

But we must attend to the process by which he arrives at this sense of contentment: before he finds the first line of the poem, he re-reads—as do we—many lines from many poems:

Master, placid are, the first sheet reads, and other sheets read, *The gods are in exile, Crown me with roses while yet others tell, The god Pan is not dead, Apollo in his chariot has been driven past, Once more, Lydia, come sit beside me on the riverbank, this is the ardent month of June, War comes, In the distance the mountains are covered with snow and sunlight, Nothing but flowers as far as the eye can see, The day's pallor is tinged with gold, Walk empty-handed, for wise is the man who contents himself with the spectacle of the world.* (Saramago 1984, 259)

In essence these lines here form another poem but one with no obvious meaning; I would argue, in fact, that they function not semantically but tropologically as a sign (or signs) of Reis/Pessoa, a sign of himself, a reminder, in fact, of himself. This cluster of quotations functions as phantasmic traces of a phantasmic presence. As he sifts through this writing, Saramago's Reis—a fictionalized fiction—marks and re-marks a spectral presence. The language and writing of this doubled spectrality delineates, perhaps resurrects is the better word, a (textual) body, a corpus, a subject: this, therefore, is "Reis" quoting, resurrecting Reis, who "is" Pessoa. Or, more precisely, these lines speak, as quotations, to the resonance and continuity of Pessoa. These lines thus take on a definitive archiolivic logic and economy. The language object—poetry—is preserved to offset Pessoa's lament that the world forgets the very object, thing, idea, it forgets: "The world is so forgetful that it even fails to notice the absence of what has been forgotten" (235). And yet, we cannot fully move away from Blanchot's notion that writing's trace works to efface the subject, works to efface writing's own function as trace. We must ask: how do these lines, now taken out of context, now functioning as fragments shoring up the subjectivity of Pessoa, evade the logic of displacement? To what extent, and surely the novel as a whole is asking this question, does the representation, re-citation, re-marking of Pessoa and Reis serve to displace rather than preserve them as subjects? For certainly one of the effects of Saramago's appropriation of Reis as subject, as character, is to call attention to the ease by which the Other—the language of the Other—may precisely be appropriated. We have thus circled back to my initial question here: Who speaks? Who is speaking in these moments of the flaring up of the trace of Pessoa?

Perhaps I can approach this question by way of a brief episode early in the novel. Reis has met Lydia, the chambermaid, for the first time and is surprised to discover that her name is the same as the figure of erotic attachment in his own poems:

Lydia, he repeats, and smiles, and smiling goes to the drawer to look for his poems, his Sapphic odes, and reads the verses which catch his eye as he turns the pages. *And so, Lydia, sitting by the hearth, Lydia, let the image be thus, Let us show no desire, Lydia, by this hour, When our autumn comes, Lydia, Come sit with me, Lydia, on the riverbank, Lydia, the most abject existence is preferable to death* . . . Like his face reflected in a tremulous mirror of water, Ricardo Reis leans over the page and recomposes old verses. Soon he will be able to recognize himself, It is I, without irony, without sorrow, content to feel not even contentment, as a man who desires nothing more or knows that he can possess nothing more . . . Ricardo Reis makes a gesture with his hands, groping the colorless air, then, barely able to distinguish the words he traces on the paper, writes, *All I ask of the gods is that I should ask nothing of them.* (Saramago 1984, 34–5)

It is, of course, this image of Reis leaning over the page, recomposing, that is crucial here, as it explicitly alludes to the Narcissus myth. But, as we might expect, Saramago's manipulation of the myth—as is true for all his rewriting of mythological tropes—is complex. The Narcissus myth is about misrecognition, is a warning about the failure to recognize the self in the world around one: Narcissus's life ends not because of a perverse love of himself necessarily—but in some ways, this is, I suppose, literally true—but a failure to recognize himself *as such*. Saramago makes it clear that Reis's narcissism is not about failing to recognize himself ("Soon he will be able to recognize himself"). His is a more spectral kind of narcissism: Saramago indicates here, by bookending the Narcissus moment with quotations from Pessoa's Reis, that his Reis is only a function of a subjectivity that precedes and exceeds him: this is a man who "desires nothing more or knows he can possess nothing more." And how does he, that is to say Saramago's Reis, arrive at this moment of emptying out? By recomposing old verses: by tracing the writing of a subjectivity *which is and is not his own*. He is a specter retracing the words of a specter (Pessoa), whose own origin is now fundamentally lost because it is dead. My questions—who speaks? who is speaking?—are unanswerable because, as is so often true of Saramago's work, the origin of that voice is endlessly deferred: Pessoa as origin is dead and in the context of the novel is a specter; this poetry, this writing, thus in some fundamental ways, is groundless, unfixed, unrooted, unclaimable.

But I wonder if the proper question here should not be, who speaks?, but, who writes? And perhaps even this question needs refining. If read from a Derridean perspective, *The Year of the Death of Ricardo Reis* confirms the idea, worked out most extensively in *Of Grammatology* and *Dissemination*, that voice—as marker of presence, truth, *logos, ousia*—while perhaps traditionally privileged over writing (writing that becomes secondary as trace or supplement to the full presence of voice) itself marks or re-marks itself as deferral and displacement of presence and origin. It strikes me that Saramago's novel puts equal pressure on the idea that neither voice nor writing could ever sustain the idea of presence, of origin, of source: he decomposes both categories and suggests that writing and voice always work as sites where full presence eludes itself. It is, however, fascinating, to see how Saramago applies hermeneutical pressure to the idea of writing here, to the status of writing, because it is clear that these poems Saramago's Reis keeps function as an archive of a preexisting writer, a writer whose writings themselves marked out a displacement of subjectivity even as they attempted to mark the presence of a real subject (Pessoa's Reis). And so, when Saramago's Reis recomposes old verses, my question should not simply be "Who writes?" (an unanswerable question) but rather, "*Who is writing?*" And I intend this question as an ontological one, not merely as factual: that is, I intend to inflect the question here as Who *is* writing? Who finds their existence "in" writing? (This, of course, is perhaps *the* central question in our next novel, *The History of the Siege of Lisbon*).

And this, of course, is the real question both for Pessoa and Saramago. What does it mean to find one's existence in writing? One answer must be that writing as such becomes the archive wherein interiority is grounded and preserved but always as a space of deferral and difference. Because at one crucial level every subjectivity in this novel—Pessoa, Reis; the authorial traces of Saramago; the specter of the real Pessoa—is marked out within the space of writing. In other words, all subjectivities find their existence in writing in this novel and as Saramago brings his Pessoa and his Reis to an end, as he tracks them into oblivion, we may wish to notice how he has worked to assert a kind of power over the idea of writing into being. He writes Pessoa and Reis into being in order to write them out in the end. But, as I have argued throughout this chapter, the very fact of having written Reis or Pessoa into being here marks *The Year of the Death of Ricardo Reis* precisely as an archive that both conserves *and* effaces the writing trace, that is, subjectivity as such. And there is indeed a subtle indication of Saramago's power—or the narrative voice's power—as the novel comes to an end. Pessoa has told Reis that the first faculty one loses when one dies—and awaits the final oblivion—is the ability to read. Pessoa has lost the ability to read; Reis as the novel reaches its end also finds himself unable to read. Presumably with this loss of the ability to read comes the loss of the ability to write (or at least the ability to interpret what one has written). If writing is the marker of interiority; if writing is the medium through which one maintains a (spectral) connection to past subjectivities and histories, we are left, as the novel concludes, with only one subjectivity in full possession of the power of writing: Saramago's narrator. And I wonder if this detail—death doubled by the loss of writing—is one way Saramago is working to shore up the final loss of Reis and Pessoa, a way of eliminating the possibility that writing continues; perhaps Saramago is arguing that what is most needful in order to die, to die properly, is to lose the ability to pluralize, to archive oneself, one's experience. For surely, writing for Pessoa, for Reis, has functioned to proliferate experience and interiorities: and surely these interiorities function only to bind oneself to the world. By removing writing from the world, as he removes subjectivity from the world, Saramago ensures that these deaths are final, complete. And yet, as always, traces of Reis, of Pessoa, can only continue in Saramago's own archive, *The Year of the Death of Ricardo Reis*, as long as there are eyes to see, as it were. I am reminded here of, and will conclude with, a passage from an interview with Derrida ("Dialanguages"). He is speaking of why he writes and links his writing, his philosophy, to memory and its preservation. Surely his words here resonate into this novel, into Saramago's very philosophical practice as a writer of fiction:

> I have a feeling there is loss when I know that things don't repeat and that the repetition I love is not possible; that is what I call loss of memory, the loss of repetition, not repetition in the mechanical sense of the term, but of resurrection, resuscitation, regeneration. So I write in order to keep. But keeping is not a dull and dead archiving. It is at bottom a question of infinite memories, of limitless memories which would not necessarily be a philosophical or literary work, simply a great repetition . . . In this sense, for me, the philosopher is above all a guardian of memory: someone who asks himself questions about truth, Being, language, in order to keep. (Derrida 1995, 144–5)

4.2 The History of the Siege of Lisbon (1989)

Literature, like the infringement of moral laws, is dangerous.
—Bataille, *Literature and Evil*

The distortion of a text is not unlike a murder.
—Freud, *Moses and Monotheism*

The History of the Siege of Lisbon begins properly, one might say, given what is to come in its narrative. The novel opens with a discussion between Raimundo Silva, a professional proofreader, and the author of the text Silva is proofreading, *The History of the Siege of Lisbon*: "The proof-reader said, Yes, this symbol is called *deleatur*, we use it when we need to suppress and erase, the word speaks for itself and serves both for separate letters and complete words" (3). And, of course, Silva, in his enigmatic act of willful defacement of the author's text, suppresses and erases the "truth" of the historical text. In large part, my task in this chapter will be to consider this act of defacement, this criminal act of historical disfiguration, in terms of its complex relation to the archive itself. We should note that at the very outset of the novel Saramago has already established the plurality of what might be called the novel's source text. we have the unnamed author's text called *The History of the Siege of Lisbon*; we have Saramago's novel of the same name; and, as becomes crucial, we will soon have Silva's defaced version of the unnamed author's text, plus his own version of that same history. *The History of the Siege of Lisbon* is a novel about the writing of history in which the proper narrative of events—call it the archive—is open to radical interrogation. Saramago's point is not simply that the event as such is open to interpretation and inflection (as in, for instance, Hayden White's arguments about the writing of history), but that the archive containing the event—the written narrative; the written history; the writing subject—itself is always already susceptible to, perhaps deserving of, defacement and displacement. I am fascinated here by how Saramago works out the relation between two central transfigurations in this novel: the historical events surrounding the siege of Lisbon (in 1147), transfigured and displaced across multiple archival/textual sites, and Silva's transfiguration from proofreader to writer. Ultimately, I wish to suggest that *The History of the Siege of Lisbon*, like *The Year of the Death of Ricardo Reis*, is a meditation on writing, on authorship, on the relation between writing and the construction of what I want here to call the archival subject, the (writing) subject who constructs himself precisely, if problematically, in relation to history.

What is fascinating then about Saramago's novel is the way he sets up a series of spectralities. We have seen in our previous chapters how the archive as such is spectral: by responding to and becoming responsible for the futurity of the event it contains (Derrida), the archive becomes a space of a kind of radical potential, of, perhaps, potentiality itself. But Saramago, as we will see, it not content merely to structure his variety of archives (the various texts in the novel) as themselves spectral or spectralizing; his pluralizing of the event of the siege of Lisbon—the siege that now must become the Event, as such—has the effect of creating that moment as groundless, without itself having any authoritative claim to the real. In other words, Saramago's novel examines the relation between spectral event and spectral archive(s): what becomes crucial thus is the figure of Silva, the passive proofreader turned active writer, for he is the one who—in his turn spectralized—haunts the interstices between event and its record, between spectral historical moment and its archived memorialization and transfiguration.

And it is Silva, in fact, who provides the term "transfiguration" here. In his exchange with the author in the opening chapter he speaks of how the Dark Ages are transformed by the act of writing and amendation, how writing and amendation are forms of transfiguration: "the age ceased to be dark when people began to write, or to amend, a task, I repeat, which calls for other refinements and a different form of transfiguration, I like the phrase . . . (5).[5] Silva's word carries with it a certain descriptive resonance in this novel because *The History of the Siege of Lisbon* is all about various acts of transfiguration: the term does allow me to think of the novel as unfolding a series of responses to the idea of the transformation of the "figure" of "figuration" as such. The idea of the figure, transfigured, extends in all directions in this novel: history as figure; writer as figure; writing as figure; Silva as figure. Because Saramago's novel explores what happens to an idea when it is transformed, translated, into something else entirely. My suggestion here is that the word "transfiguration" attains the level of a kind of master trope in the novel. If a figure is always already an idea carried across to something else,[6] this "trans" merely doubles the tropological effect of the trope. *Transfiguration* thus is a doubled trope, in other words, is maybe even the trope of tropes (the figure carried across into something else). I do not wish unnecessarily to burden this trope here, but it may do to recall that transfiguration, in its most literal sense, means transformation from one state to another more beautiful or spiritual: is this not, in fact, a form of spectralizing? Does not, for instance, the transfiguration of Christ spectralize Christ? If there is a latent theological trace in the word—and this latency itself is again a form of haunting—then we must turn our gaze on Silva and observe his place within this constellation of specters and spectralities.

If the transfiguration of Silva is the most important alteration in this novel, we should begin our analysis with his defacement of the author's history of the Moorish occupation of Lisbon and perhaps with attempting to answer this question: Why does Silva do it? Why does he alter the official history? The text he is proofreading, as he himself acknowledges, is a by-the-book repetition of a very old and well-known series of events in Portuguese history. Silva, in fact, is rather bored by the text: "In those four hundred and thirty-seven pages he did not find a single new fact, controversial interpretation, unpublished document, even as much as a fresh reading" (30). Silva has become slightly irritated with what appears to be minor factual errors (concerning the proper term for weapons; the fact that the author has suggested that Dom Afonso [the first King of Portugal] has a coat of arms), but what seems to spur him to make his fateful amendation

Archiving Melancholy: José Saramago

is the fact that the author of this history has reproduced the speech Dom Afonso made to the crusaders prior to the attack on Lisbon. This speech strikes Silva as absurd: in his estimation, it is clear that its language, with its convoluted rhetorical flourishes, is far too complex to have been constructed within the primitive form of Portuguese spoken at the time. This suspicion leads Silva into what essentially is a hermeneutical dilemma. He desires to know exactly what was actually said at this historical moment; he wishes to be able to translate properly from the various textual accounts and uncover the correct version of this discursive event: "he would be capable of renouncing something . . . in order to discover . . . some parchment, papyrus, sheets of paper, newspaper cutting, some entry, if possible, or stone engraving, as a record of what was really said, the original, as it were" (37). Silva's desires for the original, his nostalgia for the true archive, leads inevitably to his alteration of the author's manuscript. When Silva adds a crucial *Not* that denies a central historical fact—that the crusaders will help to restore Lisbon to the Portuguese—he essentially creates a spectral or phantasmic archive wherein his desire to know may be realized. His entry into writing thus is the entry into what may be termed the pure fantasy of hermeneutics: translating a desired version of history, transfiguring, violently, *archioviolithically*, what may have been into what should be.

And Silva, as we have seen previous to this moment, is temperamentally perfectly suited to this fantasy hermeneutical procedure. The second chapter of the novel opens with what appears to be the representation of Lisbon in 1147; that is, we read a description of a muezzin's call to prayer initially as if it were perhaps a description in the unnamed author's history, or even perhaps, as if we had been transported back to this historical period. It turns out, however, that the description of the muezzin is, in fact, the fantasy elaboration of Silva himself:

> the whole thing was nothing more than vague thoughts in the proof-reader's mind as he was reading and correcting what he had surreptitiously missed in the second and third proofs. The proof-reader has this remarkable flair for splitting his personality, he inserts a *deleatur* or introduces a comma where required, and at the same time, if you'll pardon the neologism, heteronomises himself. (Saramago 1989, 14)

Silva's talent for fantasy and, most precisely, for heteronomizing himself, is, of course, the talent of the author as such, is precisely what allows an author to insert himself into an event separate from himself in order to convincingly represent and reproduce it. But at this point in the narrative—that is, at this point of pure imagination—Silva is, of course, not an author; it is only with his act of defacement, this brazen, and uncharacteristic, act of mad redaction—his *Not* that denies history—that Silva has become something more than what he was; he is at this moment transfigured into an author.

And this act is a kind of madness: a madness of writing, a madness of hermeneutics, a madness of the desire to create an alternate archive: "He is exhausted, all his strength has gone into that *Not* with which he has just put at risk, not only his professional integrity, but also his peace of mind. As from today, he will live for that moment, sooner or later, but inevitable, when someone will ask him to account for this mistake" (41). Silva's fantasy of being discovered leads him to imagine his editor, Costa, revealing the mistake; the following line is crucial here because it does, in my reading, give the real reason why Silva added his *Not*, and perhaps the real reason the author, as such, writes: "if he [Costa] were to take the trouble to read the word and understand what has come to be written, the world, at that moment amended once more, he will have lived differently for one brief instant" (41). The author, in other words, has the power—and is not a resistance to an official narrative itself an act of defiant power?—to alter the world, to change the way one experiences the world; the author can, by altering the archive, transfigure his reader, if only for one brief instant.

But I want to return here to a word used to describe Silva's *Not*, how this redaction has put at "risk" his peace of mind and professional integrity. This word, "risk," is an English translation of the Portuguese verb "jogar," meaning "to play," or "to gamble."[7] The idea of gambling or risking is perfectly apt here, because, as Blanchot will have it, risk is always in play in the act of writing: a risk of all stability, a risk of subjectivity, a risk of authority. The act of writing, as Blanchot tells us, as Derrida will confirm, and as Saramago will thematize, is a dangerous one. I wish to turn briefly to Blanchot's "Literature and the Right to Death" here in order to orient our discussion to follow. Blanchot meditates on the relationship between writing and writer and posits that the space of writing resonates with a critical ontological function. First, the space of writing creates the writer as such. Blanchot speaks of the exhaustion of the writer at the moment of the creation of the sentence: "The point is that he is the author of it—or rather that because of it, he is an author: it is the source of his existence, he has made it and it makes him, it is himself and he is completely what it is. This is the reason for his joy, his pure and perfect joy" (25). As Silva writes his *Not*, he is created. He finds his true being, and I wonder if this is part of the reason he chooses to add that *Not* in the first place: he writes to call another world into being and to call himself into (true) being. But Blanchot continues. Writing, he argues, is not merely the calling into being of the single author-entity: it is to fashion a world wherein solitude as such—and Silva is essentially a solitary figure; he is a figure of pure loneliness—is banished. But writing does not fashion company in any traditional sense. There is no companionship in the writing itself; rather, writing calls the self into being as Other to itself. The creation of company—Beckett's word for this imagined community—is the creation of the radically Other self. Blanchot's words here are crucial for they speak directly to the strangeness of writing as such; I read these lines as speaking almost directly to Silva's mad act of writing:

> For me, the written volume is an extraordinary, unforeseeable innovation—such that it is impossible for me to conceive what it is capable of being without writing it. This is why it seems to me to be an experiment whose effects I cannot grasp, no matter how consciously they were produced, and in the face of which I shall be unable to remain the same, for this reason: in the presence of something other, I become other. But there is an even more decisive reason: this other thing—the book—of which I had only an idea and which I could not possibly have known in advance, is precisely myself become other. (Blanchot 1981, 34)

Blanchot's sense of the radically strange entity called the book, and the author's uncanny relation to it, a relation of what can only be a kind of compromised authority, surely does speak to Silva's compromised relationship to what now is *his* book. And this, for me, is the crucial point: with the addition of this *Not*, Silva not only creates himself as author, he claims a kind of unlawful, yet fully present, ownership of this book, this history, this archive. What becomes clear as the novel now progresses, as Silva, for reasons crucially to do with the idea of solitude and company, begins writing in earnest his own version of the history, is that the book, what Blanchot calls "this other thing," is Silva's act of self-creation. This book becomes the archive of a self that never to this point *had* been. It remains thus to consider the implications of Silva's fully immersed acts of writing and especially that act of writing's relation to what Blanchot calls the "essential solitude" of the writer.

Because if Silva's mad act of reaction, his addition of this fatal *Not*, was the act of a solitary man, his extended act of writing, what we may now term his "project," is produced fully in concert with another, Maria Sara, his editor. It is Maria who, upon the revelation that Silva has unlawfully added this *Not*, encourages Silva to continue writing the history, encourages him to write the history as he sees and imagines it: *his* history, his archioviolithic history, in other words. Maria, perhaps alone of all the characters in the novel, recognizes what Silva has done with his act of defacement; referring to the amended copy of *The History of the Siege of Lisbon* (the only copy not to be sent into the world with an erratum explaining Silva's crime) she says, "This book belongs to you, she took a long pause and added, this time putting greater emphasis on certain syllables, Let me rephrase that, This is your book" (92). It therefore follows that Maria proposes to Silva that he continue writing his own proper history. Her admiration for his past reports, his talent for what she calls his "lateral thinking" (96), together with her amusement at his act of desecration, leads her to propose that Silva write his own history. She goes on to say that Silva's addition of this *Not* "will prove the most important act in your life" (96). And indeed, it is.

Silva's initial resistance to the idea of writing his own history stems at least in part from what I believe to be his unconscious realization of the risk involved in writing: for one, his ostensibly minor act of adding one word, *Not*, has caused him to be exposed before his editorial board and, from his perspective, to Maria's teasing. But there is something altogether darker now pressing on him; Silva returns home after Maria's proposal and feels altered:

> As he ate, he had a curious feeling of alienation, as if, a purely imaginary experience, he had just arrived after a lengthy, drawn-out journey through distant lands where he encountered other civilizations. Obviously, in an existence so little given to adventures, any novelty, however insignificant for others, can seem like a revolution, even if, to cite only this recent example, his memorable desecration of the almost sacred text of *The History of the Siege of Lisbon* had not affected him in the slightest, but now he has the impression that his home belongs to someone else, and that he himself is the stranger. (Saramago 1989, 99)

Coming closely after Maria has told him that the act of writing his *Not* is the most important act of his life, that this book is now his own, and given our sense that writing always must set the self up as Other to itself, it is perhaps not surprising that Silva finds himself alienated from his own home, from his sense of security in his loneliness. Because what truly is at risk here for Silva is precisely his solitude. Recall that Silva is a man alone; there is, as the narrator has told us, "no woman in this house, nor has there ever been" (25); Silva himself has acknowledged that his bachelor status precludes any erotic entanglements. Maria's encouragement to write is an encouragement to risk, to risk this (hard-won?) solitude. He will only write because of her, and as we shall see, for her. She becomes the object of his writing, even if he is not (yet) writing directly about her; surely we have here, in Silva's decision to begin writing his own history, another confirmation of Lacan's dictum: desire is always the desire of the Other. Maria's desires here are what mobilize Silva into the position of archivist of his own imaginary history. But this act of writing, crucially, creates a community of readership. Maria, who now enters Silva's solitude, becomes a part of that solitude even as she relieves it. As Blanchot puts it in the *Space of Literature*: "The work is solitary: this does not mean that it remains uncommunicable, that it has no reader. But whoever reads it enters into the affirmation of the work's solitude, just as he who writes it belongs to the risk of this solitude" (22).

Thus Silva's question to himself, after discovering that Maria has become ill (and missing an appointment): "what have I got to do with this woman?" (188). The question, asked to himself just as he begins to conceive of a more than merely erotic attachment to her (he now perhaps is feeling something closer to real care, perhaps love), really in some crucial ways is *the* question of the novel. It is only after he conceives of his attachment to her in terms of true care that his new history of the siege of Lisbon seems to come to life. His narrative before this critical question is a rather plodding: "Raimundo Silva is well aware that his limited gifts do not match up to the task, in the first place because he is not God . . . in the second place because he is not a historian, a human category which is closer to divinity in its way of looking at things, and in the third place, an initial confession, he never had any talent for writing creative literature" (161). After Maria's illness and his realization of his care for her, Silva is able to begin structuring the narrative along parallel historical lines: his main character, Mogueime, conceives of a love for a concubine, Ouroana; the erotic fantasies of this man and woman are made to parallel the erotic fantasies and attachments of Silva and Maria in the present. Silva's archive, in other words, refracts, temporally, in the ways Derrida speaks of: the archive is not only the record of the past, but also contains a link to a futurity. The complexity in this case, however, is that Silva is the one manipulating the historical archive so that it mirrors the future (or is it that he manipulates the present so as to mirror the past?). As the narrator puts it, so perfectly describing both the operation of Silva's mind as author and as archivist-fantasist: "Raimundo Silva is going to live in two ages and in two seasons" (215). Thus, after an erotic reverie in the present in which Silva ponders Maria's body—"as for her body, the first impression is good, but bodies can only be judged when they are naked" (200)—he begins to imagine himself into the past, archiving another passionate relationship, that between Mogueime and Ouroana: "but now there was a woman washing clothes at the water's edge, Raimundo and Mogueime knew who she was, they had been told she was the concubine of the aforementioned knight Heinrich" (200–1). As the historical relationship unfolds and mirrors the present relationship, it is inevitable that Maria, after reading a portion of Silva's text, would recognize the parallel: "Who is this Ouroana, and this Mogueime, who is he . . . Raimundo Silva took two short steps in the direction of the table and came to a halt, I'm still not sure, he said and fell silent, after all, he should have guessed that Maria Sara's first words would be to inquire who these two were these, those, whosoever else, in a word, us" (235).[8]

Whatever the temporal orientation of this particular archive is, one thing is clear: there is a crucial blurring of temporalities to the point where the past and present seem to exist in a kind of spectral—but the imaginary is always spectral—simultaneity. The past inhabits the present just as the present inhabits the past. Silva's question then—what have I got to do with this woman?—must be read carefully in the context of this spectrality. The question indeed is the motivating question of the novel: it is Maria's desire for more of his History that spurs Silva into writing, that has the concomitant effect of creating him "in" company with himself as Other, with Maria as Other. That is to say, it is Maria who confers upon him his own desire, defines him as a desiring creature just as he defines himself now as a writer. It is because Silva now has desire that his archive becomes more than simply a re-vision, a re-interpretation of the past; his archive now must become an archive of the erotic, an erotic archive. That is to say, the archive now, as something "in" the past and responding to and becoming responsible for the future, must contain his desire; it becomes the crypt of his desire inasmuch as it preserves a record of his mirrored longing in Mogueime and Ouroana.

If it is a kind of hermeneutical desire that spurs Silva to insert that initial *Not*, the desire to know another way of seeing, it is erotic desire—or, crucially, its promise—that drives him now:

> He recognizes that his freedom began and ended at that precise moment when he wrote the word *Not*, that from then on a new and no less imperious fatality had got under way, and that he has no other choice than to try and understand what, having initially appeared to stem from his initiative and reflection, is now seen to have resulted from a mechanism that was, and continues to be, external, of whose functioning he has only the vaguest idea . . . He considers that the tiny tree of the Science of Errors he

planted has already given its true fruit, or promised it, which was to make this man encounter this woman. (Saramago 1989, 226)

It is, I think, part of the brilliance of Saramago to dovetail so closely hermeneutic and erotic desires in this novel, because both are about wishing to know, to be known; Silva's archive—the site of the attempt to preserve the record of these conflated, entwined desires—speaks now, especially after the broaching and mingling of desires, to the inevitable, and melancholy, possibility of the end of these desires. Because the archive, as a kind of erotic crypt, must be a response to the sense of the tenuousness of the relationship in the present moment; Silva has been absolutely solitary in the past; this present relationship, occurring, let us be clear, because of a (seemingly) arbitrary whim, has, of course, both the fragility of possibility and the fragility of unknowing: "the one says, Oh, my love, the other, may this last forever, and suddenly they were both afraid of the words they had spoken, and they embraced, the room was dark, Switch on the light, she said, I want to know if this is real" (264). The beautiful ambiguity of this anxiety—is there, in fact, a fear of this passion, this love?—and Maria's desire to know its reality, if in fact it is real, speaks, of course, both to the fear of desire and to a sense of the unreality of things, the sense that perhaps this is all a kind of fantasy (which, of course, all love is). Silva's radical sense of his ambivalence about Maria, her body, speaks also to a sense of the absence always at the core of the erotic, of the knowledge of the Other that is a part of the erotic: "Raimundo Silva had put his arm around Maria Sara's shoulder, he knew this body, he knew it, and from knowing it came this feeling of infinite strength, and, on the other hand, a feeling of infinite emptiness [*infinito vazio*], of indolent weariness" (268). In some ways thus Silva's erotic archive is a way of structuring some form of his desire to be preserved against the possibility of future loss. The archive, as we will see in my analysis of *All the Names*, always already constructs itself on the possibility of loss occurring; it looks forward to loss, as such. And thus, Silva's archive is melancholy in many senses of the term: it preserves a connection to a past (in its insistence on preserving the past, the archive is a priori melancholy) and it works as an anticipation of the loss Silva may—or may not—endure in his relationship to Maria (she does speak, lovingly, but rather ominously, about wishing to live in their passion honestly, "However long our relationship may last" [295]). It is in this sense that his initial *Not*—which leads inevitably, fatally, to his creation of the archive of his History—has indeed become the most important action in his life, inasmuch as it sets him up as imbricated—and let us always keep in mind that he writes himself into this position and *continues* to write himself into this position—within the possibility of total loss, which itself must be understood as the precondition for desire: everything has led him to this moment, but this is a moment the resonance of which sounds only within the possibility of its effacement.

In some fundamental ways, Saramago's *The History of the Siege of Lisbon* is a perfect confirmation of a crucial observation made by Derrida in *Archive Fever*. Derrida notes how the technical means of preserving history—printing, writing—in some senses alter the event of history as such: "the technical structure of the *archiving* archive also determines the structure of the *archivable* content" (17); he then adds: "the archivization produces as much as it records the event" (17). Silva's addition of his fatal *Not* is a pure and perfect example of an archiving gesture that produces the event—imaginary, defaced, but an event—as such: his archive of a possible history is a production of the past within the act of writing, of risk. But, finally, we must ask: what precisely is the event being produced here? Is the event of the novel this imaginary history? Or is it, as I do believe, and have been arguing, the production of the event of company, the event of productive melancholy? Because Silva's history alters one major detail in the history of the siege: the crusaders did not help the Portuguese conquer Lisbon. But Silva's history ends with the same outcome as the official history: Lisbon *is* taken back from the Moors. Surely a more radical act of reimagining would have seen the Moors fend off the Portuguese. Silva's narrative, however, is not about this particular act of fantasy; it is about Mogueime and Ouroana, who may return to Galicia, or who may remain in Portugal, but who do remain together. That is to say, this archive preserves the integrity of the erotic impulse in its historical and contemporary variations: "As I see it, Ouroana will return to Galicia, and Mogueime will go with her . . . What makes you think that they should go away, Difficult to say, the logical thing would be for them to stay, Forget it we're staying" (312). Silva's archive, finally, preserves the fantasy of company even as the fantasy of the archive reveals itself as only ever the product of a radically fragile economy of (shared) desire.

4.3   *All the Names* (1997)

In the work of mourning it is not grief that works: grief keeps watch.
—Blanchot, *The Writing of the Disaster*

It is my purpose here to examine the representation of the archive in José Saramago's *All the Names*. The archive, as traditionally conceived, is a location of knowledge, a place where history itself is housed, where the past is accommodated. The archive, thus, is intimately conjoined with cultural memory, with its preservation, perhaps even with its supplementation. Certainly Saramago figures the archive in these terms, terms that suggest that the archive plays a role in the continuity of a culture as a whole. But his novel suggests also that the archive is a place where history can, perhaps should, be fabricated, consciously falsified in order to preserve the integrity of individual subjects, to preserve and conserve, more specifically, the desires of individual subjects. Saramago highlights a specific truth about the archive: it always is a space of the Imaginary, a space into which desire and loss, perhaps the desire *for* loss, is projected and maintained in a kind of melancholy stasis.

All the Names traces the journey of Senhor José, a clerk in the sprawling, labyrinthine General Registry, a bureaucratic archive in which the birth and death notices of the residences of José's unnamed city are housed. It is here in the Registry that José by chance comes across the record card of a woman unknown to him (and unnamed in the text): José immediately conceives a desire to know this woman. José, who keeps a personal archive of record cards of famous people, sets off on a quest for this woman, a quest motivated by his desire to fill in the gaps of her story: José's "archive fever" thus is figured initially as a kind of narratological desire for totalizing knowledge. In the course of his journey he investigates a number of archives, the most important being the room housing the school records of this woman, and, ultimately, the General Cemetery in which he searches (in vain) for the grave marking the woman's death by suicide. The novel concludes with José falsifying the records of the General Registry: with the approval of the Registrar José makes up a false record card indicating that the woman still lives.

Saramago's novel offers a complex analysis of the archive, of a multiplicity of understandings of the archive. The archive, according to the Registrar, is a location of foundational, preservative, ethical knowledge. It is the archive that preserves, maintains, and creates, a culture's (narrative) understanding of itself. Yet, the archive is, in both examples of the Registry and Cemetery, a place where sure knowledge of beginnings and endings is continually placed under erasure precisely as the categories of life and death become confused (in the Registry, the records of the living and the dead coalesce) or where the corporeal and textual traces of ending (death) are removed (in the Cemetery, a trickster shepherd deliberately switches headstones on graves, making it impossible to locate the dead). In both the Registry and the Cemetery, mourning is rendered impossible, as the traces of the dead are obscured. Saramago's novel thus may be read as a critique of the idea of mourning itself, that mourning's working through is an absurd, perhaps unethical, attempt to forget—to kill off—the dead. As well, it is possible to see the novel as critiquing the *viability* of mourning, as suggesting that despite all efforts to work through loss, memory is persistent despite itself, perhaps *to spite* itself; mourning is an impossibility precisely to the degree that memory, and its traces, cannot be eradicated.

This, in fact, may be one way of reading *All the Names*, but it does not take fully into account the particular figuration of the relation between memory and desire in the novel. José has no memory of this woman because she is, and will remain, *fully unknown* to him. The phrase, the "unknown woman," is how José refers to the object of his quest throughout the novel. The term "unknown" (*desconhecida* in the original Portuguese) resonates on several levels, as it becomes clear that José does, in fact, know the woman's name, details of her family life, her schooling, and the circumstances of her suicide, if not the specific reasons for it. The phrase "the unknown woman" signifies, thus, that the woman is unknown to José on a more ontological, perhaps metaphysical, level (clearly it is José who is "unknown" to the woman). The impossibility of any reciprocal relationship or knowledge occurring between José and the woman signals her distance from him and hence her status as "unknown" because she is profoundly unknowable (she is dead). It is also apparent that her status as "unknown" is directly related to the fact that, as we discover, José is unable to narrate the entirety of her story because he is missing important elements of it, the location of her body, the reasons for her melancholia: she is, to borrow Freud's infamous phrase, the "dark continent" of the novel. It is crucial to notice that Saramago, through José, through whose consciousness the novel unfolds, deliberately keeps the woman a mystery to the reader: we never learn her name and the reasons for her suicide, her melancholy. The woman thus is a complete cipher to the reader. If knowledge is a component of any narrative, the woman must, because unknown, represent a troubling blank spot in José's story of his imagined relation to her. Concomitantly, the reader's vision of her, which is completely filtered through José's increasingly narcissistic perspective, is fatally skewed precisely to the degree that she becomes, uncomfortably, the blank spot in our own reading.

Thus, what becomes clear as the novel moves to a close is that the Registrar and José decide to archive, to house, as it were, *desire itself*, not memory, not the past. One is tempted to read the novel thus as a literalization of one of Freud's most puzzling suppositions. In *Beyond the Pleasure Principle*, Freud suggests that memory and consciousness have no business together: "becoming conscious and leaving behind a memory-trace are processes incompatible with each other within one and the same system" (296). If memory and consciousness are incompatible, what happens to the viability of the archive? What implications does this idea have for a reading of the archive generally? One suggestion, and one that Saramago, I think, advances, is that the idea of the phenomenal archive as a site of the organization of memory and history is an absurdity if regarded, as it tends to be, as a supplement to memory, a supplement to the conscious processes of the mind. Saramago's depiction of the archive as a threatening, chaotic, categorically confused space—a labyrinth—suggests that it resembles more the working of the unconscious mind and as such must, perhaps, be subjected to the kinds of analyses that the dream-work invites. And it is here that we may be able to reconcile the archive and Freud. If the archive is understood as a place where memory (and desire) is housed unconsciously, as a site, perhaps screen, of *spectral*, imaginary, desire rather than a space of conscious memory, of "real" history, we may be able to reconcile memory and the archive. Indeed, Derrida suggests that the archive is always already spectral: "It [the archive] is spectral a priori: neither present nor absent 'in the flesh,' neither visible nor invisible, a trace always referring to another whose eyes cannot be met" (84). Saramago, through José, certainly suggests that memory itself cannot be housed consciously (José has no memory of the woman), so a sublimation of *what would have been remembered and lost* transforms (impossible) memories into spectral, ghostly desires, desires that are dead for never having been directed toward the living, desires that are ghostly because they are now projected toward the dead. But because the authority of the archive allows, indeed *commands*, that the dead nostalgically return, the archive becomes doubly spectral, a melancholic space where ghosts are housed and desire impossibly and perpetually accommodated.

Senhor José's archive fever—and this is a novel that explores the obsessive need for the totalizing knowledge an archive *may* provide—is one that compels him to seek out the origins of his subjects, and it is this initial compulsion that structures the novel and gives it its philosophical resonance. Indeed, it is clear that Saramago is exploring the complex relation between the idea of the archive (as an authoritative seat of knowledge) and nostalgia (as a compulsion for and toward an originary, perhaps Imaginary, scene of commencement and beginning). I wish to foreground these terms, archive and nostalgia, twinned as they are (like the Central Registry and General Cemetery) by similar etymological and philosophical resonances. The term "archive" is itself a conflation of two ideas: from the Greek *arkhein* we derive the meaning "begin, to be in the first place." The term thus designates a point of origin. From *arkheion* we derive the meaning of seat, location, of authority. The *arkhons*, as

Derrida reminds us in *Archive Fever*, were superior magistrates, "those who commanded" (2). Derrida writes of these magistrates:

> On account of their publicly recognized authority, it is at their home, in that *place* which is their house (private house, family house, or employee's house), that official documents are filed. The archons are first of all these documents' guardians. They do not only ensure the physical security of what is deposited and of the substrate. They are also accorded the hermeneutic right and competence. They have the power to interpret the archives. (Derrida 1995, 2)

Ultimately thus, as Derrida notes usefully, the term archive names "at once the *commencement* and the *commandment*" (1): beginnings and authority. The archive is an authoritative site of beginnings.[9] In the case of Saramago's Central Registry, the archive records the entire arc of a life: beginning and end, birth and death.

The archive, therefore, is a site of deep nostalgia. The term nostalgia designates literally "homesickness." From the Greek *nostos* (return) and *algia* (illness), the term signifies a compulsion to return home, to the beginning, to the origin and source of what has been lost. Nostalgia is thus a deeply melancholic impulse in the sense that it strives to keep the past— and in the case of Senhor José, the *dead* past—perpetually present. My analysis of *All the Names* attempts to diagnose Senhor José's archive fever, his deep desire to discover the "truth" about this "unknown woman," as being an effect of an inability, or unwillingness, to mourn the dead, the past. Saramago's novel suggests—in a manner that resonates with Freud's notion of the melancholic desire for the past—that successful mourning is an impossibility and, indeed, something perhaps not even desirable because the dead cannot, *should not*, be separated from the living.

And indeed, it is in the archive, as site of commencement and authoritative beginnings, that Senhor José's quest begins. The Central Registry, which harbors the records of both the living and the dead, is a curious mixture of furious discipline and imminent chaos. There is a strict aesthetic ordering of space and authority within the Registry, a hierarchical ordering with distinct fascistic overtones:

> The first row of desks, parallel with the counter, is occupied by the eight clerks whose job it is to deal with the general public. Behind them is a row of four desks, again arranged symmetrically on either side of an axis that might be extended from the main entrance until it disappears into the

rear, into the dark depths of the building. These desks belong to the senior clerks. Beyond the senior clerks can be seen the deputy registrars, of whom there are two. Finally, isolated and alone, as it is only right and proper, sits the Registrar, who is normally addressed as "Sir." (Saramago 1997, 2)

The space of the Central Registry, at least the space open to public view, is strictly organized, authorized, and disciplined by the various levels of its hierarchy, each ultimately under the omnipotent, panoptical gaze of the Registrar, who embodies total authority.[10] This disciplined structure, as the Registrar makes clear, serves a larger purpose, indeed a larger moral purpose. The Registrar sees the Registry as continuing a tradition of authority and organization: the archive, in other words, serves to organize and interpret the world, morally. The Registrar puts it thus:

> I understand, as did those who were in charge of the Central Registry before me, that the preservation of the spirit, of the spirit of what I will call continuity and organic identity, must prevail over any other consideration, for if we fail to proceed along that path, we will witness the collapse of the moral edifice which, as the first and last depositories of life and death, we continue here to represent. (Saramago 1997, 172–3)

The Registrar, himself part of a genealogy of authority, figures the archive as a moral edifice because it contains—as does the crypt; the analogy is crucial—the records of beginnings and endings. The archive, like the crypt or cemetery that he deliberately evokes, contains the arche and telos of a life, is moral precisely because it houses these clear narrative trajectories. The archivist's moral authority derives from the "scrupulous" maintenance of clarity, which means maintaining a single archive that separates, "according to the law of nature" (3), the records of the dead from those of the living; the archive's moral traditions are the "foundations of our reason and our strength"(173); it is this edifice that enables the maintenance of "both our identity and our autonomy" (173).

It is clear from the Registrar's description of the mandate of the archive that reason, identity, and autonomy are at stake here, that the archive signifies the preservation of enlightenment values of subjectivity and reason (perhaps subjectivity *as* reason). Yet, crucially counterbalanced to this sense of reason, this *desire* for reason, is the condition of the archive as a labyrinth. At several points in the narrative Saramago balances the image of the disciplined archive, of conscious control, with the image of the archive as a chaotic, threatening, irrational labyrinth, a place in which unconscious fears are unleashed.[11] Despite the clerks' best attempts to organize the archive spatially and ethically (or, as the narrator puts it, "structurally and essentially" [3]), the records of the dead continually threaten to impinge on those of the living, and a general state of chaos grows at the rear of the building that begins to resemble a labyrinth or a catacomb.

As a result of this chaos, the Registrar requires that anyone going into the archive of the dead "make[s] use of Ariadne's thread" (5). Saramago's invocation of the image and myth of the labyrinth is one of several mythological references in *All the Names*. At some level, this image is perfectly resonant with the image of complexity that the archive represents: ill-lit corridors, confusing paths, a proliferation of textual detritus. The idea of the labyrinth is appropriate, however, also because it is clearly an image of controlled chaos. The labyrinth harboring the Minotaur represents the attempt to repress—but, crucially and problematically, also *maintain*—chaotic, destructive energies and impulses. We recall that the Minotaur is the result of illicit sexual congress between Pasiphae and a bull: the labyrinth, as image of the unconscious, contains the repressed libidinal energy the Minotaur represents.[12] Theseus's use of Ariadne's thread to penetrate the labyrinth and destroy the Minotaur thus is an allegory of the triumph of reason over chaos, the conscious mind's *ultimate* repression of illicit unconscious impulses that were not initially properly eliminated.

In Saramago's labyrinth, the Minotaur is translated into the idea of chaos itself (libidinal, illicit, or otherwise): this chaos seems to stand in total opposition to the reasoned discipline of the public space of the archive and the stated moral imperative of the Registrar. And yet, as we notice, this state of chaos—embodied in the image of the perpetually decreasing distance between the records of the dead and the living—is, like the Minotaur, placed and maintained in the labyrinth at the behest of Minos, scrupulously maintained by the Central Registry: order and chaos thus are in perpetual uneasy balance. To use a more specific metaphor, the boundary between order and chaos in the Registry, and, as we will see, outside the Registry, is constantly under threat, is continually always about to be blurred. Indeed, José's journey is one that explores the consequences of blurring categories of order and chaos, of rationality and irrationality, of cleanliness and filth, of the living and the dead. As we trace through this trajectory of categorical confusions, which results ultimately in José's loss of a coherent sense of self and an inability to locate the grave of the unknown woman, it becomes clear that the archive is inscribed in a matrix of categorical confusion, which inevitably results in making it impossible to mourn the (dead) past. As Saramago's central image of the blurring boundary between the records of the dead and living suggests, *All the Names* works out an analysis of the results of the inability to keep clear the distinction between the symbolic claims of the living and the dead: if this fundamental category cannot be maintained, a melancholic identification with the dead is the living subject's inevitable and intractable position.

And indeed, toward the conclusion of the novel, Saramago's narrator offers another image from Greek mythology that clarifies the melancholy trajectory of the narrative. José, after discovering that his unknown woman, a mathematics teacher, has killed herself, seeks out and discovers her apartment:

> Here lived a woman who committed suicide for unknown reasons . . . whose name while she was alive was in the Central Registry, along with the names of all the people alive in this city, a woman whose dead name returned to the living world because Senhor José went to rescue her from the dead world, just her name, not her, a clerk can only do so much. (Saramago 1997, 231)

This is a crucial passage indicating that the novel is about the crossing of boundaries and categories, of, in this case, life and death, that it is about a refusal to acknowledge the *fact* of death. In other words, Saramago makes clear that José is a figure of pure melancholy (the melancholy of the woman, like her name, is unknown): José, an ironic analogue to the melancholic Orpheus, descends into the underworld—the *archived* underworld—to rescue his Eurydice. "Mourning," as Freud notes in "Mourning and Melancholia," "is regularly the reaction to the loss of a loved person, or to the loss of some abstraction which has taken the place of one, such as one's country, liberty, and ideal, and so on" (251–2). In the process of mourning, as Freud notes, the subject—Freud favors the masculine pronoun in describing the melancholic—accepts that the "loved object no longer exists" (253) and through the painful process of mourning, where "memories and expectations in which the libido is bound to the object is brought up and hypercathected" (253), the subject becomes "free and uninhibited again" (253) by withdrawing his libidinal energies from the memory of the lost object. As Freud suggests, the subject of mourning learns to "sever its attachments to the object that has been abolished" (265) and maintain a singular identity. This process of working through, what Freud calls the "economics of pain" (252), fails in the melancholic, who is unable to work through the loss of the love object, is unable to digest the facts of loss precisely because he identifies with the object: the libido is continually working *toward* the object of loss, the memories of the loved object, and is thus unable to forget the past trauma. Freud suggests that there is an essential narcissism at work in the melancholic who is fully unable to withdraw his libidinal desires from the lost object. Instead, the lost object is incorporated: "the ego wants to incorporate this object into itself, and, in accordance with the oral or cannibalistic phase of libidinal development in which it is, it wants to do so by devouring it" (258). "Becoming" the lost object means, as Peter Homans intriguingly puts it in *Symbolic Loss*, that the melancholic "does not even have a memory of an experience of loss, cannot for that reason work through the loss" (17). Orpheus is, of course, the perfect emblem of (masculine) melancholy, refusing as he does to mourn, to work through the loss of Eurydice. Saramago gently ironizes José but in the process makes clear his filiation, his genealogical link, to Orpheus and what Julia Kristeva calls the "abyssal suffering" (*Black Sun*: 189) of the melancholic. Death is figured as a bureaucratic oblivion where the dead are scattered into various textual traces: like Isis gathering the limbs of Osiris, José is compelled to remember the textual traces of this unknown woman ("just her name"), translating her into a coherent narrative.

Importantly, Saramago signals to the reader that the process José has undergone is a perilous one: like all descents into the underworld (we think of Odysseus, Aeneas, Dante) the process is transformative. José is radically altered by his quest, radically altered not only because of the peril but because all descents, all crossings of boundaries, involve degrees of violation, transgression, and taboo. Perhaps the clearest indications that José's crossing is transformative and that penetrating the archival abyss is a dangerous task are the various forms and degrees of filth that attend his journey. Certainly filth plays a huge role in José's own sense that his subjectivity is threatened, and perhaps ruptured, by his repeated transgressive incursions into the various archives, transgressive in his mind because criminal (to gain access to the unknown woman's school records José must break into her school). The penetration of the archive is transgressive, more specifically, because these incursions must violate the taboo of disturbing the dead. In the former school of the unknown woman, José climbs into the attic in search of records: "Senhor José got up, vainly trying to brush the dust from his trousers and shirt, his face looked like the face of some eccentric clown, with a great stain on one side only" (90):

> Each movement he made, opening a box, untying a bundle, raised a cloud of dust ... In a matter of moments his hands were black ... Before going down to the kitchen, Senhor José went to the head teacher's bathroom to wash his hands, he was amazed by what he saw in the mirror,

he hadn't imagined that his face could possibly get into this state, filthy, furrowed with lines of sweat, It doesn't even look like me, he thought, and yet he probably never looked more like himself. (91–2)

José's trespass into the school produces a tangible shift in his sense of self. And, despite the fact that José at this point in the narrative does not know the unknown woman is dead, Saramago makes it clear to the reader that this violation of her school records is a kind of tomb raiding: "He was working in a kind of dream state, meticulous, feverish . . . as if he were rummaging in the remains of a tomb, the dust became grafted onto his skin, so fine that it penetrated his clothing" (91). It is this tomb dust that precipitates his transformation into someone unrecognizable, yet, paradoxically, totally himself.[13] This phrase—"it doesn't even look like me, he thought, and yet he probably never looked more like himself"—is enormously resonant: José thinks of himself as transformed; the narrative voice (not José, it seems) thinks José has at some level been restored to himself. There is a fascinating frisson set up here, as if José, after his plundering the archive, his tomb raiding, has become himself and not-himself: as if his subjectivity, or at least his apprehension of his physical appearance, is uncannily multiplied.

What is clear about Saramago's representation of the archive that is this records-tomb, is that the archive is a place of danger: it is, precisely, a space of transformation where the subject, in this case José, is pluralized and confused. Inherent in the archive, it seems, is a threat to a singular subjectivity; this threat, in fact, resonates with certain anthropological understandings of taboo. The taboo, the unclean space and unclean object, is that which confuses ontological, metaphysical, or cultural categories. As we have seen, the Registry-archive confuses the categories of the living and the dead, or, precisely, is always on the verge of doing so. The tomb of the school records becomes a tabooed space in that it initiates a subjective categorical confusion in José: at some level thus, the archive translates its danger onto the archivist thus rendering him an uncanny double of both himself and the archive.[14]

The archive's power to multiply or split the subject is a crucial component of Saramago's analysis of the relation between the archive, loss, and melancholy. First, the categorical confusion that works its way into José's sense of self is analogous to the varieties of categorical confusions that seem to attend the archive a priori. The archive, despite its ontological first principles, cannot keep the dead separate from the living: the archive's own subject position, its metaphysical compact, is split. And thus, the individual archivist inevitably begins to reflect the categorical confusions of the archive. Second, and to look ahead briefly for a moment, José's subjective displacement presages the curious physical displacement of the unknown woman. Saramago's novel, a wry critique of the quest structure, suggests that José's desired goal will never be achieved, not only because the goal is "unknown"—ontologically, to José; narratologically, to the reader—but because the quester himself is discontinuous: the quest is fractured precisely as the goal and the seeker are displaced. At a crucial level Saramago is doubling the melancholy stakes here: he is not simply suggesting that mourning is problematized by the inability to locate the object of loss; he is suggesting that mourning cannot occur if the subject of mourning, the one subjected to the sense of loss, is *himself* unable to locate himself. Saramago's irony, increasingly despairing as José passes through the varieties of archives in his impossible journey, is that it is the archive, that which signals loss in the first place, that makes the amelioration of loss (through mourning) impossible: it is while he is in the archive of the school records that José's mourning transforms into intractable melancholy precisely as his coherence as a subject who mourns dissipates. The archive, which should stand at the beginning and *end* of loss, which traditionally maintains the coherent narrative of loss in its space of memory, in Saramago operates to signal the initial (imaginary) loss and then make impossible the narrative and psychic working through of that loss: if José keeps the woman "unknown" to the reader, thus obscuring her identity and articulating her (uncomfortably) as a version of Freud's "dark continent," the archive works reciprocally to obscure José to *himself*, compelling him to become his own (dark) Other. The archive thus operates as a site signaling the impossibility of loss ever being identified with its object *as such*. As the archive displaces and ruptures José's subjectivity, and as the archive itself increasingly is marked as a space of disorder (and thus in a curious way becomes the externalized manifestation of José's displaced desire, a sort of objective correlative of that displaced loss[15]), the *coherence of loss itself* is ruptured. José thus becomes a perfect emblem of Freud's melancholic, who may know whom he has lost but not what he has lost in him ("Mourning and Melancholia": 254). Indeed, it is crucial to note that immediately following this episode José takes ill: he sees himself as a "hollow-eyed phantom" (96) and then succumbs to the flu. The narrator describes his mental state: "Senhor José did not seem like Senhor José, or, rather, there were two Senhor José's lying in bed . . . one Senhor José who had lost all sense of responsibility, another to whom this was all a matter of complete indifference" (96–7).

It is clear that the effects, physical and psychological, of the violation of the archive are dramatically unpleasant. José's sense of self being ruptured results from having the "dust" of these tombs "grafted" onto him (indeed, by bearing these traces of these records, José becomes another archive). This image of grafting speaks to the idea that the effects of this archive fever will be permanent despite José's attempts to clean himself. And yet it seems that *All the Names* as a whole advances the idea that such tabooed violations of the archive are inevitable if not, indeed, a desired and desirable event. José's compulsion to discover the truth of this woman, as we see, will lead him again into the depths of the Central Registry. José's penetration of the school-tomb and the image of dust grafted to José's skin, moreover, anticipate the larger theme of *All the Names*: the dead and the living do not, perhaps cannot, inhabit separate spaces, despite attempts to the contrary.[16] The archive (school records, the Central Registry), as a space designated as a repository of memory, is the primary locus for this categorical blurring (the memory—and, perhaps, *body*—of José become secondary spaces). As José breaks into the Central Registry a second time, the narrator makes explicit that José has embarked on a journey involving the fundamental confusion of categories. The narrator suggests that one would expect the records of the living and the dead to be kept separately because "the space designated for the dead obviously begins where the space for the living ends" (139). This, however, is not the case. We discover that the Central Registry, in its attempt to accommodate increasing numbers of records, inevitably cannot keep the records separate; the records merge. Here now, in the Central Registry, "where the living and the dead share the same space" (140), where José's musings on "the light and the dark, on the straight and the labyrinthine, on the clean and the dirty" (146) suggest that such definitional thresholds and categories are losing their clarity, the claim of the archive to totalizing authority is weakened. What the narrator calls the "deontological laws of the Central Registry" (160), the claims to clarity and order, clearly are being violated, not only by José's tomb raiding, but by the very organization—spatial, temporal, and ethical—of the Central Registry itself.

This violation, moreover, is given official sanction by the Registrar himself. In his speech to the astonished clerks, the Registrar discusses what he calls the "double absurdity of separating the dead from the living" (176). Having received what he calls two "premonitory warnings" (175) about this absurdity, the Registrar offers an argument for the official merging of the records. His argument, one that suggests the need for what I call the "melancholy archive," is that the dead must not be forgotten. It is the Registrar's assertion that the dead must be kept in the midst of the living that allows me to suggest that the archive, at least in his view, operates as a site of protracted and inevitable melancholy. The archive, and I speak generally here, functions to preserve the memory of the dead, the past. The archive's mandate is melancholy in the Freudian sense that it preserves, rather than destroys (by working through), the memory of the dead. By positing the figure of the melancholy archive, I am suggesting that the culture of memory is melancholic, that archives work actively against the working through of trauma, the past, of history: the archive does not allow working through to occur precisely because its mandate is set against what Freud calls the normal process of mourning.

Derrida's summary of these Freudian principles in *The Ear of the Other*, drawing as it does on the work of Abraham and Torok, is useful here, as it points specific attention to the mechanisms of melancholy.[17] Derrida is discussing the "question concerning the crypt" (57) and its relation to the processes of mourning and melancholy:

> The metaphor of the crypt returns insistently. Not having been taken back inside the self, digested, assimilated as in all "normal" mourning, the dead object remains like a living dead abscessed in a specific spot in the ego. It has its place, just like a crypt in a cemetery or temple, surrounded by walls and all the rest. The dead object is incorporated in this crypt—the term "incorporated" signaling precisely that one has failed to digest or assimilate it totally, so that it remains there, forming a pocket in the mourning body. (Derrida 1988, 57)

The Registrar's idea of maintaining a close contact between the records of the living and the dead transforms the archive into a crypt. And perhaps this makes sense on some level because the archive as a *cultural* (rather than individual) repository is charged with keeping memory (of the dead) alive. As the Registrar puts it to the clerks: "Just as definitive death is the ultimate fruit of the will to forget, so the will to remember will perpetuate our lives" (177). The mandate of the archive, the melancholy archive, is to keep the knowledge of the dead alive. There is, of course, a series of paradoxes at work in the Registrar's plan: in order to perform the successful work of memory that is the function of the melancholy archive, the "deontological" laws of the archive have to be violated. Indeed, as the Registrar himself notes, by making an explicit comparison between the Central Registry and the Cemetery, the Registry will become a kind of transgressive space precisely as the records of the dead and the living are kept together in what he calls the "historic archive." (177). The melancholy archive, violating taboo and custom, simultaneously violates the foundational claims, the classificatory logic, of the archive proper. Taboos of custom and archival law are violated in order for the memory of the dead to be maintained: the archive has become crypt as the dead return to the space of the living.

It is not, of course, accidental that the Registrar makes reference to issues of "hygiene" in his speech. Recall that he has suggested that two premonitory warnings have effected his reevaluation of the purposes of the archive: the first was a suggestion by a lowly clerk to reorganize the archive of the dead in order to facilitate access to the most recently dead. The second was the loss and near death of a genealogist who became lost in the archives and was forced to survive by eating old documents (4–5). The Registrar, however, makes oblique reference to a third warning: it is clear to the reader, and of course to José, that José is the third warning, that his illness (during which he was cared for by the Registrar) and change in personal cleanliness, have alerted the Registrar to the dangers inherent in keeping the dead and living separate. In order to accommodate the melancholy of José, in order to protect the physical hygiene of the archivist, the logic of the archive, its classificatory logic, must be altered. The Registrar's final personal remark to José is, therefore, one that makes perfect sense: "then the Registrar said, That beard" (179). Given that the Central Registry will now merge the records, the outward signs of individual transgressions (filth, unkempt clothing, beards) must be removed: the individual's taboos have now become those of the archive.

The archive, as defined by the Registrar, fulfills a deeply melancholic impulse: it keeps the memory of the dead alive by introjecting their records into the space of the living. In Jean Baudrillard's terms, the dead are brought back into symbolic circulation. In *Symbolic Exchange and Death*, Baudrillard makes positive reference to Foucault, whose analyses of the discourses of exclusion, what Baudrillard calls "a genealogy of discrimination" (126), have helped us understand the logic of cultural value. In texts such as *Madness and Civilization*, Foucault has succeeded in analyzing the logic of "othering," but, Baudrillard suggests, a crucial Other has been ignored. The one Other that precedes and exceeds all others is death itself:

> There is an irreversible evolution from savage societies to our own: little by little, *the dead cease to exist*. They are thrown out of the group's symbolic circulation. They are no longer beings with a full role to play, worthy parties in exchange, and we make this obvious by exiling them further and further away from the group of the living. (Baudrillard 1993, 126)

The Registrar's speech, authorizing as it does the reintegration of the dead and the living, recognizes (I would suggest on the strength of José's transfiguration) the need for the dead to play a role in maintaining some kind of balance: "we need them," (177) he says. Thus, the Registrar, again acting against the traditional mandate of the archive, and indeed, the cultural devaluing of the dead, wishes to reintegrate the symbolic values of the dead and the living. If, as Baudrillard suggests, modern culture eradicates the signs of the dead (cemeteries are "hidden"; the dead are "obliterated" [126]) and the dead themselves are "thrown into a radical utopia" (126), the Registrar works against this prejudice by creating another space to house and revitalize the symbolic value of the dead.

The Registrar's implicit comparison between the Central Registry and the Cemetery recalls Michel Foucault's analysis of the heterotopia. In "Of Other Spaces," a lecture anticipating aspects of Baudrillard's analysis of the cemetery in *Symbolic Exchange and Death*, Foucault defines the heterotopia as a physical place/space with particular, almost uncanny characteristics:

> There are also, probably, in every culture, in every civilization, real places—places that do exist and that are formed in the founding of society—which are something like counter-sites, a kind of effectively enacted utopia in which the real site, all the other real sites that can be found within the culture, are simultaneously represented, contested, and inverted. (Foucault 1984, 24).

Foucault gives several examples of these heterotopias, these counter-sites: "In the so-called primitive societies, there is a certain form of heterotopia that I would call crisis heterotopias, i.e., there are privileged or sacred or forbidden places, reserved for individuals who are, in relation to society and to the human environment in which they live, in a state of crisis: adolescents, menstruating women, pregnant women" (24). These places see the subject in crisis undergoing some kind of transformation. Victor Turner would refer to these places as "liminal spaces" because the subject, as s/he undergoes the process of transformation, is neither one thing nor another: in *The Forest of Symbols* Victor Turner writes that the liminal stage is "a process, a becoming" (94). During the process, however, the subject is "rendered down" (96); that is, the subject is identified with "nothing," placed in a sense under erasure: "In so far as a neophyte is structurally 'dead,' he or she may be treated, for a long or short period, as a corpse is customarily treated in his or her society" (96). José's transformation into self and not-self that occurs because of his tomb raiding in his archive makes clear that the archive is a site where subjectivity is multiplied or, which may in fact, amount to the same thing, threatened with erasure. The space of the heterotopia is a space of transformation and crisis where the subject—the understanding of what constitutes subjectivity itself—is placed under particular pressure. Certainly, though perhaps not immediately obviously, the unknown woman feels these pressures acutely. Although José's transformations and melancholia are the ostensible focus of the text, it is the woman—her (unknown) melancholia, her (unknown) life—that provides the narrative energy of the text. And, of course, we should be clear that her transformation from named and known woman into unnamed and unknown woman signifies that *she* will be perpetually in a liminal stage, a stage that for José will be only temporary, or temporary until the next quest begins. Foucault's analysis of the "strange heterotopia of the cemetery" (25) suggests that it is here, in the cemetery, where the question of the subject, paradoxically, is most at stake; Saramago's irony—and I do believe it to be an irony rather than a willful ignoring of the unknown woman's claims to subjectivity—is that the subject whose identity is most at stake, the woman, is the subject fully hidden, encrypted, from the reader.

If the heterotopia as a counter-site challenges traditional cultural norms, including a singular definition of the self, it is also, according to Foucault's "second principle" of the heterotopia, a place that can serve multiple functions "according to the synchrony of the culture in which it occurs" (25). The heterotopia is a space the parameters and definitions of which are fluid. The cemetery, as a heterotopia, is, as Foucault suggests, "capable of juxtaposing in a single real place several spaces, several sites that are in themselves incompatible" (25). Like the heterotopic Central Registry, which confuses categories of living and dead, the cemetery offers itself as a space that intermixes temporalities, that eternalizes loss: "[T]he cemetery is indeed a highly heterotopic place since, for the individual, the cemetery begins with this strange heterochrony, the loss of life, and with this quasi-eternity in which her permanent lot is dissolution and disappearance" (26). The cemetery is not, as one may intuitively expect, a site of mourning. Instead, because it makes loss permanent, because it eternalizes the remains of the dead by marking their place in its archive, the cemetery becomes a melancholic space.

A similar emphasis is placed on the Cemetery in Saramago's novel. My reading of the archive that is the Central Registry should indicate, however, that the Registry already functions as an anticipation of the General Cemetery, if it is not an analogue of it. The Registry-archive itself thus functions as a kind of heterotopia primarily because it serves as this "counter-site" to the values of its society. The Registrar's claim to enact in the Central Registry a mixing of the dead and the living, which "beyond these walls, law, custom and fear do not allow" (177), draws specific attention to the archive as a space of contestation and inversion: the archive is, to borrow Foucault's description of the cemetery, "a place unlike ordinary cultural spaces. It is a space that is however connected with all the sites of the citystate or society or villages, etc., since each individual, each family has relatives in the cemetery" (25). In one of José's imagined conversations, we read the following description of the Central Registry where clerks and deputies are

> Accustomed to making links between causes and effects, since that is essentially what underpins the system of forces which, from the beginning of time, has ruled in the Central Registry, where everything was, is and will continue to be forever linked to everything, what is still alive to what is already dead, what is dying to what is being born, all beings to all other beings, all things to all other things. (Saramago 1997, 130)

The rhizomatic, decentered Central Registry, as this description suggests, is a place of authorized (ethical) connection, a melancholic space in which the dead and the living are intimately and *eternally* conjoined.

Such a description, of course, fits that of the General Cemetery in *All the Names*. To emphasize that the heterotopic archive of the Central Registry is connected to that of the General Cemetery, Saramago indicates that the façades of both buildings are identical "twin sister[s]" (180). Moreover, the interior space of the Cemetery's main building is identical to that of the Registry; it has identical counters and shelves as well as an identical arrangement of staff under the panoptical gaze of a "keeper" (185). It is clear that Saramago wishes us to view the Cemetery as another kind of archive, an archive on a continuum with the Central Registry. And certainly, in an obvious sense, the cemetery (speaking generally) is a melancholy archive: the arrangement of the dead in space, ordered with plot numbers and headstones, headstones recording birth and death dates, gives the narrative of a life in miniature: "the General Cemetery is a perfect catalogue, a showcase, a summary of all styles, especially architectural, sculptural and decorative, and therefore an inventory of every possible way of seeing, being and living that has existed up until now" (192). José thinks that "a cemetery like this is a kind of library which contains not books but buried people" (195), that the headstone is "the summary of a whole book that had proved impossible to write" (194).[18]

And, as if to solidify the connection between both archives, Saramago's Cemetery is figured as another labyrinth.[19] The General Cemetery is a sprawling, chaotic, rhizomatic structure that, like the Central Registry, is constantly growing (and thus, paradoxically, "alive") and, crucially, encroaching on the space of the living. Moreover, the organizational principles of the Cemetery are identical to the philosophical principles outlined in the Registrar's speech. Initially, the Cemetery was surrounded by a wall that would be demolished and rebuilt as the Cemetery grew:

> One day, it must be close to four centuries ago, the then keeper of the cemetery had the idea of leaving it open on all sides, apart from the area facing onto the street, alleging that this was the only way to rekindle the sentimental relationship between those inside and those outside . . . He believed that, although walls served the positive aims of hygiene and decorum, ultimately they had the perverse effect of aiding forgetfulness. (Saramago 1997, 180–1)

The language of this passage is close to the words used by the Registrar. Both the keeper of the Cemetery and the Registrar argue for a kind of rule of remembrance: the archive becomes a space of permanent memory. Moreover, the Cemetery, precisely as it works to connect (if not exchange) the symbolic energies of the dead with the imaginary desires of the living, precisely, that is, as it eternalizes loss by introjecting death into life, denies the work of mourning by transforming itself into a heterotopic space of melancholy.

Where the Central Registry has begun to confuse the records of the living and the dead (violating archival principles), the Cemetery, too, or at least that space where suicides are buried, is a space of confusion. José, after tracking through the labyrinth that is the Cemetery, thinks he has discovered the unknown woman's grave, only to discover that a shepherd has made it his peculiar mission to switch the headstones of the dead. It is, thus, not possible to know with any certainty where the dead rest. José remonstrates indignantly with the trickster shepherd, arguing that the shepherd has violated civil law and general principles of decorum (not to mention the classificatory laws of the archive):

> But in the name of decency, you should have a minimum of respect for the person who died, people come here to remember their relatives and friends, to meditate or pray, to place flowers or to weep before a beloved name, and now it seems, because of one mischievous shepherd, the person lying there has another name entirely, these venerable mortal remains don't belong to the person they were thought to belong to, that way you make death a farce. (Saramago 1997, 205)

The shepherd's ethical counterargument—"Personally, I don't believe one can show greater respect than to weep for a stranger" (205)—is a powerful one, not simply because it speaks to a larger principle of sympathy, but because it cuts to the heart of Senhor José's melancholy quest: he has indeed wept for a complete stranger, a woman referred throughout the text as the *unknown* woman.[20] José seems to recognize the resonance of the shepherd's ethic: "The shepherd asked, Were you a friend or a relative of the person you came to visit, I didn't even know her, And despite that you came looking for her, It was precisely because I didn't know her that I came looking for her' (206). The unknown woman thus remains fully and finally unknown because her final resting place cannot be found. The archive that is the Cemetery, because violated, because its classificatory principles are transgressed, fails to reveal to José the *origin* of his desire: the body of the woman. We may assume that if the body had been located a process of normal mourning could have been enacted, but as it stands, the quest cannot be concluded: mourning cannot occur.

All the Names ends with a turn of events not unsurprising given the melancholy tone and organizational principles that have articulated the narrative. José manages to find the unknown woman's apartment, her homely origins as it were. But here, of course, is only absence, absence doubly signaled by the presence of her voice on her answering machine, a voice working to deny José's desire for nostalgia, for an imagined home with this woman: "The answering machine came on, a female voice said the telephone number, then added, I'm not at home right now . . . "(232). Her voice, "grave, veiled" (233) can only function as a spectral origin, a ghost voice of an unknown and now fully unknowable woman, forever denying José his desire for home: "I'm not at *home*" (emphasis mine). This voice speaking these "definitive words" (233) of absence conjures an entire life forever out of José's reach. The unknown woman's apartment, her furniture, her clothes that give off "a smell of absence" (233), these are the trace remains of a life animated by the spectral answering-machine voice. Indeed, Saramago emphasizes the unbridgeable chasm between José's corporeal desires and these spectral traces when José is briefly seized by the idea of spending the night in the woman's bed, listening to her voice: "I'm not at home, she'll say, and if, during the night, lying in her bed, some pleasant dream excites your old body, as you know, the remedy is to hand, but you'll have to be careful not to mess up the sheets" (233). It is precisely José's "memory of his old darned socks and his bony white shins with their sparse hairs" (234) that convinces José to quit the apartment without spending the night. José's own body serves to remind him of the impossibility—the fruitlessness—of his corporeal desires: he is thus compelled to leave the unknown woman in her apartment, which is thereby transformed into another archive. Her voice remains among the traces of a life signaling the critical spectral dialectic of absence/presence that animates the archive: "a trace always referring to another whose eyes cannot be met" (Derrida: *Archive Fever.* 84). In Lacanian terms, the unknown woman is a variation of the *object petit a*. She is the Imaginary "nothing" that constitutes the desires of the self (José). Lacan's notion of the Imaginary, one of the three registers structuring the psyche, itself is articulated by a sense of melancholic "loss." The Imaginary, a fundamentally narcissistic register (Registry/Registrar), creates itself out of the subject's sense of loss of the "Ideal-I." As a narcissistic register, the Imaginary is where fantasy images of the self and the ideal Other are projected. My argument is that the archive—the phenomenal archive; the archive that is always the embodiment of a culture's desire—too is a function of loss, indeed has no meaning separated from loss. It is because something has been lost—or is always in danger of being lost—cultures, memories, records—that archives are needed. The archive grounds loss both in its initial raison d'être and in the manner by which loss is eternalized.

The final moments in the novel concretize Derrida's notion that the archival trace is an eternal one: *always* referring to other traces. The Registrar, after hearing of Jose's failure to locate the body of the unknown woman, suggests José create a false record card for the woman, one that omits any information about her death:

> Do you know what is the only logical conclusion to everything that has happened up until now, No, sir, Make up a new card for this woman, the same as the old one, with all the correct information, but without a date for her death, And then, Then go and put it into the archive of the living, as if she hadn't died. (Saramago 1997, 237–8)

Although José knows the date and manner of the unknown woman's death, her actual death certificate has been lost: without this official, authoritative, archival material, an archival possibility exists that the woman is alive. More precisely, the gap in the archival record is another space opening itself up to allow José to continue his narrative, his melancholic quest: in other words, Jose's desire for loss initiates desire itself. And thus, the final image of the novel is of José setting out once again into the heart of the labyrinthine archive:

> Senhor José went into the Central Registry, walked over to the Registrar's desk, opened the drawer where the flashlight and Ariadne's thread were

waiting for him. He tied the end of the thread around his ankle and set off into the darkness. (Saramago 1997, 238)

This final image is one that sees the archive transformed into a fully melancholic space by the process of disavowal (*Verleugnung*[21]): when mourning cannot occur, when the dead cannot be put to rest, melancholy becomes a way of maintaining a full connection to loss. Derrida describes unsuccessful mourning: "I lose a loved one, I fail to do what Freud calls the normal work of mourning, with the result that the dead person continues to inhabit me, but as a stranger" (*Ear.* 58). The loved one becomes other, becomes "a living dead" (58) in melancholy. Derrida here is describing the loss of a known loved one: but José's loss is of a stranger to begin with, which leads to a kind of double othering of the known woman: she is always a stranger, estranged by the process of melancholy, which keeps her alive in death, alive and soon to be lost *again* in the archive of the Central Registry. The desire of melancholy, the desire *for* melancholy, is the aporetic desire for the ever-retreating object: melancholy eternalizes loss and thus eternalizes desire. And it is here, as the woman, a textualized Eurydice once more, is again embedded in the archive, housed in the nostalgic space of the labyrinth, that José, who before thinks that "Nothing in this world makes any sense" (234), is given the opportunity once again to inscribe the lineaments of his own desire against the textual traces of the archived, unknown Other.

Conclusion

Reality, that about which nothing should ever be known or heard of, would thus be in an essential relation with the secret.

—Derrida, *Fors*

How then does one conclude an analysis of the archive and melancholy? How does one come to a conclusion about these figures? In some ways, the most appropriate way to end would be simply to do that: end. To offer no conclusion. To let the analysis of the melancholy archive as it is represented in the work of Auster, Murakami, Mitchell, and Saramago stand as the final word. Why? Because, as Derrida, at the outset of *Archive Fever* reminds us, the archive is not about conclusions: it is about beginnings and the future. The archive may, in fact, stand as the antithesis of the idea of the end as such (we might here remind ourselves how Mitchell, in *Cloud Atlas*, also repudiates the idea of the end of the novel-as-archive by inserting his ending in the center of the text). We could put this another way and suggest that the archive, far from being about ends, is about continual states of transformation, of transfiguration, of becoming; it is, moreover, a small step to notice how melancholy too is a state not of ends but of being in continual relation to the debts and weights of history: the melancholic subject is defined by a dynamic relation to the past rather than a confirmed step beyond definitional thresholds. We need only think of several central characters from the novels we have analyzed here to confirm the truth of the idea of the archive's inconclusive ontology: recall Auster's Nick Bowen, trapped forever in the archive of the Bureau of Historical Preservation; or Mr. Blank, forever traced into the archive of Fanshawe's novel; think of the unnamed woman in Saramago's *All the Names*, deliberately cast back into the archive, lost again within the crypt of desire and melancholy; of the narrator in Murakami's *Hard-Boiled Wonderland*, trapped asymptotically within a death that can never arrive but that for him has already come; of the tribe in Mitchell's "Sloosha's Crossin'" themselves in perpetual thrall to a figure, Sonmi-451, who cannot be known but who is archivally maintained in melancholy relation to the present moment; think, finally, of Mitchell's Miyake, having shaken off one dominant fantasy, now in hot pursuit of his melancholy ninth dream. Each of these characters is in a state of inconclusion, their narratives never to be ended, their archival impulses fully articulating them as *yet to be*.

It follows from this premise that the archive is something yet to be, that the archive as such cannot be known: a thing in the process of becoming cannot be known, at least as a complete thing. In this sense, the archive unfolds, as I have argued in various ways, in strict relation to the notion of the secret: the truth of the archive is its hiddenness, its secrecy. And we might simply remind ourselves that here we have been analyzing *literary* representations of the archive, literary representations of the economy of melancholy as they unfold within an understanding of the secret archive. It is, perhaps not surprisingly, Derrida who argues that the literary object, in fact, is a priori the best kind of secret, that the literary text can only, should only, be understood as a secret forever withholding itself from full view, forever refusing to disclose. But this refusal to disclose takes place, as Derrida reminds us in his reading of Baudelaire's "The Counterfeit Money" (*Given Time:* 1), in the paradoxical openness of the literary: nothing is hidden from us in the literary text, he suggests; it is all there for us to see, yet something, some kernel of the real of the literary, resists our interpretive gaze, confounds our desire to know. Derrida puts it thusly in *On the Name*: "There is in literature, in the exemplary secret of literature, a chance of saying everything without touching upon the secret" (29). The literary text, in other words, becomes crypt, becomes archive, allowing itself to be read, but never giving itself up to our desire. The reader's desire, thus, in relation to the secrecy of the literary text, enters into (yet) another condition of what we might call hermeneutic melancholy: we are forever in pursuit of a secret that cannot be found, a secret that is lost because never known in the first instance. I am fascinated to notice how novels about the archive, about secrecy, about hiddenness, encourage readings that are in their turn as melancholic as the literary texts themselves; perhaps more precisely, I am fascinated to notice how these novels produce readings that must become records, traces, archives of a kind of (melancholy) failure to fully comprehend the original archive.

The archive, its subject, its secret, and now we might add, its interpretation, are in states of becoming, in states of secret becoming. To conclude, therefore, about the archive, its secrecy, its melancholy, would be to act in something approaching bad faith. Only a conclusion offered in secrecy, that is to say, a conclusion that disguises or effaces its traces, would be appropriate.

But this is an impossibility. And thus, any interpretation of the archive—its representation by the author; its subsequent reading by me—is a violation, a defacing, of the response and responsibility to the archive's demand. Derrida speaks of the archioviolitic drive of the archive, the death drive at the heart of the archival impulse that "bequeaths no monument . . . no document of its own" (11). Perhaps, finally, any reading of the archive can only ever be a monument, a document, of the archive's melancholy betrayal.

Notes

Introduction

[1] Carolyn Steedman describes a similar puzzlement over Derrida's use of the term "archive" in her reading of *Archive Fever* in *Dust: The Archive and Cultural History* (1–16).

[2] We may recall here, for instance, the traditional—and traditionalist—assumptions of, for instance, Sir Frederic Kenyon, the director of the British Museum. In *Libraries and Museums* (published in 1930), Kenyon writes: "The study of history not only widens our mind by increasing our interests, but contributes to the stability of our civilization by its record of the actions of men . . . " (quoted in Eugenio Donato's "The Museum's Furnace": 222). Didier Maleuvre makes a similar point about the function of the museum in *Museum Memories*: "museums are institutions devoted to the protection, preservation, exhibition, and furtherance of what a community agrees to identify as works of artistic or historical value" (9).

[3] In *The Archaeology of Knowledge* Michel Foucault defines the archive in terms that draw attention to the archive as a *system* of authority. For Foucault, the archive does not consist of the texts a culture organizes to make sense of itself, nor is it the physical structures housing the various documents of a culture. Rather, the archive is "first the law of what can be said, the system that governs the appearance of statements as unique events" (145). The archive is a system of thought that, according to Foucault, precedes and exceeds (and thus eclipses) the physical and metaphysical presuppositions of the *idea* of the archive: "it [the archive] is *the general system of the formation and transformation of statements*" (146). Didier Maleuvre continues from Foucault and notes: "the museum takes part in the process of societal rationalization that controls beings by immobilizing their identity, or by simply postulating an identity" (11).

[4] Derrida uses the term "hauntology" in *Specters of Marx* to refer to the specter who does not, he suggests, "belong to ontology, to the discourse on the being of beings, or to the essence of life or death" (51).

[5] In "Melancholy and the Act" Slavoj Zizek characterizes this reading of melancholy: "In the process of loss, there is always a remainder that cannot be integrated through the work of mourning, and the ultimate fidelity is the fidelity to this remainder: Mourning is a kind of betrayal, the second killing of the (lost) object, while the melancholic subject remains faithful to the lost object, refusing to renounce his or her attachment to it." (658)

[6] In their introduction to *Loss: The Politics of Mourning,* David L. Eng and David Kazanjian draw important attention to the many resonances, real and potential, of

the idea of melancholia. In their reading of Freud's "Mourning and Melancholia," they suggest that melancholia is a "mechanism of disavowal and a constellation of affect" (3). But they also wish to reclaim the positive aspects of the concept, to "depathologize" melancholia's attachment to the object of loss. Thus, they suggest that melancholia works actively to maintain history, to keep it alive in the present: "For instance, we might observe that in Freud's initial conception of melancholia, the past is neither fixed nor complete. Unlike mourning, in which the past is declared resolved, finished, and dead, in melancholia the past remains steadfastly alive in the present" (3–4). In their reading of melancholy, "the past is brought to bear witness to the present" (5) and thus is a means to an ethical relation to history.

[7] Mary Anne Doane expresses this point eloquently: "For what is archivable loses its presence, becomes immediately the past. Hence, what is archivable is not so much a material object as an experience—an experience of the present" (*The Emergence of Cinematic Time*: 82).

[8] I would draw a distinction between my sense of the subject-as-archive and what Diana Taylor calls "embodied memory." In *The Archive and the Repertoire* Taylor wishes to suggest that when memory is performed, and embodied, it somehow "exceeds the archive's ability to capture it" (20). For Taylor, the archive seems only ever to be a material thing: film, document, text. Because the film of a performance is not the performance itself, the archive fails. On a (very) basic level, I agree with this, but I wonder if Taylor is not too quick to discount the idea of the subjectivity—as opposed to the materiality—of performed memory. I wonder, that is, if a performance offers (at least) a trace of a preceding consciousness.

[9] Giorgio Agamben, although writing in a different theoretical register than Derrida and Blanchot, would perhaps agree about the end results of the archive for the subject. In *Remnants of Auschwitz* Agamben, drawing, as always, on Foucault (here, from *The Archaeology of Knowledge*), writes about the archive and the subject: "The archive's constitution presupposed the bracketing of the subject, who was reduced to a simple function or an empty position; it was founded on the subject's disappearance into the anonymous murmur of statements" (145).

[10] Paul Auster has won many awards, including the Prix France Culture de Litterature Etrangere and the Prince of Asturias Award; Haruki Murakami has won the Franz Kafka Prize and the Jerusalem Prize; David Mitchell's *Ghostwritten*, *number9dream*, and *Cloud Atlas* were shortlisted for the Man Booker Prize and *Ghostwritten* won the John Llewellyn Rhys Prize; José Saramago, of course, won the Nobel Prize for literature in 1998. It is perhaps worth mentioning here that Mitchell cites both Auster and Murakami as influences on his own work: he goes as far as to mention both writers in *Ghostwritten* (47; 262)

[11] Paul Ricoeur translates this key line as: "Archive as much as you like: something will always be left out" (*History, Memory, Forgetting*: 403). Nora's original French reads: "Archivez, archivez, il en restera toujours chelque chose!" (xxviii). While Ricoeur at times cites Nora approvingly, he is more cautious in his appraisal of the negativity of the archive: "every plea in favor of the archive will remain in suspense, to the degree that we do not know, and perhaps never will know, whether the passage from oral to written testimony, to the document in the

archive, is, as regards its utility or its inconvenience for living memory, a remedy or a poison, a *pharmakon*" (168).

12. In *Existence and Being* Heidegger writes, in language and image anticipating Blanchot: "Because our *Da-sein* projects into Nothing on this basis of hidden dread, man becomes the 'stand-in' (*Platzhalter*) for Nothing" (343).

13. I will, in my reading of Mitchell, argue that the archival subject is, in fact, a posthuman subject. My sense of the posthuman, worked out in *Beckett: A Guide for the Perplexed*, "Borges and the Trauma of Posthuman History," "Archives of the End," and "Posthuman Melancholy," begins with the idea that the subject is always already produced by systems—discursive, psychoanalytical, linguistic—that precede and exceed him. If it is true that the subject has always been *subject to* forces defining him at his own limits, then the idea of an integrated, self-coincidental, fully responsible (ethically or otherwise) subject is pure fantasy.

Chapter 1

1. Zimmer calls the silent film a "dead art, a wholly defunct genre" (15).
2. This is, of course, not to say that cinema—and especially early cinema—does not give the impression of the real. I quote Mary Anne Doane, as she summarizes early responses to the cinema: "While photography could fix a moment, the cinema made archivable duration itself. In this sense, it was perceived as a prophylactic against death" (*The Emergence of Cinematic Time*: 22).
3. From Derrida's *Echographies of Television*: "A specter is both visible and invisible, both phenomenal and nonphenomenal: a trace that marks the present with its absence in advance" (117).
4. Alma, not surprisingly given her knowledge of Mann's life, is writing his biography.
5. This last title, of course, being that of one of Auster's own novels.
6. *The Inner Life of Martin Frost* as a story, as a film, has an uncanny genealogy: it was written originally, in 1999, as a film script; Auster then incorporated that script into *The Book of Illusions*; in 2007, Auster wrote and directed a film version of his story; and in 2008, he published an illustrated version of the story with artist Glenn Thomas.
7. *Ekphrasis* is defined, in simplest terms, as "the verbal representation of visual representation" (Grant Scott, "The Rhetoric of Dilation": 301). Peter Wagner's Introduction to *Icons—Texts—Iconotexts: Essays on Ekphrasis and Intermediality* gives an extensive, and useful, overview of the term as it functions in eighteenth- and nineteenth-century art. James Heffernan's essay "Entering the Museum of Words" (included in Wagner's book) is particularly useful for its discussion of ekphrasis as the "translation of visual art into words" (262): ekphrasis thus is revealed to be art about the hermeneutics of art. J. Hillis Miller, intriguingly, moves to suggest, in good post-structuralist fashion, that the distinction between image and word is a binary much in need of deconstruction (*Illustration*: 75).
8. Earlier in the novel we have learned that Zimmer himself has contemplated writing a book on artists who have renounced their art.
9. For another reading of this line, see Peacock's "Carrying the Burden of Representation" (66) and *Understanding Paul Auster* (166).

10 No metal gymnastics are required, also, to hear the German word for death, *Tod*, in Zimmer's son's name.
11 I would, therefore, disagree with Debra Shostak, who writes that Zimmer's relation with Mann and his films begins a process of "working-through" and recovery from his loss (79).
12 I am reminded of Stephen Cheeke's analysis of the etymology of the term ekphrasis. He draws attention to the fact that in its original sense the term meant "digression" (*Writing for Art: The Aesthetics of Ekphrasis*:19). How far away are we from the idea of displacement and deferral here?
13 *Oracle Night* has the structure of a retrospective recollection: Orr in 2002 describes events—and stories; precisely, he is rewriting stories—that have taken place twenty years previously. This retrospective structure makes it clear that Orr is still trying to comprehend the events of the past, is trying, more precisely, to comprehend his place and role within these events; in this sense, it is true to say that Orr is still in mourning for his life twenty years after the events he describes in the narrative proper.
14 In the final paragraphs of *Inhibitions, Symptoms, and Anxiety*, a text produced nine years after "Mourning and Melancholia," Freud seems to gloss over the economic problems of mourning—"We know of yet another emotional reaction to the loss of an object, and that is mourning. *But we no longer have any difficulty in accounting for it*" (172: emphasis mine).
15 Beckett's text reads "I have given myself up for dead" (1: 103).
16 And indeed this is certainly a strong fantasy among Auster's own characters: *The Locked Room* (1986) is about another disappearing man, Fanshawe; in *Ghosts* (1986), Auster retells Nathaniel Hawthorne's Wakefield, a precursor to Hammet's Flitcraft; *Leviathan* (1992) is yet another story of a disappearing man.
17 In *Unclaimed Experience* Cathy Caruth argues that the instance of trauma, the precipitating event of shock, is not immediately knowable to the subject: the event of trauma, she writes, "is experienced too soon, too unexpectedly, to be fully known and is therefore not available to consciousness" (4).
18 In their introduction to *Loss*, Eng and Kazanjian argue for the depathologizing of melancholy, suggesting that melancholy has an ethical economy: "while mourning abandons lost objects by laying their histories to rest, melancholia's continued and open relation to the past finally allows us to gain new perspectives on and new understandings of lost objects" (4).
19 *Nachtraglichkeit* is a term, as Laplanche and Pontalis indicate, that Freud uses often but never actually defines. It is commonly defined as "deferred action" or as "a revision" of past experiences. Laplanche and Pontalis argue that the term is best understood in relation to the experience of trauma: the event of trauma cannot in itself be understood until a point in the future; the meaning of the event is deferred until its significance can be assimilated (112).
20 A study remains to be written on Auster's mastery of the précis. His narratives often take the form of the recounting—in summary or précis—of events or stories. At times, these summaries read as bare plot outlines or film treatments. There is something uncanny about this. At once it seems as if Auster is not committed to the idea of constructing a fully realized world (he wishes only to convey the important plot points); and yet this précis structure works to suggest a world

Notes

we never see; in other words, Auster's use of the précis manages to spectralize yet animate the worlds just behind his narrative summaries.

[21] In *Paul Auster*, Mark Brown argues that this passage reflects Auster's own beliefs about the origins of stories and the relative passivity of the author (96).

[22] "The Storyteller."

[23] We hear clear echoes of the opening of Beckett's *Molloy* in this passage.

[24] For a reading of early Auster with Blanchot, see Joseph Tabbi's *Cognitive Fictions*, Chapter 4.

[25] Brendan Martin perhaps overstates when he comments on Auster's self-referencing novels: "Auster . . . does indeed write the same book, or more accurately, interchangeable versions of Auster's first and most obvious postmodern work, *The New York Trilogy*" (144); this is apropos of Zimmer's resemblance to Quinn of *City of Glass* (1985).

Chapter 2

[1] ἀ-λήθεια (aletheia) is the Greek word for "truth" and translates as "not being hidden."

[2] For another reading of Murakami's interrogation of the "material," see Matthew Strecher's "Beyond 'Pure' Literature."

[3] For a fascinating analysis of Murakami, the core consciousness, and its relation to magical realism, see Matthew Strecher's "Magical Realism and the Search for Identity in the Fiction of Murakami Haruki."

[4] In his reading of Derrida's notion of the secret, J. Hillis Miller reminds us that, for Derrida, the true secret, "if there is such a thing, cannot ever, by any means, be revealed" (*Topographies*: 309). Derrida puts it thus: "the secret remains there impassively, at a distance, out of reach"; he is particularly insistent on the muteness of the secret: "the secret will remain secret, mute, impassive" (*On the Name*: 27). Perhaps Derrida is thinking of one of the etymologies of the term secret. Sissela Bok reminds us that the term comes from the Greek *arretos*: "At first, it meant the unspoken; later it came to mean also the unspeakable" (*Secrets*: 7). Derrida's fullest treatment of the secret comes in *Given Time* where he argues that the secret is the fundamental principle of all literature. For a fascinating (and entertaining) deployment of Derrida's theories of the secret, see Tom McCarthy's *Tintin and the Secret of Literature*.

[5] I have argued something similar in "Does Mourning Require a Subject?"

[6] See also Freud in "The Uncanny": "but no human being really grasps it [the fact of his own death], and our unconscious has as little use now as it ever had for the idea of its own mortality" (242).

[7] In its classic formulation—I think here of Freud's case studies—psychoanalysis works to help the subject move past inhibiting trauma: in this sense, the process is a form of mourning. In Part IV of *Studies on Hysteria*, for instance, Freud speaks of how the hysterical patient is able to conjure images—pictures—of the past in order to free herself from their claims; once the patient is able to speak of the importance of this image, Freud writes, "the picture vanishes, like a ghost that has been laid" (281).

[8] At this point of writing, an English translation of *1Q84* is not available.

[9] We may also trace the story of Izanagi and Izanami into Murakami's novel: this being essentially the Japanese version of the Eurydice myth (Strecher: *Haruki Murakami's The Wind-Up Bird Chronicle*: 17–18).

[10] And, as we will see, some events in the novel actually do take place outside of ordinary reality; Toru's exploration of a parallel world suggests a different level of being as well as a different order of temporality.

[11] For a fascinating analysis of the trope of the digression, see Ross Chambers' *Loiterature*, especially "Towards a Poetics of Digression."

[12] For a magisterial analysis of the Nomonhan Incident, see Alvin D. Coox's *Nomonhan: Japan Against Russia, 1939*.

[13] Mamiya's experience in the well is clearly a traumatic one; prior to being cast down the well, Honda, already it seems in 1939 something of a prophet, has predicted that Mamiya will not die in Mongolia, but can only die in his homeland.

[14] It is useful to keep in mind here that "Toru" literally means "to pass through," as Jay Rubin notes in *Haruki Murakami and the Music of Words* (208).

[15] For an account of well imagery in Murakami generally, see Susan Fisher's "An Allegory of Return: Murakami Haruki's *The Wind-Up Bird Chronicle*."

[16] The well, as much as being an archive, or encouraging the archival impulse, is also a conduit, a link between the real world and a parallel world, a darker, more dreamlike world (it bears more than a passing resemblance to the Freudian unconscious): Kumiko has vanished into this parallel world.

[17] In *Beyond the Pleasure Principle* (1920), Freud describes traumatic neuroses, which are articulated within the logic of *Nachtraglichkeit*, as presenting a "symptomatic picture" similar to hysteria (281).

[18] For a related reading of Toru's "quietism," see Myles Chilton's "Realist Magic and the Invented Tokyos of Murakami Haruki and Yoshimoto Banana."

[19] In *Unclaimed Experience*, Cathy Caruth writes:

> [T]he wound of the mind—the breach in the mind's experience of time, self, and the world—is not, like the wound of the body, a simple and healable event, but rather an event that . . . is experienced too soon, too unexpectedly, to be fully known and is therefore not available to consciousness until it imposes itself again, repeatedly, in the nightmares and repetitive actions of the survivor." (Caruth 1996, 3–4)

Trauma, she argues, is "*not known* in the first instance" (4) and this results in the peculiar temporality of the condition of trauma. See also the analysis of the temporality of trauma in LaCapra's *Writing History, Writing Trauma*, Judith Herman's *Trauma and Recovery*, Geoffrey Hartman's *The Longest Shadow: In the Aftermath of the Holocaust*, and Shoshana Felman and Dori Laub's *Testimony: Crises of Witnessing in Literature, Psychoanalysis, and History*. For an exploration of the temporality of trauma as it plays out in the noncorporeal subject, see my essay "Does Mourning Require a Subject? Samuel Beckett's *Texts for Nothing*."

[20] Freud writes: "The symptomatic picture presented by traumatic neurosis approaches that of hysteria in the wealth of its similar motor symptoms" (281). The "motor symptoms" (282) of hysteria are explained "by fixation to the moment at which the trauma occurred" (282).

[21] See Hayden White's *Metahistory* and *The Content of the Form* for fully elaborated arguments about the fictionalized element of historical writings.

[22] Eng and Kazanjian offer a "counterintuitive" (5) reading of melancholy, one that attempts, counter to Freud, to depathologize melancholy: "While mourning abandons lost objects by laying their histories to rest, melancholia's continued and open relation to the past finally allows us to gain new perspectives on and new understandings of lost objects" (94). They ask a provocative question: "Might we say that the work of mourning remains becomes possible through melancholia's continued engagement with the various and ongoing forms of loss—as Freud writes 'of a loved person' or 'some abstraction which has taken the place of one, such as one's country, liberty, an ideal, and so on?"

[23] It is useful to keep in mind Nietzsche's tracing of the term guilt and his admonition to remember that guilt is a moral concept with material origins: "the basic moral term *Schuld* (guilt) has its origin in the very material term *Schulden* (to be indebted)" (*The Genealogy of Morals*: 194).

[24] For a reading of the idea of "criminality" and the gas attacks, see Mark Seltzer's "Murder/Media/Modernity."

[25] One story in *after the quake* functions as a clear instance of wish fulfillment. "superfrog saves tokyo" imagines how an earthquake threatening to destroy Tokyo is averted by the combined efforts of a hapless banker (Katagari) and a giant frog. This text clearly, perhaps too clearly, functions as a kind of exorcism of guilt, as it plays out Murakami's impossible desire to have saved Kobe from disaster.

[26] If mourning is predicated on an understanding of trauma *as* trauma, it is clearly a process intimately connected to the function of narrative. Narrative—as a process of both knowing and telling—allows the epistemological working though that mourning requires: the event must be *known* as event and communicated as such.

[27] In "Mourning or Melancholia: Introjection *versus* Incorporation" Nicholas Abraham and Maria Torok suggest that the crypt contains the traces of trauma, the "objectal correlative" (130) of loss: "Inexpressible mourning erects a secret tomb inside the subject. Reconstituted from the memories of words, scenes, and affects, the objectal correlative of the loss is buried alive in the crypt" (130).

[28] We might, after Baudrillard, refer to the absence of the past and the future as "the unlimited suspending of the end" (*The Illusion of the End*: 7).

Chapter 3

[1] Compare on this point Philip Griffiths: he argues that *Ghostwritten*, despite mobilizing contemporary postmodern theories of the effaced subject, ends up reinstating "the unfashionable value of individuality" ("On the Fringe of Becoming": 92)

[2] The Fellowship is clearly based on the Aum Shinrikyo cult, which unleashed a terrorist attack on the Tokyo subway system in 1995. In an interview with Leigh Wilson, Mitchell refers to an article he had read concerning a fugitive member of that cult: the article, which inspired the first chapter of *Ghostwritten*, is characterized as a "stem cell for a narrative" (95).

[3] A quasar is defined by the Oxford English Dictionary as a "massive and extremely remote celestial object."

4. Indeed, is there a better description of a ghostwriter—or the object of the ghostwriter's discourse, the *ghostwritten*—than that found in Blanchot's thinking?
5. Indeed the murderer—Punsalmaagiyn Suhbataar—appears again in Mitchell's *number9dream*.
6. The noncorpum receives his name from Jorge Luis Borges, with whom the noncorpum has written "some stories" (166). It is clear that the noncorpum, specifically in its inability to forget ("I am apparently immune to age and forgetfulness" [165]), is the inspiration for Borges's story "Funes, the Memorious."
7. An ancestor of Mo Muntervary's, Fiacre Muntervary, appears in Mitchell's latest novel *The Thousand Autumns of Jacob de Zoet*. He, like Mo, is on the run from an authority figure after escaping from an Australian penal colony.
8. In this sense, as Eugen Weber would remind us, I am drawing on the popular meaning of the term apocalypse, meaning "doomsday" and, interestingly, "disaster" (*Apocalypses*: 29). Mitchell will rely on the true meaning of the term, "revelation," in *Cloud Atlas*.
9. This uncanny return to the human is implicit in the term "posthuman," of course: the idea of the "human," as such, is never too far from any fantasy of leaving the human subject behind; even in the most radicalized version of the posthuman—cyborgs, nonmaterial subjectivities—the idea of the human is there, if only to orient our reading of this aftereffect that is the posthuman. I argue this point at some length in my reading of the Beckettian posthuman in *Beckett*; I make a related argument in "Posthuman Melancholy: Digital Games and Cyberpunk." Iain Chambers is surely correct to note: "To be post-humanist does not mean to renounce the human; on the contrary, it announces something that is more human precisely through its attempt to exit from the abstract confines and controls of a universal subject who believes that all commences and concludes with such a self" (*Culture After Humanism*: 26).
10. James Berger makes a similar point in *After the End: Representations of the Apocalypse*: "Very few apocalyptic representations end with the End. There is always some remainder, some post-apocalyptic debris, or the transformation into paradise" (34).
11. "Structure, Sign and Play in the Discourse of the Human Sciences": 292.
12. The structure and effect of *Cloud Atlas* reminds me of Fredric Jameson's description of the effect of J. G. Ballard's dystopian novels: "Its multiple mock futures serve the quite different function of transforming our own present into the determinate past of something yet to come" (*Archaeologies of the Future*: 288). Surely Jameson is touching here upon the spectral messianicity of the science fiction novel as such.
13. Compare my reading of the structure of Mitchell's narrative with that of Richard Bradford; he speaks of the novel's structure as creating "a deliberate though not gratuitous distortion of historical perspective" (*The Novel Now*: 62). Compare also Carol Watts, who reads the novel as an intermedial experiment; her implication that *Cloud Atlas* functions as a kind of montage (160) is fascinating ("On Conversation"). Gerry Smyth reads the novel through the idea of musical form: *Cloud Atlas* should, he argues, be seen as a fluid, musical interweaving of voices and "key human impulses": "it is precisely music's ability to embody and to represent those impulses that accounts for the central role it is afforded in this particular text" (*Music in Contemporary British Fiction*: 58)

[14] In "The Anorexic Ruins" Jean Baudrillard comments on the effects, or indeed, *affect*, of the apocalyptic postmodern: "Postmodernism is the simultaneity of the destruction of previous values and their reconstitution. It is restoration in distortion" (41). This phrase, restoration in distortion, does, I think, perfectly characterize the "end" of Mitchell's narrative logic.

[15] Slavoj Zizek is surely thinking about Benjamin when he notes that the terrorist attacks in New York on 9/11 were "libidinally invested": "That is the rationale of the often-mentioned association of the attacks with Hollywood disaster movies: the unthinkable which happened was the object of fantasy" (15–16).

[16] In this sense, by alerting us to the weight of history on the present, Mitchell acts (archivally) on Benjamin's appeal in Thesis V: "For every image of the past that is not recognized by the present as one of its own concerns threatens to disappear irretrievably" (*Theses on the Philosophy of History*: 255)

[17] *The English Novel in History*.

[18] And yet, as Kermode reminds us, all narratives end: "it is one of the great charms of books that they have to end" (23). The question Mitchell's novel asks, just as do those of Robbe-Grillet or Beckett (both of whom Kermode analyzes in *The Sense of an Ending*), is: *where*, precisely, is an ending? Mitchell, it seems to me, has given us (at least) two endings: the temporal end that is the central narrative of the post-apocalypse, and the actual end, page 509 (of my edition).

[19] For the sake of immediate clarity, let me add here a brief plot outline of "Sloosha's Crossin.'" The only story not divided into two halves, "Sloosha's Crossin'" takes place in a distant post-apocalyptic Hawaii. It is narrated by Zachry, a member of a preindustrial tribe called the Valleysmen, forty years or so after the facts he relates. His story largely is about the coming of Meronym, a member of a group called the Prescients: the Prescients have managed to survive the nuclear apocalypse and have also managed to retain and develop technological and scientific advances (their ship, for instance, is run by fusion energy; Meronym has advanced weaponry and a device, the orison, which is a holographic transmitter and recorder). The Prescients have come to Hawaii in search of a suitable location to settle, given that their own country has been struck by plague. Zachry befriends Meronym; together they explore the island. During the course of this exploration, Meronym reveals to Zachry that Sonmi, the Valleymen's deity, was only a real, material being, a clone. (The Valleysmen worship Sonmi and the implication is that they are descendents of the ancient Korean peoples who created Sonmi: the Valleysmen, it is revealed, have arrived in Hawaii some time after the Fall, the nuclear apocalypse). The Valleysmen are attacked and enslaved by a rival tribe, the Kona; Zachary is rescued by Meronym, who takes him to Maui. The story ends with Zachry's son revealing to an audience of (we presume) listeners his father's orison, which shows Sonmi speaking in a language that cannot be understood. The Valleysmen have survived and flourished on Maui; Sonmi's power as a deity continues.

[20] In *The Art of the Motor*, in a chapter entitled "Terminal Art," Paul Virilio—the preeminent thinker of the end—wonders about what art looks like after we have exhausted the "world's being" (70), that is, after the apocalypse, after the human.

[21] Virilio: *Pure War*: 34.

[22] I am reminded here of Norman Cohn's analysis of Jewish apocalypticism of the second and third centuries. Cohn notes that, contrary to the biblical prophets, whose visions came to them in words, the apocalyptic writers favored the visual image: "To a much greater extent than the prophets, an apocalyptist commonly received his revelations in visual form" (164). Mitchell's conclusion here, his apocalyptic vision, is, we notice, one transmitted through the visual. Mitchell's conclusion also reminds me of Kermode's analysis of the parables of Christ in *The Genesis of Secrecy*, specifically, his emphasis on the hiddenness of the message of the parables (see Chapters One and Two). The parables' meaning is, of course, open to those who can comprehend: Sonmi, on the other hand, stands as a perfect image of radically opaque significance.

Chapter 4

[1] Reis is considered to be one of Pessoa's three main heteronyms: Alberto Caeiro and Alvaro de Compos are the others.
[2] Mark Sabine reads *The Year of the Death of Ricardo Reis* largely as Saramago's explicit critique of Reis's political apathy: "Saramago effectively raises Pessoa from the dead to do his bidding, namely to participate in mounting a critique of Reis's philosophical stance as both morally questionable and physically unsustainable" (38).
[3] This is Lacan's subtitle for his seminar on *Antigone*, "The Essence of Tragedy" (Seminar 7: *The Ethics of Psychoanalysis*). For a fascinating analysis of Reis's relationship with death, see David Frier's *The Novels of Jose Saramago* (183ff.).
[4] The translation in the novel is as follows: "I stand firmly upon the foundation of the poems I fashioned" (191).
[5] In the original, the phrase is "outra transfiguração."
[6] Any figure, or metaphor, is a carrying across of one idea to another; metaphor (Gk: *metapherein*) means "to carry across." "Transfiguration"—trans + figure = across + *figura*—thus doubles the idea of the figure as such.
[7] I am indebted to Rhian Atkin for her help in teasing out the meanings of Saramago's verb.
[8] Compare this to Mary L. Daniel's reading in "Ebb and Flow: Place as Pretext in Jose Saramago's Novels," especially page 35.
[9] In *The Archaeology of Knowledge* Michel Foucault defines the archive in terms that draw attention to the archive as a *system* of authority. For Foucault the archive does not consist of the texts a culture organizes to make sense of itself, nor is it the physical structures housing the various documents of a culture. Rather, the archive is "first the law of what can be said, the system that governs the appearance of statements as unique events" (129). The archive is a system of thought that, according to Foucault, precedes and exceeds (and thus eclipses) the physical and metaphysical presuppositions of the *idea* of the archive: "it [the archive] is *the general system of the formation and transformation of statements*" (130).
[10] An interesting reading of the Registry's structure can be found in Naomar Almeida-Filho's "Saramago's *All the Names* and the Epidemiological Dream" where he links it to the "social observatories" (743) of epidemiological analysis.

11. Indeed, in his exploration of the depths of the Registry José suffers a "violent attack of claustrophobia" (146). In his anxiety he flashes back to a nightmare that obsessed him in his youth: he is enclosed in a dark space in which a stone, or what appears to be stone, gradually increases in size to the point of encompassing him.
12. In "Minds, Archives, and the Domestication of Knowledge," John Hunter writes that the archive is "the product of a desire to impose limits on the alienating immensity of the information that is available to be known" (201). Compare my reading of the Minotaur with that of Rhian Atkin ("From Theseus to Daedalus").
13. Note that it is the narrator who gives us the sense that José looks more like himself. José is puzzled by his appearance: the narrator is not.
14. In *Purity and Danger*, Mary Douglas writes: "[O]ur pollution behavior is the reaction which condemns any object or idea likely to confuse or contradict cherished classifications" (36). The taboo arises, in short, when an object defies hermeneutical understanding.
15. In "Mourning or Melancholia: Introjection *versus* Incorporation" Nicholas Abraham and Maria Torok suggest that the crypt contains the traces of trauma, the "objectal correlative" (130) of loss: "Inexpressible mourning erects a secret tomb inside the subject. Reconstituted from the memories of words, scenes, and affects, the objectal correlative of the loss is buried alive in the crypt" (130).
16. Carolyn Steedman's *Dust* is instructive here: "This is what Dust is about; this is what Dust is: what it means and what it is. It is not about rubbish, nor about the discarded; it is not about a surplus, left over from something: it is not about Waste. Indeed, Dust is the opposite thing to Waste, or at least, the opposite principle to Waste. It is about circularity, the impossibility of things disappearing, or going away, or being gone" (164).
17. In his Foreword to Abraham and Torok's *The Wolf Man's Magic Word*, Derrida suggests that "cryptic incorporation always marks an effect of impossible or refused mourning" (xxi) precisely because the crypt—actual, linguistic, or psychic—always negotiates with the dead, keeps the dead within the symbolic circuit. The crypt, in other words, is a space of melancholy inasmuch as it keeps the dead alive.
18. This reference to the headstone as a narrative refracts out into the narrative of *All the Names* as a whole. Indeed, the entire narrative hinges on a kind of "impossibility": José's search for this unknown woman will be endlessly deferred as her remains, textual and corporeal, are deliberately displaced. José's comment also looks to his own narrative procedures: the journal he keeps, which records the ostensible events of the narrative proper (and thus works as yet another archive), operates to "double" the impossibility.
19. We are also informed that the General Cemetery and the Central Registry share the same motto: the narrative voice informs the reader that "some deplorable lapse of memory" prevented it from telling the reader that the motto of the General Registry, like that of the Cemetery, is "All the Names" (184).
20. In "On Language as Such and on the Language of Man," a profoundly resonant essay analyzing mourning's relation to language, Walter Benjamin suggests that the name, or naming as such, always indicates a relationship to mourning: "To be named—even when the namer is Godlike and blissful—perhaps always remains an intimation of mourning" (330). At a crucial level the woman's status as "unknown"

is related to her not having a name in the text (a name given at any rate to the reader; it is clear that José must know her name). In Benjaminian terms, perhaps, she resists the intimation of mourning precisely as she resists being named. It should be noted, moreover, that namelessness proliferates throughout *All the Names* (initiating what is surely one of the most obvious ironies in the text): we are in an unnamed city; José is known only by his first name. The narrator makes clear that although José does have "very ordinary" (7) surnames, people tend to only to remember his first name: José is thus figured as a complete cipher. See, on this episode, Bev Hogue's "Naming the Bones," especially page 136.

21 Freud's concept of disavowal (*Verleugnung*) is perhaps best known from his essay "Fetishism" (1927) where it is linked to trauma of the boy's perception of woman not having a penis. The fetish object is "a substitute for the woman's (the mother's) penis that the little boy once believed in and—for reasons familiar to us—does not want to give up" (152–3). On a more general level, the fetish arises at the moment that a disavowal of knowledge occurs; this moment, as Freud notices, shares some similarities to "the stopping of memory in traumatic amnesia" (153). My reading of José's disavowal would necessarily figure the archive as the fetish object, substituting as it does for the "real" knowledge of the unknown woman's disappearance.

Bibliography

Primary Sources

Auster, P. (2002), *The Book of Illusions*. New York: Picador.
— (2003), *Oracle Night*. New York: Henry Holt.
— (2004), *Collected Poems*. New York: Overlook.
— (2006), *Travels in the Scriptorium*. New York: Henry Holt.
Mitchell, D. (1999), *Ghostwritten*, New York: Vintage.
— (2001), *number9dream*, London: Hodder and Stoughton.
— (2004), *Cloud Atlas*, Toronto: Vintage.
Murakami, H. (1993), *Hard-Boiled Wonderland and the End of the World*. Alfred Birnbaum (trans). New York: Vintage.
— (1998), *The Wind-Up Bird Chronicle*. Jay Rubin (trans). New York: Vintage.
— (2000), *Underground: The Tokyo Gas Attack and the Japanese Psyche*. Alfred Birnbaum and Philip Gabriel (trans). New York: Vintage.
— (2002), *After the Quake*. Jay Rubin (trans). New York: Vintage, 2002.
Saramago, J. (1984), *The Year of the Death of Ricardo Reis*. Giovanni Pontiero (trans). New York: Harvest.
— (1989), *The History of the Siege of Lisbon*. Giovanni Pontiero (trans). New York: Harvest.
— (1997), *All the Names*. Margaret Costa (trans). New York: Harvest.

Secondary Sources

Abraham, N., and M. Torok (1994), "'The Lost Object—Me': Notes on Endocryptic Identification." In *The Shell and the Kernel: Renewals of Psychoanalysis*. Nicholas Rand (ed). Chicago: U of Chicago P. 139–56.
— (1994), "Mourning or Melancholia: Introjection *versus* Incorporation." In *The Shell and the Kernel: Renewals of Psychoanalysis*. Nicholas Rand (ed). Chicago: U of Chicago P. 125–38.
— (1994), "Notes on the Phantom: A Complement to Freud's Metapsychology." In *The Shell and the Kernel: Renewals of Psychoanalysis*. Nicholas Rand (ed). Chicago: U of Chicago P. 171–6.
— (1994), "The Topography of Reality: Sketching a Metapsychology of Secrets." In *The Shell and the Kernel: Renewals of Psychoanalysis*. Nicholas Rand (ed). Chicago: U of Chicago P. 157–61.
Adorno, T. (1978), *Minima Moralia: Reflections from Damaged Life*. E. F. N. Jephcott (trans). London: Verso.

Agamben, G. (1999). *Remnants of Auschwitz: The Witness and the Archive*. Daniel Heller-Roazen (trans). New York: Zone Books.

Almeida-Filho, N. (2004), "Saramago's *All the Names* and the Epidemiological Dream." *Journal of Epidemiology and Community Health* 58:9, 743–46.

Atkin, Rhian. (2007). "From Theseus to Daedalus: Saramago, Sr. José, and the Reader in the Labyrinth of *Todos os Nomes*." *Portuguese Studies* 23:2, 191–207.

Bachelard, G. (1994), *The Poetics of Space*. Maria Jolas (trans). Boston: Beacon.

Bataille, G. (1988), *Guilty*. Bruce Boone (trans). Venice: Lapis.

— (1997), *Literature and Evil*. Alastair Hamilton (trans). London: Marion Boyars.

Baudrillard, J. (1989), "The Anorexic Ruins." In *Looking Back at the End of the World*. Dietmar Kamper (ed). New York: Semiotext(e).

— (1993), *Symbolic Exchange and Death*. Iain Hamilton Grant (trans). London: Sage.

— (1994), *The Illusion of the End*. Chris Turner (trans). Stanford: Stanford UP.

— (1996), *The Perfect Crime*. Chris Turner (trans). London: Verso.

— (2002), The Spirit of Terrorism and Requiem for the Two Towers. Chris Turner (trans). London: Verso.

Beckett, S. (2006), *Texts for Nothing. Samuel Beckett: The Grove Centenary Edition. Volume IV, Poems, Short Fiction, and Criticism*. New York: Grove, 295–339.

Benjamin, W. (1936), "The Work of Art in the Age of Mechanical Reproduction." In *Illuminations*. Hannah Arendt (ed). New York: Schocken. 217–51.

— (1950), "The Storyteller." In *Illuminations*. Hannah Arendt (ed). New York: Schocken. 83–109.

— (1950), "Theses the Philosophy of History." In *Illuminations*. Hannah Arendt (ed). New York: Schocken. 253–64.

— (1978), "On Language as Such and on the Language of Man." *Reflections: Essays, Aphorisms, Autobiographical Writings*. Edmund Jephcott (trans). New York: Schocken Books.

Berger, J. (1999), *After the End: Representations of the Post-Apocalypse*. Minneapolis: U of Minnesota P.

Blanchot, M. (1981), "Literature and the Right to Death." In *The Gaze of Orpheus*. P. Adams Sitney (ed). New York: Station Hill. 21–62.

— (1982), *The Space of Literature*. Ann Smock (trans). Lincoln: U of Nebraska P.

— (1992), *The Step Not Beyond*. Lycette Nelson (trans). Albany: SUNY.

— (1995), *The Writing of the Disaster*. Ann Smock (trans). Lincoln: Nebraska.

Bok, S. (1989), *Secrets: On the Ethics of Concealment and Revelation*. New York: Vintage.

Boulter, J. (2004), "Does Mourning Require a Subject? Samuel Beckett's *Texts for Nothing*" *Modern Fiction Studies* 50.2: 332–50.

— (2005), "The Melancholy Archive: José Saramago's *All the Names*" *Genre* XXXVIII: 115–43.

— (2008), *Beckett: A Guide for the Perplexed*. London: Continuum.

— (2009), "Borges and the Trauma of Posthuman History." In *Cy-Borges: Memories of the Posthuman in the Work of Jorges Luis Borges*. Stefan Herbrechter and Ivan Callus (eds). Lewisburg: Bucknell UP, 126–47.

— (2009), "Archives of the End: Embodied History in Samuel Beckett's Plays." In *Samuel Beckett: History, Memory, Archive*. Sean Kennedy and Katherine Weiss (eds). London: Palgrave, 129–49.

— (2010), "Posthuman Melancholy: Digital Games and Cyberpunk." In *Beyond Cyberpunk: New Critical Perspectives*. Graham Murphy and Sherryl Vint (eds). London: Routledge.
Bradford, R. (2007), *The Novel Now: Contemporary British Fiction*, Oxford: Blackwell.
Brown, M. (2007), *Paul Auster*. Manchester: Manchester UP.
Butler, J. (1997), *The Psychic Life of Power: Theories in Subjection*. Stanford: Stanford: Stanford UP.
Caruth, C. (1996), *Unclaimed Experience*. Baltimore: Johns Hopkins UP.
Chambers, I. (2001), *Culture After Humanism*. London: Routledge.
Chambers, R. (1999), *Loiterature*. Lincoln: U of Nebraska P.
Cheeke, S. (2008), *Writing for Art: The Aesthetics of Ekphrasis*. Manchester: Manchester UP.
Chilton, M. (2009), "Realist Magic and the Invented Tokyos of Murakami Haruki and Yoshimoto Banana." *Journal of Narrative Theory*. 39:3, 391–415.
Cohn, N. (2001), *Cosmos, Chaos and the World to Come: The Ancient Roots of Apocalyptic Faith*. New Haven: Yale UP.
Connor, S. (1996), *The English Novel in History, 1950–1995*, London: Routledge.
Coox, A. (1985), *Nomonhan: Japan Against Russia, 1939. Volume One*. Stanford: Stanford UP.
Daniel, M (1990), "Ebb and Flow: Place as Pretext in the Novels of José Saramago." *Luso-Brazilian Review* 27:2, 25–39.
De Certeau, M. (1986), "Psychoanalysis and Its History." In *Heterologies: Discourse on the Other*. Brian Massumi (trans). Minneapolis: U of Minnesota P. 3–16.
— (1988), *The Writing of History*, Tom Conley (trans). New York: Columbia UP.
Derrida, J. (1978), "Structure, Sign, and Play in the Discourse of the Human Sciences." In *Writing and Difference*. Alan Bass (trans). Chicago: U of Chicago P. 278–93.
— (1984), "No Apocalypse, Not Now (full speed ahead, seven missiles, seven missives)" *Diacritics* 14:2: 20–31.
— (1986), "Foreword: Fors: The Anglish Words of Nicholas Abraham and Maria Torok." *The Wolf Man's Magic Word: A Cryptonymy*. Nicholas Rand (trans). Minneapolis: U of Minnesota P. xi–xlviii.
— (1988), *The Ear of the Other: Otobiography, Transference, Translation*. Christie McDonald (ed). Lincoln: U of Nebraska P.
— (1992), *Given Time: I. Counterfeit Money*. Peggy Kamuf (trans). Chicago: U of Chicago P.
— (1993), *Aporias*. Thomas Dutoit (trans). Stanford: Stanford UP.
— (1994), *Specters of Marx: The State of the Debt, the Work of Mourning, and the New International*. Peggy Kamuf (trans). London: Routledge.
— (1995), *Archive Fever: A Freudian Impression*, Eric Prenowitz (trans). Chicago: U of Chicago P.
— (1995), "Dialangauges." In *Points... Interviews, 1974–1994*. Elisabeth Weber (ed). Stanford: U of Stanford P. 132–55.
— (1995), *The Gift of Death*. David Wills (trans). Chicago: U of Chicago P.
— (1995), *On the Name*. Thomas Dutoit (trans). Stanford: Stanford UP.
— and D. Stiegler. (2002), *Echographies of Television*. Jennifer Bajorek (trans). Cambridge: Polity.
Doane, M. (2002), *The Emergence of Cinematic Time: Modernity, Contingency, the Archive*. Cambridge: Harvard UP.

Donato, E. (1979), "The Museum's Furnace: Notes Toward a Contextual Reading of *Bouvard and Pécuchet.*" In *Textual Strategies: Perspectives in Post-Structuralist Criticism,* Josué V. Harari (ed). Ithaca: Cornell UP. 213–38.

Douglas, M. (1966), *Purity and Danger: An Analysis of Concepts of Pollution and Taboo.* London: Routledge.

Eng, D. L., and D. Kazanjian (2003), "Introduction: Mourning Remains." In *Loss: The Politics of Mourning.* David L. Eng and David Kazanjian (eds). Berkeley: U of California P. 1–25.

Fisher, S. (2000), "An Allegory of Return: Murakami Haruki's *The Wind-Up Bird Chronicle.*" *Comparative Literature Studies* 37:2, 155–70.

Foucault, M. (1972), *The Archaeology of Knowledge.* A. M. Sheridan-Smith (trans). London: Routledge.

— (1973), *The Order of Things: An Archaeology of the Human Sciences.* New York: Vintage.

— (1984), "Of Other Spaces." *Diacritics.* Spring (1986): 22–7.

Freud, S. (1959), "The Question of Lay Analysis." In *The Standard Edition of the Complete Psychological Works of Sigmund Freud. Vol. 20.* James Strachey (ed). London: Hogarth. 177–258.

— (1961), "Fetishism." In *The Standard Edition of the Complete Psychological Works of Sigmund Freud, Vol. 21.* James Strachey (ed). London: Hogarth P. 149–57.

— (1984), *Beyond the Pleasure Principle. The Penguin Freud Library. Volume II.* Angela Richards (ed). London: Penguin. 269–338.

— (1984), "The Ego and the Id." In *The Penguin Freud Library. Volume 2.* Angela Richards (ed). London: Penguin. 339–407.

— (1984), "Mourning and Melancholia." In *The Penguin Freud Library. Volume 2.* Angela Richards (ed). London: Penguin. 245–68.

— (2001), "Civilization and Its Discontents." In *The Standard Edition of the Complete Psychological Works of Sigmund Freud. Vol. 21.* James Strachey (ed). London: Vintage. 55–145.

— (2001), "Inhibitions, Symptoms and Anxiety." In *The Standard Edition of the Complete Psychological Works of Sigmund Freud. Vol. 20.* James Strachey (ed). London: Vintage.

— (2001), "The Interpretation of Dreams." In *The Standard Edition of the Complete Psychological Works of Sigmund Freud. Vol. 4–5.* James Strachey (ed). London: Vintage.

— (2001), "Moses and Monotheism." In *The Standard Edition of the Complete Psychological Works of Sigmund Freud. Vol. 23.* James Strachey (ed). London: Vintage. 1–137.

— (2001), "Thoughts for the Times on War and Death." *The Standard Edition of the Complete Psychological Works of Sigmund Freud. Vol. 14.* James Strachey (ed). London: Vintage. 273–302.

— (2001), "Remembering, Repeating, and Working-Through." In *The Standard Edition of the Complete Psychological Works of Sigmund Freud. Vol. 12.* James Strachey (ed). London: Vintage. 145–56.

— (2001), "Studies on Hysteria." In *The Standard Edition of the Complete Psychological Works of Sigmund Freud. Vol. 2.* James Strachey (ed). London: Vintage.

— (2001), "The Uncanny." In *The Standard Edition of the Complete Psychological Works of Sigmund Freud. Vol. 17.* James Strachey (ed). London: Vintage. 217–56.

Frier, D. (2007), *The Novels of José Saramago.* Cardiff: U of Wales P.

Griffiths, P. (2004), "'On the fringe of becoming': David Mitchell's *Ghostwritten*." In *Beyond Extremes: Reprasentation und Reflexion von Modernisierungsprozessen im zeitgenossisschen britischen Roman*. Stefan Glomb and Stefan Horlacher (eds). Tubingen, Narr. 79–99.

Hammett, D. (1989). *The Maltese Falcon*. New York: Vintage.

Heffernan, J (1996), "Entering the Museum of Words: Browning's 'My Last Duchess' and Twentieth-Century Ekphrasis." In *Icon—Texts—Iconotexts: Essays on Ekphrasis and Intermediality*. Berlin: Walter de Gruyter. 262–80.

Heidegger, M. (1949), *Existence and Being*. Werner Brock (ed). Chicago: Gateway.

— (1962), *Being and Time*. John Macquarrie (trans). Harper: San Francisco.

Hogue, B. (2006), "Naming the Bones: Bodies of Knowledge in Contemporary Fiction." *Modern Fiction Studies* 52:1, 121–42.

Homans, P. (2000), "Introduction." In *Symbolic Loss*. Peter Homan (ed). Charlottesville: UP of Virginia. 1–40.

Hunter, J. (2002), "Minds, Archives, and the Domestication of Knowledge." In *Lost in the Archives*. Rebecca Comay (ed). Toronto: Alphabet City. 199–215.

Jameson, F. (2005). *Archaeologies of the Future*. London: Verso.

Kermode, F. (1979), *The Genesis of Secrecy: On the Interpretation of Narrative*. Cambridge: Harvard UP.

— (2000), *The Sense of an Ending*. Oxford: Oxford UP.

Kristeva, J. (1989), *Black Sun: Depression and Melancholia*. Leon S. Roudiez (trans). New York: Columbia UP.

Lacan, J. (1981), "The Line and Light." In *The Four Fundamental Concepts of Psycho-Analysis*. Jacques-Alain Miller (ed). New York: Norton.

— (1992), *The Ethics of Psychoanalysis, 1959–1960. The Seminar of Jacques Lacan Book VII*. Jacques-Alain Miller (ed). New York: Norton.

Laplanche, J., and J.-B. Pontalis. (1973), *The Language of Psychoanalysis*. Donald Nicholson-Smith (trans). New York: Norton.

Maleuvre, D. (1999), *Museum Memories: History, Technology, Art*. Stanford: Stanford UP.

Martin, B. (2008), *Paul Auster's Postmodernity*. New York: Routledge.

McCarthy, T. (2006). *Tintin and the Secret of Literature*. London: Granta.

Miller, J. H. (1992), *Illustration*. Cambridge: Harvard UP.

— (1995), *Topographies*. Stanford: Stanford UP.

Nietzsche, F. (1956), *The Birth of Tragedy and the Genealogy of Morals*. Francis Golffing (trans). New York: Doubleday.

Nora, P. (1989), "Between Memory and History: Les Lieux de Mémoire." *Representations. Special Issue: Memory and Counter-Memory*. (Spring) 26: 7–24.

Peacock, J. (2006), "Carrying the Burden of Representation: Paul Auster's *The Book of Illusions*." *Journal of American Studies*. 40:1, 53–69.

— (2010), *Understanding Paul Auster*. Columbia: U of South Carolina P.

Pessoa, Fernando. *A Little Larger than the Entire Universe: Selected Poems*. Richard Zenith (ed). London: Penguin.

Ricoeur, P. (2004), *Memory, History, Forgetting*, Kathleen Blamey and David Pellauer (trans). Chicago: U of Chicago P.

Rubin, J. (2002), *Haruki Murakami and the Music of Words*. London: Harvill.

Sabine, M. (2002), "Re-incarnating the Poet: Pessoa, the Body, and Society in José Saramago's *O ano da morte des Ricardo Reis*." *Journal of Romance Studies* 2:2, 37–52.

Scott, G. (1991), "The Rhetoric of Dilation: Ekphrasis and Ideology." Word and Image 7: 301–10.
Seltzer, M. (2002), "Murder/Media/Modernity." *Canadian Review of American Studies.* 38:1, 11–41.
Shostak, D. (2009), "In the Country of Missing Persons: Paul Auster's Narratives of Trauma." *Studies in the Novel.* 49:1, 66–87.
Smyth, G. (2000), *Music in Contemporary British Fiction: Listening to the Novel,* London: Palgrave.
Steedman, C. (2002), *Dust: The Archive and Cultural History.* New Brunswick: Rutgers UP.
Strecher, M. (1998), "Beyond 'Pure' Literature: Mimesis, Formula, and the Postmodern in the Fiction of Murakami Haruki." *The Journal of Asian Studies* 57:2, 354–78.
— (1999), "Magical Realism and the Search for Identity in the Fiction of Murakami Haruki." *Journal of Japanese Studies* 25:2, 263–98.
— (2002), *Haruki Murakami's The Wind-Up Bird Chronicle.* London: Continuum.
Tabbi, J. (2002), *Cognitive Fictions.* Minneapolis: U of Minnesota P.
Taylor, D. (2003), *The Archive and the Repertoire.* Durham: Duke UP.
Tew, P., F. Tolan and L. Wilson (eds) (2008), *Writers Talk: Conversations with Contemporary British Novelists,* London: Continuum. 88–104.
Turner, V. (1967), *The Forest of Symbols: Aspects of Ndembu Ritual.* Ithaca: Cornell UP.
Virilio, P. (1995), *The Art of the Motor.* Julia Rose (trans). Minneapolis: U of Minnesota P.
— and S. Lotringer. (1983), *Pure War.* Mark Polizzotti (trans). New York: Semiotext(e).
Wagner, P. (ed). (1996), *Icon—Texts—Iconotexts: Essays on Ekphrasis and Intermediality.* Berlin: Walter de Gruyter.
Watts, C. (2005), "On Conversation." In *Literature and the Visual Media.* David Seed (ed). Cambridge: Brewer. 142–62.
Weber, E. (1999), *Apocalypses.* Toronto: Vintage.
Zizek, S. (1989), *The Sublime Object of Ideology.* London: Verso.
— (2000), "Melancholy and the Act." *Critical Inquiry* 26: 657–81.
— (2002). *Welcome to the Desert of the Real.* London: Verso.

Index

Abraham, N. 39, 60–2, 87, 95, 192, 196
Adorno, T. W. 99
  Minima Moralia 99
Agamben, G. 187
  Remnants of Auschwitz 187
Almeida-Filho, N. 195
  "Saramago's *All the Names* and the Epidemiological Dream" 195
apocalypse 16, 113–14, 116, 133–4, 138, 193–4
  post-apocalypse 131, 194
Atkin, R. 195–6
Aum Shinrikyo cult 192
Aum Shinrikyo gas attacks 16
Auster, P. 3–4, 8, 15–16, 18–19, 23, 183, 187–90
  The Book of Illusions 15–16, 19, 23–33, 48, 50, 188
    archival quest in 26
    as a decrypter of secrets 33
    and *The Inner Life of Martin Frost* 28–30
    mourning in 24
  City of Glass 52, 190
  The Country of Last Things 33, 51, 56
  Ghosts 33, 189
  Leviathan 33, 189
  The Locked Room 33, 52, 189
  "The New York Trilogy" 190
  Oracle Night 15–16, 19, 23, 33–50
    as an archive of memory 41
    as an articulation of *Nachtraglichkeit* 48
    as a critique of mourning 34
    loss in 33, 39
    mourning as a narcissistic process 38
    narrative and mourning, link between 34
    symbolic death, mourning of 36, 49
    trauma and time, relation between 44
  Travels in the Scriptorium 15–16, 19, 23, 50–8
    as an archive of the revenant 57
    Blank as an archive of unknowing 51
    as a narcissistic novel 50

Ballard, J. G. 193
Barthes, R. 72
Baudelaire, C. 184
  "The Counterfeit Money" 184
Baudrillard, J. 93, 98, 175–6, 192
  "The Anorexic Ruins" 194
  The Illusion of the End 98
  The Spirit of Terrorism 93
  Symbolic Exchange and Death 175–6
Beckett, S. 35, 189–90, 193–4
  Stories and Texts for Nothing 35
Benjamin, W. 196–7
  "On Language as Such and on the Language of Man" 196
Berger, J. 193
  After the End: Representations of the Apocalypse 193
Blanchot, M. 8–14, 53–4, 84, 91, 93, 105–6, 108, 112, 130, 187, 190, 193
  The Space of Literature 53
  The Writing of the Disaster 8–10, 84, 130

Boulter, J. 199–200
Bradford, R. 193
Brown, M. 190
  Paul Auster 190
Butler, J. 6
  The Psychic Life of Power 6

Caruth, C. 189, 191
  Unclaimed Experience 189, 191
Chambers, I. 193
Chambers, R. 191
Chateaubriand, F-R. 25
  Memoires d'outré-tombe 25
Cheeke, S. 189
Chilton, M. 191
  "Realistic Magic and the Invented Tokyos of Murakami Haruki and Yoshimoto Banana" 191
City of Glass 33
Cohn, N. 195
Connor, S. 134
consciousness 7, 9, 19, 38–9, 59, 61–9, 76, 81–2, 108, 114–15, 122, 133, 164–5, 187, 189–91
Coox, A. D. 191
  Nomonhan: Japan Against Russia 191
crypt, the 3, 6–7, 23–4, 35, 39–40, 42, 47, 61–2, 64, 71, 76–7, 79, 83, 87–8, 95, 97, 99, 121, 141, 143–5, 147, 160–1, 167, 174–5, 183–4, 192, 196

Daniel, M. L. 195
  "Ebb and Flow: Place as Pretext in Jose Saramago's Novels" 195
De Certeau, M. 131–3
  "Psychoanalysis and Its History" 132
  The Writing of History 133
Derrida, J. 1, 3–4, 7–8, 10–14, 17–18, 20, 24–5, 37, 42, 55, 97, 114–15, 118, 126–7, 133, 135–8, 140–1, 165–6, 174, 181–8, 190, 196
  Archive Fever 1–3, 5, 136, 166, 181, 183
  The Ear of the Other 1, 6, 97, 174
  The Gift of Death 49

Given Time 190
Specters of Marx 1, 37, 136, 186
The Work of Mourning 1
digression 71–3, 76–7, 81, 123, 128, 189
disavowal (*Verleugnung*) 182
Douglas, M. 196
  Purity and Danger 196

ego 2, 5–6, 30, 39, 42, 61–2, 65, 87, 97, 170, 174
Ekphrasis 29, 188–9

Fisher, S. 191
  "An Allegory of Return: Murakami Haruki's The Wind-Up Bird Chronicle" 191
Foucault, M. 101–2, 175–7, 186–7, 195
  The Archaeology of Knowledge 186, 195
  Madness and Civilization 175
  "Of Other Spaces" 176
  The Order of Things 101–2
Freud, S. 1–3, 5–7, 11–2, 21–2, 34, 38, 45–6, 48, 62, 68–9, 81, 85, 88, 95, 104–5, 108, 112, 116–17, 119, 140, 164, 166, 172, 182, 186–7, 191–2, 197
  Beyond the Pleasure Principle 1, 11, 41, 46, 85, 164, 191
  The Ego and the Id 6
  "Fetishism" 197
  Inhibitions, Symptoms, and Anxiety 189
  The Interpretation of Dreams 67, 108
  "Mourning and Melancholia" 21, 23, 34, 39, 88, 117, 172, 186, 189
  Studies on Hysteria 190
  "Thoughts for the Times on War and Death" 67
Frier, D. 195
  The Novels of Jose Saramago 195
futurity 3–4, 55, 114, 135, 138, 153, 159

Griffiths, P. 192
guilt 15–16, 28, 45, 48, 50–1, 53, 55–9, 65–6, 83–6, 89, 92–4, 97–9, 122, 192

hauntology 186
Heffernan, J. 188
　"Entering the Museum of
　　Words" 188
Hegel, G. W. F. 19
Heidegger, M. 60, 69, 78, 188
　Being and Time 60, 188
heteronym 9, 142, 144, 146, 195
heterotopia 176–7
history 3–20, 22–3, 40, 43–5, 48,
　59–60, 71–6, 79, 81, 83, 89, 93–5,
　98–104, 108, 111, 114–16, 119,
　122–3, 126–8, 131, 133–4, 136,
　138–41, 147, 153–63, 165, 174,
　183, 186–7, 194
Hogue, B. 197
　"Naming the Bones" 197
Hunter, J. 196
　"Minds, Archives, and
　　the Domestication of
　　Knowledge" 196

Jameson, F. 193
Japan, Murakami's views on 83, 98–9

Kenyon, F. 186
Kermode, F. 134, 194–5
　The Genesis of Secrecy 195

Lacan, J. 13, 181, 195
Levinas, E. 9
loss 1–9, 12–13, 15, 17, 20–4, 28–34,
　37, 39–41, 43, 49, 59–62, 64, 66,
　69, 73, 75–8, 81, 87–9, 91, 95–7,
　100–3, 112, 117–19, 122, 129,
　131–3, 145, 151–2, 161–4,
　168–72, 175, 177, 179, 181–2,
　186–7, 189, 192, 196
Loss: The Politics of Mourning (by Eng
　and Kazanjian) 89
"The Lost Object—Me" (by Torok and
　Abraham) 39, 60

Maleuvre, D. 186
Martin, B. 190
McCarthy, T. 190
　Tintin and the Secret of Literature 190
melancholy 3, 5–6, 10, 16–17, 21, 23,
　25, 30–1, 40, 43–4, 48, 54, 69–70,
　76, 78, 82, 86, 89, 95–6, 98–100,
　103–4, 112, 114, 117, 119, 132–3,
　143–5, 161–4, 169–75, 178–80,
　182–7, 189, 192, 196
memory 1, 3–4, 7–9, 12–13, 15–18, 23,
　25, 31, 33, 35, 38, 40–2, 44–5,
　48–51, 61–2, 77, 84, 87, 89, 95–6,
　99, 102, 104–10, 114, 116–20,
　122, 126, 131–2, 134, 138, 141,
　145, 152, 163–5, 169–70, 172–5,
　179–80, 187, 196–7
Mitchell, D. 3–4, 8, 14, 17, 19, 102, 105,
　101–39, 183–4, 187–8, 193–4
　Cloud Atlas 8, 14, 17, 102, 130–9, 183,
　　187, 193
　　central event in 136
　　central narrative of 131, 137
　　function of future in 133
　　six individual narratives of 130
　Ghostwritten 9, 14, 17, 102–16, 187
　　central narrative of 108
　　final narrative of traumatic
　　　return 116
　　imagined death in 105–6
　　as a meditation on memory and
　　　identity 109
　　two fantasies of 113
　　weaving of subjectivities in 115
　number9dream 14, 17, 102, 116–30,
　　187, 193
　　as a critique of Freudian
　　　melancholy 119
　　as a novel about nostalgia 118
　　the Oedipus paradigm in 118, 123
　*The Thousand Autumns of Jacob de
　　Zoet* 193
mourning 1–3, 5–7, 21–5, 28–32,
　34–44, 47–9, 61–2, 66, 68–70,
　83, 86–9, 92, 94–7, 102, 117–18,
　131–2, 143, 163–4, 166, 169, 172,
　174, 177, 179–80, 182, 186–7,
　189–90, 192, 196–7
Murakami, H. 3–4, 8–9, 16–17, 19,
　59–100, 183, 187, 190–2
　1Q84 190
　after the quake 59, 83–100
　　as displaced narrative 85

Index

the Oedipal paradigm in 90, 92
Murakami, H. *Continued*
  Hard-Boiled Wonderland and the End of the World 16, 59, 60–70, 92, 183
    as an allegory of secrecy 69, 71
    as an analysis of split subjectivity 61
    shuffling in 64
  Underground 8–9, 16, 59, 83–100
    as an attempted representation of guilt 84
    as a narrative of mourning and purification 95
  The Wind-Up Bird Chronicle 14, 16, 18, 59, 70–83, 191
    as an archive of history and personal trauma 75
    linear historical narrative in 72
    as a version of the Eurydice myth 72, 82

Nachtraglichkeit 48, 81, 116, 189, 191
narrative, economy of 34
The New York Trilogy 34
Nietzsche, F. 17, 136, 192
Nomonhan Incident 73, 81, 191
Nora, P. 12–13
nostalgia 7, 25, 43, 115, 118, 125, 134, 141, 143, 155, 165–6, 180

Peacock, J. 188
  "Carrying the Burden of Representation" 188
  Understanding Paul Auster 188
psychoanalysis 104, 132

quantum cognition 110, 113, 115, 119

Ricoeur, P. 116–17, 131, 187
  Memory, History, Forgetting 116, 131
Robbe-Grillet, A. 194
Rubin, J. 191
  Haruki Murakami and the Music of Words 191

Sabine, M. 195
Saramago, J. 3–4, 8–9, 17, 119, 140–83, 195–7
  All the Names 18, 119, 140–1, 162–83, 196
    as a critique of mourning 164
    Registry-archive 171, 173, 176–8, 181–2
    representation of archive in 163
  The History of the Siege of Lisbon 8, 14, 18, 140–1, 152–62
    transfiguration in, various acts of 154, 156
    writing 156–7
  The Year of the Death of Ricardo Reis 8, 14, 17–18, 142–52
    Reis as subject 142
    voice vs. writing 150–2
    writing as a ground of being 147
Schuld (guilt) 192
secret 23, 26–8, 30, 32–3, 51, 53–4, 59–61, 64, 68–72, 74, 76, 78–9, 83, 91, 127, 134, 139, 184, 190, 192, 196
secrecy 33, 59, 68–9, 70, 184
Seltzer, M. 192
  "Murder/Media/Modernity" 192
The Shell and the Kernel (by Abraham and Torok) 87
Shostak, D. 189
silent film 188
Smyth, G. 193
specter 5, 14, 25, 33–5, 41, 49, 53, 56, 140, 142, 150–1, 154, 186, 188
spectrality 4–5, 25, 27, 127, 138–40, 149, 160
Steedman, C. 186, 196
  Dust: The Archive and Cultural History 186, 196
Strecher, M. 190
  "Magical Realism and the Search for Identity in the Fiction of Murakami Haruki" 190
  "Beyond 'Pure' Literature" 190
subjectivity 8–10, 12, 15, 22, 35, 37, 56–7, 61–3, 69, 76, 79, 82, 96, 102–4, 107–8, 110–1, 113–15, 119, 142–5, 149–52, 156, 167, 170–2, 176–7, 187

subjectivity without any subject 9–11, 13, 105–6, 108, 112–13

Tabbi, J. 190
  Cognitive Fictions 190
Taylor, D. 187
Tennyson, A. 128
terrorism 16, 94, 96–9, 103–4, 106–7, 116, 192, 194
Torok, M. 39, 60–2, 87, 95, 192, 196
trauma 1, 3, 5–11, 13, 15–17, 21–3, 26, 31, 33–4, 37–49, 59–62, 64–6, 68–9, 74–5, 81–7, 89, 91–7, 99–100, 102, 104–6, 109, 116–17, 119, 121, 123, 133, 141, 148, 170, 174, 189–92, 196–7

unconscious, the 15, 22–3, 31, 34, 59, 67–70, 74–5, 80, 82, 108, 112, 117, 122, 165, 168, 190–1

Virilio, P. 138, 194
  The Art of the Motor 194

Wagner, P. 188
Watts, C. 193
Wells, H. G. 44
  The Time Machine 44
White, H. 191
  Metahistory and The Content of the Form 191
Wilson, L. 192
writing 8, 13–14, 23, 34, 38, 41, 43, 49, 52–3, 84, 86, 89, 91, 99–100, 125, 133, 142, 145, 147, 149–60, 162

Yerushalmi, Y. 3, 5
  Freud's Moses 3

Zizek, S. 36, 186, 194
  "Melancholy and the Act" 186
  The Sublime Object of Ideology 36